DISABILITY HATE CRIMES

This book is dedicated to Wally

Disability Hate Crimes
Does Anyone *Really* Hate Disabled People?

MARK SHERRY
University of Toledo, Ohio, USA

ASHGATE

Published by
Ashgate Publishing Limited
Wey Court East
Union Road
Farnham
Surrey, GU9 7PT
England

Ashgate Publishing Company
Suite 420
101 Cherry Street
Burlington
VT 05401-4405
USA

www.ashgate.com

British Library Cataloguing in Publication Data
Sherry, Mark, 1966-
   Disability hate crimes : does anyone really hate disabled people?.
   1. People with disabilities--Abuse of--Great Britain.
   2. People with disabilities--Abuse of--United States.
   3. Hate crimes--Great Britain. 4. Hate crimes--United States.
   I. Title
   364.1'5'087-dc22

Library of Congress Cataloging-in-Publication Data
Sherry, Mark, 1966-
   Disability hate crimes : does anyone really hate disabled people? / by Mark Sherry.
      p. cm.
   Includes bibliographical references and index.
   ISBN 978-1-4094-0781-2 (hardback) -- ISBN 978-1-4094-0782-9 (ebook) 1. People with disabilities--Crimes against. 2. People with disabilities--Crimes against--Great Britain. 3. People with disabilities--Crimes against--United States. 4. Hate crimes. 5. Hate crimes--Great Britain. 6. Hate crimes--United States. I. Title.
   HV6250.4.H35S54 2010
   364.15087--dc22

2010006002

ISBN 9781409407812 (hbk)
ISBN 9781409407829 (ebk)
Reprinted 2011

Printed and bound in Great Britain by the
MPG Books Group, UK

Contents

List of Graphs

List of Tables

Foreword

It is a rare academic tome that can move a reader through a gamut of emotions; however, Dr. Sherry has accomplished this feat with this book. In *Disability Hate Crimes: Does Anyone* Really *Hate Disabled People?* Dr. Sherry answers the question with an unequivocal 'Yes'. This book breaks the taboo of discussing hate crimes against people with a wide range of disabilities. As Dr. Sherry clearly demonstrates through his case examples and analysis of FBI hate crime statistics and statistics from the United Kingdom, the problem of hate crimes against this highly vulnerable population is widespread and rampant. I loathed the fact that I was comfortably ignorant of the size and scope of the problem and Dr. Sherry's book made me aware of a heinous phenomena that I did not want to think about. The reader is simultaneously repulsed and yet compelled to continue reading. It awoke my moral outrage. I read this book in two sittings.

The use of case examples runs the risk of becoming sensationalistic; however, Dr. Sherry treats the victims with dignity and respect. The stories are used to illustrate that no single disability is spared from hate crimes. The descriptions of the crimes are graphic. They are not done so to titillate the reader. Rather, they are vivid in their detail to demonstrate the raw and base hatred involved. The victims were specifically targeted because of their disability. What is shocking is not only the rage that is exemplified by these assaults, but how widespread this hatred appears to be. Dr. Sherry gives countless examples of websites and blogs that call the public to action in the killing of people with disabilities that range from autism to Williams Syndrome. These warped 'calls to action' are reminiscent of the Social Darwinism of the late nineteenth and early twentieth centuries with the eugenics movement and the 'final solution' rhetoric of the Nazi era.

As an educator of individuals with a variety of disabilities, I have heard countless stories from my own students that involved harassment, bullying, economic exploitation, and assault. As individual stories it is difficult to absorb the magnitude of the problem. Dr. Sherry's use of aggregate data makes the answer to the question in the title of his book crystal clear. Yes, someone does really hate people with disabilities. It is not just a handful of deviant individuals who perpetrate these crimes. The problem is an epidemic that does not know national borders. Although the stereotype may be that these crimes are committed by hoards of teenage gang members, the truth is that the vast majority of these crimes are committed by adults. Through Dr. Sherry's analysis we learn that the crimes are rarely done in isolation. Often they are done in a campaign of terror against people with disabilities and with multiple perpetrators involved. No single race, class, gender, or region is not involved in perpetrating these hate crimes. One shocking statistic still lingers in my mind: Victims of disabilities-related hate crimes are 30 times more likely to be sexually assaulted than any other type of hate crime. They are also more likely to be urinated upon and defecated upon than victims of other types of hate crimes. This dehumanization is abhorrent.

What is equally valuable in *Disability Hate Crimes: Does Anyone* Really *Hate Disabled People?* is Dr. Sherry's contextual analysis. Language, as Dr. Sherry aptly points out, has 'the power to wound' as well as the power to heal. Our current usage of language may be responsible for the under-reporting and the under-prosecution of these crimes. Why do we call the theft of a person's money or property 'economic exploitation' when the victim of this crime is a person with a disability and the perpetrator is a caregiver? The term 'economic exploitation' seems more benign and consequently draws lighter criminal sentencing. Perhaps this example seems like a superficial semantic exercise; however, as Dr. Sherry demonstrates, the language we as helping professionals use permeates the judicial system. The very professionals who are charged with protecting individuals with disabilities are reluctant to charge criminals with hate crimes. Rarely are these crimes prosecuted. Furthermore, the disparities in sentencing are outrageous. When the murder victim has a disability, the length of the criminal sentences are a fraction of what they would be had the victim been neurotypical or able-bodied. This fact is unacceptable.

One would think that after reading such a book, the reader would be left enervated, depressed, and demoralized. This is not true with *Disability Hate Crimes: Does Anyone* Really *Hate Disabled People?* Dr. Sherry provides a concluding chapter with his own call to action that is both practical and inspiring. *Disability Hate Crimes: Does Anyone* Really *Hate Disabled People?* is a seminal piece of work in the area of disability rights. Hopefully, this book will spark the consciousness of the masses and will one day be regarded as a cornerstone in the disability civil rights movement. This book should be required reading for educators, attorneys, judges, law enforcement officials, social workers, medical professionals, therapists, and policymakers. If you are not moved emotionally and called to action after reading this book, then you were not paying attention.

Ernst VanBergeijk, Ph.D., M.S.W.
Associate Dean and Executive Director
New York Institute of Technology
Vocational Independence Program

Preface

Writing this book has, in many ways, burned my soul with pain. It has been a long, tough ordeal. I have heard so many horrifying stories of unimaginable cruelty. Sometimes, it has been hard to continue because I've been overwhelmed by the violence, anger, abuse and pain. But I have continued, because I think it is important to bear witness to this under-recognized social problem, and the victims deserve their pain to be acknowledged. For many years, I have wanted to write something that recognized those who suffered, those who survived, those who didn't survive, and those who barely survived. I have spoken, written and advocated about this issue for over 10 years, in many different countries. Disability hate crimes are a global problem. I have spoken to countless victims, survivors, advocates, lawyers, law enforcement officers, academics and others about this problem. I've spoken to some people who were so tortured by their experiences that they subsequently killed themselves. I've spoken to others who continued to feel the pain throughout their lives, a pain that was not necessarily diminished by the passing of time. And some people have told me about their resilience, and the ways that being identified as a 'survivor' has helped them recognize their own strengths, and has reminded them that their lives are not defined by the heinous crimes which have been committed against them. I've also listened to family members of people who have been killed, as well as others who have had other types of crimes committed against them. I have wanted to pay tribute to all of these people; but I don't exactly know how. I hope that simply bearing witness to their pain is a start.

But this is not a book that was only created out of pain. I have also been inspired, and I want to pay tribute to those people who've shared with me their experiences of going public, breaking the silence, becoming advocates, and saying 'no' when they saw injustice occurring. These people are human rights champions. They have taught me a lot too. One of the things that has most inspired me has been the way so many of these people are 'in it for the long haul'. It is easy, when you hear about injustice, to get fired up for a day, a week, or even a month. But to see people who have been advocating about various forms of crime and injustice in the lives of disabled people for decades, and who remain strong and committed, has sometimes given me the courage to continue when it all seemed too hard. There is a scene in the movie *The Bodyguard*, which stars Kevin Costner and Whitney Houston, where Costner, who plays a bodyguard, is asked what famous people he had protected. He mentions a few people, including Ronald Reagan. 'Reagan got shot', is the reply. Costner fires back, 'Not on my watch'. This scene has been an inspiration for me for years. It captures the feelings I get when I am around these disability advocates. They may not be able to tackle every form of abuse, every crime, every injustice in the lives of disabled people – but they do what they can. Every day, they make a difference. They consistently and loudly advocate against injustice when they see it. I hope this book does not demoralize readers. Instead, I hope it renews their determination to say 'Not on my watch' every time they have the opportunity. And if you are not one of this group already, perhaps the book will inspire you to become one. I hope so.

I also wanted to reach out to people who are suffering right now because they have been victimized. So many people have spoken to me in person, sent emails, and contacted me over the years, usually in extreme pain. I've often wanted to say more, or do more, but usually I've just listened and in my own way shared the pain. I have been contacted by so many people who felt they were at their breaking point; and I want to send a message to people who are reading this book because they find themselves in that situation. I hope you are in a safe position now. Please prioritize getting safe above everything else. And once you are safe, physically and emotionally, never forget that you have the right to be treated with respect and dignity always. If you are the victim of a crime, please report it, and get someone else to help you go through the process – a friend, a disability advocate, a lawyer or someone else you trust. Don't think that you have to do everything yourself. People are often victimized because they are isolated; finding support can be a lifesaver.

I do want to say something about the language I've used in the book. Sometimes, I've quoted hate speech extensively. Vile, obnoxious, hurtful, pain-inflicting hate speech. There was a time when I once did all I could to avoid such language. I would give entire talks on this topic without even quoting any of these words once. And people would always, always, disbelieve me. No matter what I said about crime rates, patterns of victimization, or bias in the selection of victims, people would object. They would suggest that I'd misunderstood the topic; that 'No one actually hates disabled people' or 'No one actually hates people with disabilities' (depending on their preferred language). And I was deeply influenced by the arguments of critical race theorists about 'assaultive speech' and 'words that wound' – believing (at the very least) that we need to be very careful about recirculating such words lest we further insult those who have already been victimized (Matsuda et al., 1993). But I have changed my mind. I just felt that no one believed me – *no one believed me* – when I said that so many people hated disabled people. So now this book contains lots of hate speech. Too much, you might even say. Even if you still find it objectionable, I hope you understand my rationale.

The next issue also concerns language – language around disability. I have found this issue quite difficult in this book – unlike another one I wrote a few years ago on brain injury (Sherry, 2006). In that book, I adopted (and then problematized) a fairly straightforward distinction between impairment (various forms of medical conditions) and disability (the forms of social exclusion, prejudice and discrimination aimed at people with those conditions). This is the preferred 'social model' approach in Britain, and it also has some supporters in Australia, Canada, and the US. But my work with people in other countries – and in particular, other legal systems – has made it difficult to continue with a strict adherence to one preferred terminology ahead of others. I would be dealing with some laws, policies, groups and even cultures that referred to 'people with disabilities' and others which referred to 'disabled people'; it was impossible to maintain my own preferred terminology when discussing particular cases and particular laws.

Likewise, I have chosen to use the term 'disablism' to describe prejudice against disabled people, as opposed to 'ableism', which is sometimes used. 'Ableism' is a term which seems far more popular in the US, whereas 'disablism' is more popular in the UK. The reason I have chosen to use 'disablism' as my preferred terminology, however, has very little to do with national allegiances. Rather, it is based on my own assessment of the literature on disability hate crimes. The most common terminology which has been used by disability advocates is 'disablism' and I want to honor that choice. Admittedly, the UK disability movement (and in particular, the magazine *Disability Now*) has been far more active on the issue of disability hate crimes than the disability movement of any other nation. But my choice has simply been decided by the weight of numbers: there have been probably more publications about disability hate crimes in the UK over the last five years than the rest of the world combined.

I have chosen to focus mainly, but not exclusively, on disability hate crime in the United States and the United Kingdom in this book. The reason for a focus on the United Kingdom is that the disability movement there has produced so much literature; the 'Getting Away with Murder' report by *Disability Now* alone is one of the most significant documents ever written by disability advocates on this issue. I do identify gaps in the report in this book, but my criticisms should not be misunderstood: this was a phenomenal, groundbreaking publication. On the other hand, my focus on the United States stems from the fact that the FBI has the largest database on disability hate crime in the world. In discussing particular legal rulings, or particular aspects of the FBI database, I have had no choice but to use the established categories. For instance, the FBI database consistently uses the term 'mental and physical disabilities', and I have used that term when citing this database.

I believe that some terms concerning disability are deeply biased and offensive – and yet they are present in many laws and policies which I will be discussing, so I have no choice but to re-use them here. For instance, there are laws that describe people as 'retarded', 'mentally incompetent', 'handicapped', 'deaf and mute', and so on – terms that are probably regarded as problematic by many people in the disability movement, and yet I find myself (sometimes, uneasily) using this language when I discuss particular occasions where people were charged for crimes that specifically use these terms. I feel I had no choice – to accurately report the crimes with which people have been charged, I often had to use language which I regarded as deeply offensive.

Fundamentally, defining disability is a political issue. There are so many different legislatures and organizations that define disability differently, it is impossible to get a consistent definition (particularly in a cross-cultural context). Some legislation provides definitions, but case law and government policies also determine eligibility requirements that may be somewhat different. This means that the legal defense of someone charged with a disability hate crime sometimes questions whether the victim is actually disabled – a form of secondary victimization, for some people (particularly those with invisible disabilities). The issue at trial sometimes becomes 'Was the victim really disabled?' as opposed to 'Was a disability hate crime committed?' This is a particular problem in those cases where the victim is attacked for not 'being disabled' but using resources (such as parking spots) which are set aside for disabled people.

I have also made a genuine effort to keep the cases I discuss relatively recent ones, and many excellent examples which occurred more than five years ago have been left out. The vast majority of crimes which are discussed have therefore occurred relatively recently, at the time of writing. I have consulted many sources – not just conducting interviews with police officers, victims, the families of victims, judges, prosecutors, advocates and others, but also immersing myself in court documents and transcripts. I have also consulted thousands of press clippings about cases – not just to get additional insights into (or comments about) the crimes, but sometimes … just to see a picture of a person who has been murdered. I never forgot that these are stories about real people, some of whom lost their lives in the crimes I discuss.

I hope you read this book and feel motivated to do something about these awful crimes. I feel drained and, as I said before, like my soul has been burned with pain. Many more people need to take action in order to address this neglected issue. Please take up this issue yourself. Please do something about this awful problem. I pass the baton to you.

Mark Sherry
December 2009

Acknowledgements

I would like to thank those who helped me as I wrote this book. My wife Molly Sherry stayed with me, all through the night on many occasions, as I was writing. She also helped me gather the information for the tables and graphs from multiple sources. But far more importantly, she emotionally supported me as I wrote on a topic which was brutal on many levels. She was with me through the nightmares that I had as I was writing, and sometimes when she got involved with some of the cases, had nightmares of her own. In terms of her input to this book, I am incredibly indebted to Molly for her support, love, kindness, and generosity. In terms of her broader contribution to my life and my emotional health, it's impossible to express what she means to me, and how she makes my life better every single day. Thank you, sweetheart.

I want to thank two of my students as well. Dustin Godenswager, who will one day be a fine lawyer, did a great deal of research on US cases with me. I often gave him little more than a newspaper clipping that mentioned a particular crime and he would return with a copy of the ruling from the court. My Graduate Assistant, Holly Renzhofer, was also invaluable with her assistance. She contacted many law enforcement officials and district attorneys and set up interviews for me, and was also able to get them to provide the relevant public documents for me. Holly also did Internet research on some cases. What incredible research skills Dustin and Holly have! I am glad to know them and to have been their teacher; I know both of them will be incredibly successful in their careers.

There were many attorneys, prosecutors, police department representatives, disability agencies, and victims who provided me with information and documents. I would like to thank all of them for their generosity and openness.

I also want to say something to my family and Aussie mates. I miss you and I get so homesick; you are always in my heart. And so are the basic ideas of principled advocacy which I learned in Australia – particularly the importance of 'being there' for vulnerable people over the long run in order to make a genuine difference in their lives. It is easy for people to advocate on behalf of someone for a couple of weeks, or even for a year. But to see people who have been advocates for many years (and sometimes decades), with their principles and commitment intact, renews my faith in the human spirit.

Finally, I want to thank Dr. Ernst VanBergeijk, who not only wrote the Foreword to this book, but also gave me the opportunity to be the Fall 2009 Commencement Speaker for the students in the Vocational Independence Program at the New York Institute of Technology. Ernst is exactly the kind of person we need running disability programs: committed, caring, smart, and deeply passionate. He is clearly loved by his students and he makes a genuine difference in their lives. Thank you, Ernst, for writing the Foreword, and for the amazing work you are doing at NYIT.

Chapter 1

Introduction

This book aims to show that disability hate crimes do exist, that they have unique characteristics which distinguish them from other hate crimes, and that more effective policies and practices can be developed to respond to and prevent them. Disability hate crimes are a global problem. They are often violent and hyper-aggressive, with life-changing effects on victims, and they send consistent messages of intolerance and bigotry. The book will discuss many disability hate crimes, but will also document the widespread nature of disability hate speech. Of course, there is a significant difference between hate speech and hate crimes, because it is rarely a crime to slur disabled people. Hate speech often occurs in the commission of a hate crime – indeed, it can be an important piece of evidence that the act is not simply a random crime, but is directed at an individual because of a particular identity.

This book discusses cases of disability hate crime from around the globe, but focuses in particular on the US and the UK. The disability movement in the UK has responded to this problem with far greater energy than the US disability movement. In the UK, disability organizations have held public meetings, published numerous reports, organized task forces, liaised with local councils, police and prosecutors to raise community awareness of the problem, and have been active in publicizing cases. There are many links on the websites of disability organizations which give people information about what to do if they are the victims of disability hate crimes. Hundreds of disability organizations have held community meetings about disability hate crimes. Multi-agency hate crime reporting centers have also been pilot-tested in some areas and other projects have been funded to develop new ways for victims of hate crimes to report them, including a 'Stop Hate UK' phone line. Additionally, disability advocates have instructed local authorities on how to produce hate crime information reporting forms in accessible formats – including 'easy read' options. On the other hand, US disability organizations have been far less intent on raising awareness (either in the disability movement or in the wider community). Instead, a small number of (leaders of) disability organizations petitioned Congress to pass the *Matthew Shepard Act*, which included disability in hate crime legislation, and a smaller number have discussed the problem in their newsletters, but none waged the sort of focused long-term campaigns which have been carried out by their UK counterparts. It has been the UK disability movement, in general, which has publicized disability hate crimes and raised the profile of this issue on the global arena. Nevertheless, the FBI hate crime database is the longest-running and most comprehensive database on disability hate crime in the world, so it deserves detailed attention. Even though the book will suggest that it has many flaws, the FBI database is still very useful in identifying patterns in the overall incidence of disability hate crime.

One fairly well-known British disability hate crime involved the vicious murder of Brent Martin by Marcus Miller, William Hughes and Stephen Bonellie in August 2007 (*Times Online Law Reports*, 2008). Martin had a learning disability and a psychiatric impairment and believed that Miller, Hughes and Bonellie were his friends. The three men took advantage of his vulnerability and his desire to be loved and have friends. After Martin was released from a long period of psychiatric hospitalization, they encouraged him to spend his £3,000 savings on alcohol and cigarettes. But when his money ran out in less than three months, their behavior towards him changed. On the night he was killed, Martin reportedly asked his sister if he could borrow some money and told her if he did not buy 'the lads' alcohol they were going to 'kick his head in' (Burton, 2008). On that night, the three men bet each other £5 that they could knock Martin out first (Minchin, 2008). Miller hit Martin first, knocking him unconscious and splitting his lip. Then Bonellie said, 'watch this, knockout with an uppercut' and knocked Martin to the ground. The assaults continued at several locations throughout the night. Hughes also took his turn at beating Martin. Indeed, after hitting Martin, Hughes turned to Bonellie and said, 'You go and kick him all over' (Burton, 2008). All three had hit Martin and kicked him in the ribs and head. Martin was also head-butted. He died from these head injuries and a post-mortem revealed that he had been hit in the head at least 18 times before his death (Whitfield, 2008).

Martin apologized to the perpetrators on numerous occasions while they attacked him. He even told these 'friends' that he loved them and that they were his 'mates'. However, their relentless attacks continued. One of the murderers told the others: 'I am not going down for a muppet'. (Muppet is a very derogatory term commonly used in the UK to disparage someone else's intelligence.) Prosecutor Toby Hedworth said at trial: 'They behaved like a pack of animals as they repeatedly punched, head-butted, kicked, stamped on Brent Martin, who never lifted an aggressive finger towards one of them, and they did so until he was dead. They did so for their own sport' (Pearson, 2008). Eyewitnesses reported Martin screaming 'Nah, nah, no please' as he was beaten. A girl with the group went to check on Martin, who was breathing shallowly and lying in a pool of blood. Hughes then stomped on his head and ribs before Martin's unconscious body was propped against a parked car. The final act of humiliation was that they left Martin lying semi-naked by pulling down his underpants (Burton, 2008). Brent Martin died two days later. Unfortunately, Brent Martin's case was never prosecuted as a disability hate crime. But his brutal murder spurred many disability organizations to lobby for increased awareness and recognition of disability hate crimes. It was the disability hate crime *par excellence* for them – particularly typical because it was not even recognized as one.

For disability advocates, Brent Martin's murder is actually the classic example of a disability hate crime. It's a crime – a murder! He was targeted, before and during the crime, because of his disability. There was evidence of disability bias (references to 'a muppet') during the commission of the crime by the perpetrator. Throughout the world, disability organizations recognized this was a disability hate crime and shared their sorrow and anger. And yet the courts never listened. Brent Martin's brutal murder was not a teaching moment for the courts. It was not a wake-up call. The murder was not recognized by the courts as a hate crime, and the murderers avoided the longer sentences which would have been associated with recognition of the murder as a hate crime. But the pattern of legal injustice, which seems to be so characteristic of disability hate crimes, did not stop there. Far from it, alas.

The three young men who had been convicted of Brent Martin's murder were initially sentenced to life imprisonment, with a nonparole period of 18 years for Bonellie, 15 years for Miller, and 22 years for Hughes. However, they appealed and their sentences were reduced on the grounds that the murder did not involve 'sadistic conduct'. Mr Justice Goldring, giving the judgment of the Court of Appeal, Criminal Division, acknowledged that Martin 'was systematically attacked, tormented, humiliated and finally beaten by the appellants whom he misguidedly believed to be his friends' but ruled that their conduct did not amount to 'sadistic conduct' as defined by paragraph 5(2)(e) of Schedule 21 to the Criminal Justice Act 2003 so as to attract a 30-year minimum term for life imprisonment (*Times Online Law Reports*, 2008). The type of 'sadistic conduct' referred to in that paragraph, the Court ruled, 'contemplated a significantly greater degree of awareness of pleasure in the infliction of pain, suffering or humiliation' than the perpetrators of the Brent Martin murder displayed.

Another case which was not officially recognized as a disability hate crime, but which disability activists strongly believe was such a crime, involved the brutal attack on Ricky Whistnant, an African-American man with bipolar disorder who lived in Hartford, Connecticut. Whistnant died in 2003 after a group of five boys, aged 12 to 14, jeered at him, taunted him and finally beat him in the lobby of his apartment area. One of the perpetrators threw a bottle of soda so hard at Whistnant that when it struck his head, he fell sideways and hit his head on a windowsill as he collapsed. One of the attackers poured soda on him as he lay on the ground; others kicked him. Another pulled his pants down. Whistnant died. The entire attack was captured and recorded by security cameras. Disability advocates called it a murderous hate crime. However, an autopsy found that Whistnant had an enlarged heart and diabetes, so his attackers were not charged with murder. (The Fatality Review Board for Persons with Disabilities later disagreed and determined that Whistnant's death should have been classified as a homicide because the taunting and assault had fatally activated his physical disabilities, including a severe breathing disorder.) (Staff *Associated Press*, 15 June 2005).

Whistnant had previously earned the Peter Kirsche Award for Self-Advocacy from the Arc, Connecticut, and was a strong self-advocate around disability issues. His friends in the local self-advocacy group began to campaign on the issue of disability hate crimes. Some of them wrote a public letter to local newspapers about his death:

Ricky Whistnant was killed because he was different. We find this whole tragedy absolutely uncalled for. It makes us angry and hurt because we thought the world had grown up. It's not like we're living in medieval times when people with disabilities were always being made fun of and experienced segregation and discrimination. We need to advocate for living together in peace. If we lived in harmony and peace Ricky would have been more accepted in his community. We have to make our streets and homes safe. And get tougher hate crime legislation so this doesn't happen to people with disabilities. It doesn't make any sense. We can't believe nobody knew what was going on, that people were harassing him. The guy was just out buying his groceries. We can't believe nobody helped him. We are sorry for Ricky's family and friends. We are sorry for their loss. We think that people with disabilities need to set an example for the community by how we treat each other. We need to make sure our government and programs that look out for people's lives do not cut supports for people with disabilities. We have to seriously look at how society is treating people with disabilities. We want justice. We have the right to not be beaten up, picked on, called names and murdered. We want people to be nice to us and if something is wrong sit down and talk about the problem. We want to believe that if we report that something is wrong that people will listen and take action. This kind of behavior cannot be tolerated. People have the right to be safe. Society needs to be completely educated on what having a disability is like. We want to educate the public, especially teenagers and children, that people with disabilities are people first (Self-Advocates Becoming Empowered, 2005).

Many disability hate crimes involve the theft of money or valuables. This was the case for a crime carried out by Katholeen R. Toeder (a 59-year-old woman who has the following aliases: Katholeen R. Redfren, Katholeen R. Klingaman, Katholeen R. Astle, Katholeen R. Weishoff, and Katholeen R. Cohoon). Toeder had been hired as a caregiver in October 2006 to provide healthcare and household help to Karen Rahn of Mazomanie, Wisconsin. Karen Rahn and her husband, Richard, owned an antique store and while Rahn was dying of cancer, Toeder stole more than $25,000 of antiques from Rahn's home over a six- to eight-month period. Toeder sold the antiques to other antique stores. The stolen property consisted of antique dolls and toys, beaded bags, mechanical banks, and a pitcher. Toeder told these stores that someone in her family had passed away and she was trying to get rid of the property. She was charged with theft of moveable property (worth more than $10,000) and with a hate crime enhancer, because the reason that she stole from Rahn was that Rahn was disabled by her cancer. The maximum penalty for this crime, with a hate crime sentence enhancement, is 10 years of prison and extended probation to 15. However, Toeder's plea deal meant that she was only sentenced to six months in prison, with a 10-year probation. In addition, Toeder was ordered to have no contact with the victim's husband, to file timely tax returns, to make regular restitution payments, and to pay toward the restitution half of any tax refund she received each year. Toeder's six months in prison for this hate crime was served after she finished a sentence for burglary in another country.

A report on disability hate crime in Northern Ireland in 2009 found that although there were very low rates of disability hate crimes reported by the Police Service of Northern Ireland (70 in 2005–2006, 48 in 2006–2007, and 49 in 2007–2008), other reports indicated much higher rates of such crimes. For instance, the Northern Ireland Survey of people with Activity Limitations and Disability indicated that 8% of disabled men and 5% of disabled women had experienced some form of hate crime. In the UK, self-reported disability hate crimes are higher: the disability charity Leonard Cheshire indicated that 1 in 11 disabled people had been the victim of a hate crime (Pitt, 2009).

Of course, disability hate crimes are not confined to the US or the UK. In Christchurch, New Zealand, in January 2009, a near-blind man with an intellectual disability was attacked by three men. The victim was not only punched and knocked to the ground; he was followed and was subjected to demeaning slurs about his identity. Even when he fled to a nearby bus stop, his attackers followed and continued their verbal abuse about his disability. They knocked him to the ground again. This case had many of the classic characteristics of a hate crime: a vulnerable person, alone, attacked by multiple perpetrators who use hateful language about the person's identity. There was ample evidence that the crime was motivated by disability hatred: anti-disability slurs were voiced throughout the commission of the crime. Additionally, the perpetrators were strangers to the victim, emphasizing the fact that it was the person's disability identity, rather than any other characteristic, which was the target of the crime (Francis, 2009, p. 3; Thomas and McKenzie-McLean, 2009).

In Melbourne, Australia, in 2006, a group of 12 boys who called themselves 'The Teenage Kings of Werribee' made a DVD which they sold for $5 around various schools. Some of the DVD was later distributed on YouTube (*Today Tonight*, 2006). It showed them victimizing a girl with developmental disabilities. Although this was not officially classified as a disability hate crime (since disability hate crime law does not exist in Australia), it clearly fits the definition. Two of the boys had previously been communicating with the girl over MSN Messenger and had arranged to meet her at a shopping center. When she arrived, the 12 boys took her to a local river, urinated on her, set her hair on fire and indecently assaulted her. Her disability was the major reason she was targeted. On the video, one boy stated, 'What the fuck, she's the ugliest thing I've seen'. The group of boys surrounded the girl chanting 'The Victim', who was then spat upon. After she performed oral sex on two of the boys, they slapped her head with their genitals, pushed her head, poked her with sticks, and bared their bottoms at her.

Her violent sexual exploitation was recorded and sold to school children throughout Melbourne. Some sections of the DVD were posted on YouTube. As the attack gained media attention, Jarred Magnabosco, one of the attackers, gave a series of media interviews. A person claiming to be Magnabosco commented on the film's website that 'I'm proud 2 say people. im part of CUNT – THE MOVIE

(CTM) GOTTA support it! its a good cause.channel 7 fuck yer!' [grammar mistakes in original] (Houlihan and Metlikovec, 2006). The teenage girl was in counseling for months after the incident. Her father said she had been 'hoodwinked, tricked, manipulated' and she was dealing with a great deal of shame (Davis and Wallace, 2006). Unfortunately, even people who allegedly condemned the actions of the perpetrators often engaged in forms of disrespect towards the teenage woman who was 'the victim'. For instance, two Facebook groups condemning the rapists were established, but one of them contained the following derogatory comments about the young woman's disability: 'The problem with this film is that some of the Kings of Werribee got a girl from Geelong who the media widely refer to as mentally retarded, slight learning disability or other pc terms to imply that she is to put it blunty [sic] stupid academically'. Despite such prejudicial comments about the victim, this group has 43 members as of November 2009 (Facebook Group, 2009).

Eight of the boys involved in making this DVD were subsequently charged. None were charged with rape. All of them avoided youth detention. Seven of the eight boys had convictions recorded with various crimes including assault, manufacturing child pornography, and procuring sexual penetration by intimidation. They were ordered to participate in a rehabilitation program for male adolescents regarding positive sexuality (Miletic, 2006; Shtargot, 2007). One of the people who attacked this young woman (and attended this rehabilitation program) later released a CD full of grammatical errors where he criticized 'cunts who judges us', saying they can all 'get fucked'. He defiantly sung 'You're gunna to love cunt: the movie' and 'It's Werribee until I'm locked up. Why don't you go and find out what we done'. Another lyric seems to refer to avoiding jail for the attack: 'I'm still untouched. When hair got flamed. They didn't show her nude, when you look, you look, on YouTube' (Dowsley and Healey, 2009). The young man who filmed the movie (who incidentally threw the woman's jacket into a river and said she would 'have to go topless') also made a public statement later that he wanted to be an independent film maker (Roberts, 2008). Many of the people involved in the DVD became active on social networking websites across the Internet. Some had more than 500 friends on these sites. On one such website, someone claiming to be the producer of 'Cunt: the movie' also stated 'You probably know me best by my fucked up, illegal movie, which I find funny and do not regret at all' (Crawford, 2006).

The fact that these perpetrators were able to avoid detention is not an aberration, alas. One study in Massachusetts found that from 1997 to 1999, the state examined 342 crimes against disabled people. Only 18 (5%) of these cases ended with a conviction. This low conviction rate compares very poorly to the conviction rate for nondisabled people during the same period, which was 70% (Mishra, 2001). In North Carolina, a similar study revealed that although 192 state employees had been sanctioned for abuse, neglect or stealing from disabled clients, charges were filed in just 13% of cases (Biesecker and Raynor, 2008). And when it comes to disability hate crime in particular, it is very rare for the crime to be actually labeled a 'hate crime'. Even if it is labeled a disability hate crime, it is very rare for perpetrators to be charged. Even if they are charged, it is very rare for perpetrators to be found guilty. Even if they are found guilty, it is very rare for them to be incarcerated. Even if incarcerated, the chances are that they will get a light sentence. Even if they get life imprisonment, which is almost unheard of, their nonparole period will almost certainly be reduced as a result of appeals. The sentences for disability hate crimes never seem to fit the crime. This is the cycle of injustice which surrounds disability hate crimes in the legal system.

A common form of disability hate crime is to take a person's disability aid away from them – for instance, to grab a blind person's cane, or to take the walking frame of a person with a mobility impairment. It is also common to hear stories of people being tipped out of their wheelchairs or mobility scooters, sometimes resulting in death (Staff *BBC News*, 2007b; Staff *Skegness Standard*, 2007; Staff *Taranaki Daily News*, 2009; Staff *The Danbury News-Times*, 2009; Valk, 2007). In one case, the assistance dog of a wheelchair user was kidnapped and ransomed, but the abductor then vanished and did not return the dog (Kelsey, 2007). In other cases, assailants have stolen the speech-generating device of people with cerebral palsy (*KNBC.com*, 2007; *Radio New Zealand*, 2009). The prescription medications of a disabled person have also been targeted (Staff *Newark Post*, 2009). Another time, an 80-year-old man's walker was taken away from him, which made him fall and break his hip (Staff *eNews Park Forest*, 2007). One victim was threatened with a knife and had her wheelchair pushed into a wall by her boyfriend (Montijo and Lilibeth, 2009). But even when the specific object which is attacked, destroyed or stolen is a symbol of the person's disability, it is rare for these cases to be officially recognized as a disability hate crime. Another example where the object of the crime was clearly disability-related (but no one called it a disability hate crime) involved the vandalism of accessible vehicles at a Colorado Springs nonprofit agency which transports disabled people. The attacks on these accessible vans began with vandals breaking windows, stealing tires, and siphoning gas from the accessible vehicles. Two additional elements of this vandalism are important: first, there were numerous occasions on which these accessible vehicles were targeted (and a pattern of repeated victimization suggests deliberate targeting of the victim) and second, this pattern of crime victimization escalated (which is also typical of many hate crimes). In October 2009, the vandals slashed the tires on nine vehicles, far more than ever before, and they also doused one vehicle with foam from a fire extinguisher and removed a wheelchair from one of the vans and played with it in the parking lot. However, the disability organization which was targeted in the crime did not recognize this was a disability hate crime. Melissa DeSutter, the organization's community relations manager, told the *Colorado Springs Gazette*, 'It just seems like such a senseless act of vandalism on such a really awesome organization' (St. Louis-Sanchez, 2009).

Disability hate crimes take many forms. One common form of disability hate crime is for a perpetrator to confront a disabled person, deny that they are 'really disabled' and then proceed to harm them. For instance, in October 2009, a 47-year-old blind man in Washington, Tyne and Wear (England) was kicked and beaten unconscious because his attacker refused to believe he could not see. The victim, Paul Metters, had left his white cane and his guide dog with a friend as he went to the restroom, and an unknown attacker commented, 'You are not fucking blind', and began kicking and punching him (Staff *Mirror.co.uk*, 2009). Metters awoke in hospital and could not identify his attacker. It is actually quite common for blind victims to be assaulted and robbed (Staff *BBC News*, 2007a; Staff *Reporter Europe Intelligence Wire*, 30 March 2006). Another case made the headlines in February 2003 because the blind victim was not only robbed and assaulted, but was also thrown into a canal before a passerby helped him out of the water (Staff *BBC News*, 2003).

There have been many news stories in recent years of blind people being attacked and victimized. Usually, the victims of such crimes are elderly blind women. For instance, in Perth, Australia, in July 2009, a blind woman who uses a walking stick was pushed from behind, falling to the ground, and then she was kicked and robbed (Staff *AAP*, 2009). In June 2009, Ann Stratford, a 58-year-old blind woman from Swindon, England, was deliberately targeted by a thief because he saw her white cane. The 31-year-old perpetrator, Brian Whelehan, was eventually arrested and jailed for 10 months for this crime. He admitted that he targeted Stratford because of her white cane. The judge, Neil Ford QC, specifically mentioned Whelehan's reason for victimizing Stratford in his decision. Judge Ford commented, 'On June 27 this year you robbed Ann Stratford as she was walking near her mother's house. You robbed her of her handbag and the reason you targeted her as your victim was because she had a white stick' (Court, 2009). Unfortunately, there was no recognition of the fact that deliberately targeting someone because they were blind meant that the case was a disability hate crime.

Another sign that a crime may indeed be a hate crime is when a particular person or group is repeatedly targeted by perpetrators. Like other hate crimes, some of the criminals who victimize disabled people are repeat offenders. Beatrice Bunnenberg, a 92-year-old blind woman from Yonkers, New York, made the news in 2006 after she was robbed and mugged four times by the same perpetrator; many other senior citizens in the residence where she lived had also been robbed. On the fourth occasion, she was assaulted as well. She told the media, 'Like a rubber doll, just took me and threw me up against the wall and then he ripped open my nightgown and I said, "oh my God, what's he gunna do?" I thought maybe he was going to kill me' (Staff *WABC-TV/DT*, 2006).

Sometimes, a disability organization can be the target of a hate crime. Typical examples from the UK include vandals spray-painting hateful slurs on buses used to transport disabled people associated with the Myriad Centre, a day center in Worcester, in October 2009 (Staff *Berrow's Worcester Journal*, 2009); vandalism against a bus which was used to transport disabled children at the Phoenix school in Peterborough, UK, in November 2007 (Dundon, 2007); and the stoning of windows at the 'Thistle Organization', a Scottish disability residential home, in October 2008 (*Disability Now*, 2008). Of course, such vandalism is not confined to the UK. In July 2008, a center for disabled people in Even Sapir, a community on the outskirts of Jerusalem, was torched by arsonists (Sanai, 2008). The center, run by the volunteer charity organization House of Wheels, mainly serves people with muscular dystrophy and cerebral palsy and had been the target of opposition from some local residents who complained that a disability organization in their area would reduce property values. Similar protests had occurred in other areas where the House of Wheels announced plans to establish disability organizations. Fortunately, the center in Even Sapir was able to reopen three months after this hate crime.

Another case involved Mark Joe Levison, a South Seattle man, who pled guilty to malicious harassment after threatening to burn the home of an autistic child. In July 2008, he told the child's mother, 'Keep your fucking retarded son in the house or the backyard like a dog; if you don't I'll burn the (child's) room down' (L.A. Jones, 2008). The family had only moved into the house two weeks earlier and the child's mother, Acquinnette Engen, said, 'I was terrified'. According to police, Levison, 48, also said, 'I pay $1,000 a month rent and shouldn't have to see that idiot spinning around and staring at my house' (Pulkkinen, 2008). Levison was again arrested a few months later for similar behavior. One report indicated that he had repeatedly threatened to burn down the home, had also taken to imitating the autistic child and had challenged the child's father to a fight. Levison had a prior conviction for breach of peace in an unrelated incident, and had been previously charged with assault and criminal trespass, as well as other misdemeanors and felonies (Staff *Seattle Times*, 2008a). He pleaded guilty in November 2008 to one count of malicious harassment, a felony, and one count of attempted malicious harassment, a misdemeanor. Levison was sentenced to nearly four months in jail, as well as a one-year suspended sentence that could be imposed if he violated the conditions of his release during the next two years. Levison was also ordered to undergo substance abuse treatment and anger management classes; he was a self-described 'alcoholic' and told the judge, 'When I'm sober, I would never say words like that' (Staff *Seattle Times*, 2008b).

People with many different types of impairments have been the victims of hate crimes. A woman with speech and mobility impairments was verbally and physically assaulted in Lincolnshire, England, in February 2009 when she was exercising her dog. The 44-year-old was in Wellhead Park, Bourne, when two teenagers began using disability hate speech against her. They taunted her with words such as 'spastic', and were calling out 'What's wrong with you?' and then they tipped over her mobility scooter and ran off. Lincolnshire Police spokesman James Newall said at the time, 'This is an absolutely disgusting crime that would have deeply shaken the woman. The references to her disability do aggravate the nature of the crime. This puts it into the hate crime category, which is very serious' (Morrish, 2009). Newall commented in a personal interview that there was a big appeal in the local media for witnesses, but no one came forward and no one was ever charged. 'Either no one saw it or no one was prepared to come forward', he said.

Another hate crime where such taunts were used occurred in 1999 in Oklahoma, USA, where a man with cerebral palsy was taunted with quite similar hate speech. Among the slurs which were said to him were, 'You belong in the trash, you cripple'. The hate speech accompanied a hate crime – in this case, he was stuffed into a trash can. The victim was unable to call for help because of his speech impairment (Consortium for Citizens with Disabilities, 1999). Another case where hate speech accompanied a crime occurred in Waterford, England, in August 2007. In that case, one handicapped parking sign was removed, another was vandalized with various hateful slurs painted all over it and the car of a man with a learning disability was egged. The graffiti on the handicapped parking sign was interesting – physically written onto the parking sign (itself a symbol of one socially marginalized identity) were homophobic and racist comments. The comments illustrate the interlocking nature of many prejudices. A base coat of white paint covered the handicapped parking sign and on top in blue spray paint were such slurs as 'dick sucker', 'fudge packer' and 'nigger lover'. The handicap sign was being used by an openly gay black man with a learning disability; his medical advocate (who is not gay) is white (Michael, 2007).

Valerie Gillespie, the mother of a 14-year-old Canadian boy with a developmental disability, accused a Paratransit driver of committing a hate crime against her son in May 2009. The case involved a boy who cannot control the amount of mucous in his mouth and as a result spits as he clears his mouth. He was riding in a Paratransit van operated by 'Pat and the Elephant'. Paratransit vans provide door-to-door transportation for disabled people. The boy attempted to clear his mouth as he exited the vehicle. As a result, sputum got on the van's door. The driver wiped the sputum off the van door and then wiped it over the boy's face, saying he would 'teach the boy a lesson'. The boy's mother, Valerie Gillespie, said her son was traumatized by the event. The man, Palo Victor Szerman, pleaded guilty in Prince Edward Island Provincial Court to assaulting Gillespie's son. Szerman was not charged with a disability hate crime, but pled guilty to assault. Judge John Douglas gave Szerman a conditional discharge, six months suspension, instructed him to write a letter of apology to the mother, and ordered that he donate $400 to a children's disability charity. Szerman was not fired from his job; his employer, Pat and the Elephant, transferred him temporarily to a position where he drove for disabled adults, and promised to return him to his position driving for disabled children in the following fall, after a 'cooling off period' (Staff *CBC News Canada*, 2009). Some disability advocates suggest that this case was another example of incredibly lenient penalties for those convicted of crimes against disabled people.

Another hate crime involved people with developmental disabilities in Cheektowaga, New York. Four perpetrators made numerous slurs about the victims' disabilities as the victims left a McDonald's restaurant. They then followed the victims from the restaurant. The perpetrators drove three cars, two of which pursued the victims' car closely, while the third stayed some distance behind. One of the cars, driven by 18-year-old Sean Kwiatkowski, came dangerously close to hitting the victims' car. As they fled their tormentors, the victims' car crashed. The victims suffered minor injuries but their car was heavily damaged (Watson, 2007). Three of the perpetrators were initially charged with a felony hate crime, and Kwiatkowski was indicted by a grand jury of the felony hate crime of reckless endangerment, but through a plea deal Kwiatkowski was found guilty of a misdemeanor count of reckless endangerment (Gryta, 2008). As an 18-year-old, he was given a 'youthful offender conviction' – sealing the records of the case and removing the criminal record from his name.

On August 16, 2009, members of the Owego Police Department in New York arrested another alleged perpetrator of a hate crime after a series of assaults on someone with a cognitive impairment. Patrick D. Hayward was accused of shooting the 31-year-old victim with a BB gun, striking the victim with a tire iron and golf club, and sexually abusing the victim. He was charged with two counts of felony assault in the second degree, one count of assault in the third degree (hate crime), one count of menacing in the second degree (hate crime), two counts of reckless endangerment in the second degree, and misdemeanor counts of 'endangering the welfare of a mentally incompetent person', criminal possession of a weapon and forcible touching. Hayward was arraigned in the Village of Owego Court and remanded to the Tioga County jail in lieu of $25,000 cash bail. The case is ongoing at the time of writing.

It seems that 'soft' sentences are routine when the victim is disabled. One well-known disabled crime victim was Christine Lakinski, a 53-year-old woman with cognitive and physical disabilities and a chronic digestive condition. She had been the victim of abuse and disability harassment all her life, and her death was no different. She had fallen and lay actively dying from pancreatic failure outside her home in Hartlepool, in northeast England. Anthony Anderson, who lived across the street from Lakinski, saw her dying on the ground. But Anderson did not call an ambulance. Instead, he doused her in cold water and shaving foam before finally urinating on her motionless and dying body. Then he and others covered her body with some laminate flooring which she had been carrying. Others watched as Anderson urinated on the dying woman, including one of Anderson's friends who videoed the incident on his cell phone. Anderson shouted, 'This is YouTube material!' (Staff *Northern Echo*, 2008). An autopsy showed that Lakinski died from natural causes (pancreatic failure) and Anderson, 27, was simply charged with 'outraging public decency'. He was sentenced to three years in prison (Staff *Daily Mail*, 2007b). This was a sentence which many disability advocates considered far too lenient. Nevertheless, Anderson exercised his right to appeal the sentence. His appeal was dismissed.

The act of urinating upon the victim is an incredibly disturbing but not uncommon occurrence associated with some disability hate crimes. Urinating often happens to a vulnerable (and usually unconscious) victim at the end of a disability hate crime. It involves acting out a sadistic and sociopathic fantasy that completely debases the victim through a smelly, degrading, violent, and sexual act. The fact that such public urination is associated with (usually male) genital exhibition further demonstrates the intent to dehumanize, objectify, violate and sexually degrade the victim. Victims are violated, demeaned and dominated through the connection of human waste and hyperviolent physical and sexual aggression. The smell, as well as the wetness of the urine, soaks the body. Urination also symbolizes sexual domination – the naked genitals being exposed and used as a weapon against a victim. Using urine, rather than defecation, seems to suggest a closer connection to the act of sex – but it is indeed a particular kind of rageful, hyperviolent, sadistic sex. Like the hate crime itself, the act of urination encapsulates a degree of disdain, disrespect, coercion and violence that harms the victim physically, psychologically and sexually. It also underlines the dangerousness of perpetrators.

Another illustration of the hyperviolent nature of many disability hate crimes involved the violent attack on Kerri Delacruz, a 38-year-old woman with Degenerative Joint Disease in 2009. She had been the victim of harassment for six months prior to this attack, but this crime was a significant escalation of the previous attacks. The attackers began by violently killing her Yorkshire Terrier dog, knifing it and leaving its body hanging by a pole in the garden. Delacruz, who lives in Liverpool, England, was then attacked. Four people, roughly aged between 14 and 21, took turns in slashing her body with a five-inch kitchen knife. They slashed Delacruz across the breasts, face, back, and hands. She received 14 stitches to the wounds on her breast, eight stitches on her cheek, and six on her hand. There should be no doubt this was a hate crime: the perpetrators swore at her and said she was a 'spastic' who 'should've been drowned at birth'. One said, 'What will happen if we cut the metal out of your spine?' (leaving Delacruz stunned and confused about their knowledge of her medical history). On three occasions they re-cut the wounds that they had already inflicted on her breasts (Johnson, 2009; Staff *CBS News Los Angeles*, 2009; Staff *Mail Online*, 2009).

Some unique forms of crimes have arisen as disabled people have been specifically targeted for attack. For example, the 'Coping With Epilepsy' website, a peer support forum for people living with epilepsy, was attacked by hackers during November 2007 (Coping With Epilepsy, 2007). November is Epilepsy Awareness Month. The hackers posted hateful messages, pornographic images, and also images which flashed quickly in an attempt to trigger seizures. The organization issued a press release which is quite instructive in terms of the ways disability hate crime is perceived by victims. Although this hacking was targeted specifically at a group of disabled people, during a month aimed to increase disability awareness, and specifically sought to create a seizure among people with epilepsy, it was apparently not recognized as a disability hate crime. Instead, Bernard Ertl, the Coping With Epilepsy Administrator, is quoted in the press release as saying, 'It was just a bunch of very immature people delighting in their attempts to cause people misery'.

This was not the only time that people had maliciously targeted people with epilepsy over the Internet in this way. A few months later, in March 2008, the website of the Epilepsy Foundation was attacked by hackers who used a script to post hundreds of messages embedded with flashing animated gifs (a particular kind of computer animation), also designed to trigger seizures. The next day, the hackers returned, using JavaScript to redirect users' browsers to a page with a more complex image designed to trigger seizures in both photosensitive and pattern-sensitive epileptics. One victim was RyAnne Fultz, 33, who reported having her worst seizure in a year as a result of the images. The whole website of the Epilepsy Foundation had to be temporarily shut down while the offending measures were removed and better security procedures were adopted (Poulsen, 2008). Again, the disability organization did not seem to recognize the attack as a hate crime. Instead Eric R. Hargis, president and CEO of the Epilepsy Foundation, described it as 'an act of vandalism' (Epilepsy Foundation, 2008). There is a significant difference between an act of vandalism and a hate crime – they demand different responses from law enforcement, for instance – but this point seems to have eluded disability advocates in this case.

Blind people have also been the victims of disability hate crimes. One blind victim who has spoken publicly about her experiences is Heather Owens from Belfast, Ireland. When there was a debate about including disability in hate crime laws in 2004, Owens told the *Belfast Telegraph*, 'I have had fireworks thrown into my garden and have been verbally abused on several occasions because of my blindness … Too often in the past such incidents have been brushed under the carpet, or there has been little point in reporting them' (Grattan, 2004). As Owens said, many disabled people are repeatedly victimized – and repeat victimization is itself one possible indicator that a criminal act is not random, but may instead be motivated by bias. Like Owens, another blind woman, Skye Banning from Australia, has also spoken about being repeatedly targeted. Banning was mugged for the sixth time in January 2007 near her home in the Sydney suburb of Bondi and suffered severe facial injuries. Banning did not refer to her experiences as hate crimes, but her comments did reveal some of the effects of repeat victimization. 'You almost get worn down by it happening all the time … it just seems to happen all the time and it seems that when you're disabled you've got to live with it', she said. Importantly, Banning had never reported her previous muggings and robberies, because she could not give a description of the perpetrators (Rich, 2007).

The connection between disability and homelessness is well established, so it would be remiss not to acknowledge the hundreds of hate crimes which have been reported against homeless people. In the US, many of these crimes are documented in the annual report 'Hate, Violence and Death on Main Street USA: A Report on Hate Crimes and Violence against People Experiencing Homelessness'. The 2008 report indicates that their organization alone has recorded 880 violent attacks on homeless people in the last 10 years, including 244 murders – with many crimes that are shocking in their brutality (National Coalition for the Homeless, 2009). For instance, the organization has identified cases of people being set on fire, shot, beaten to death, run over, kidnapped and even beheaded. An earlier report on hate crimes against homeless people had included the case of 50-year-old Doug R. Dawson, an amputee wheelchair user from Spokane, Washington, who was attacked and burned to death in June 2006 (National Coalition for the Homeless, 2007). This was not considered a disability hate crime, however, even though the offender had no grievance against Dawson and had not even spoken to Dawson prior to setting him on fire. Dawson had newspaper underneath him in his wheelchair, and witnesses said he and the wheelchair 'lit up like a candle'; his body was so badly burned that (at first) medics did not even realize that a human being was involved (Jamieson, 2006). Interestingly, in terms of the poor treatment of homeless disabled veterans, just before Dawson was set alight, he had been refused entry to the Union Gospel Mission (a homeless shelter) on the grounds that his disability meant he would not be able to do the chores normally required of people who sleep at the Mission (Levine, 2006).

Even if there is evidence of disability bias, and a case is regarded as a disability hate crime, there are no guarantees that those charges will go to trial or that they will be successfully prosecuted. For instance, on April 12, 2006, Patrick John Dizon Solis, 23, and Michael Douglas Rama, 25, cornered a mentally disabled adult in a restroom at Jossen Vocational Academy in Anaheim, California. They slapped the man repeatedly and recorded the attack on Rama's cell phone video camera. Solis was the primary caregiver of the victim, who appears on the video shrieking and cowering in fear. Both Solis and Rama were charged with a hate crime. However the judge, the Honorable David Hoffer, dismissed the hate crime charges and enhancements that had been filed against both Solis and Rama (Pulkkinen, 2008; Staff *Seattle Times*, 2008). Solis pleaded guilty to a misdemeanor count of battery and a felony count of false imprisonment of a dependant adult and was sentenced to 90 days in jail. Rama pleaded guilty on February 22, 2008 to one misdemeanor count of permitting a dependant adult to be injured. (Rama had previously participated in the abuse of another dependant adult on March 22, 2006 and had also recorded that incident on a cell phone video camera. In that video, someone is laughing in the background.) Rama co-operated with the prosecution in the Solis case and was sentenced to 30 days' imprisonment. But neither of these convictions was officially recorded as a disability hate crime.

The case of Levi Kielsmeier was another one where charges were initially laid indicating that the crime involved a disability hate crime, but the hate crime charges were dropped. Kielsmeier was 15 and, along with 13-year-old Coby John Winters, he committed numerous crimes against Lloyd Sterns, a 44-year-old developmentally disabled man. (Two other boys participated in some of the actions against Sterns at various times in the day as well.) They burned some of Sterns' property, including books, magazines, a coffee basket, and coffee percolator parts. Some of the items burned while others melted and were thrown on the floor. Sterns had to stomp out some of these fires, and they left holes and scorch marks on the floor. The boys also threw kitchen knives in a door, pushed Sterns into a running shower, duct-taped Sterns' arms together, operated a lawn mower in the living room and hinted that they would use it to run over Sterns' feet, and then forcefully poured mouthwash into Sterns' mouth. They also called Sterns derogatory names, put their hands down his shirt, pinched his nipples, and broke some of his upstairs windows. Sterns asked them to leave his home on many occasions. After some time, they did leave – but they returned on two occasions that day, committing more crimes when they did. The first time they returned, they defecated on a table and urinated on the floor. Then they rubbed feces in Sterns' hair, claiming it was good for him. Kielsmeier pulled Sterns' shorts down and laughed at him. They also tried to spray insecticide into Sterns' eyes. The boys left, but returned a second time. When they returned, Sterns had gone to a nearby lake and was returning home. They followed him, trying to shove him into the lake, and nearly running him over with a moped. Kielsmeier again pulled Sterns' pants down. They also raised their fists at him. Although Kielsmeier was initially charged with a disability hate crime, these charges were not pursued. He was simply convicted of the delinquent acts of arson, burglary, criminal mischief, assault while participating in a felony, and trespass. Sterns is another disabled crime victim who has not *officially* been affected by hate crime.

A low rate of prosecution is not unique to disability hate crimes. In general, there is a very low rate of prosecution and conviction for hate crimes. Boston has been cited as a national model for hate crime investigations, and yet a study of 452 hate crimes in Boston between 1983 and 1987 found that approximately 85% of offenders were not arrested, and charges were dropped against one-third of those arrested. For a total of 452 incidents, many of which were extremely violent, only five individuals were sent to jail (Levin and McDevitt, 2002).

Often a crime which is initially regarded as a hate crime is eventually reclassified as a different type of criminal act – one with lesser penalties. This can occur for various reasons. For instance, one case which was initially framed as a disability hate crime, but was reclassified as a misdemeanor assault, involved a violent attack on a student with a prosthetic leg in Cape Girardeau, Missouri. The victim was Michael Williams, 18, a senior at Cape Central High School. Williams was standing in a parking lot when a car pulled up with two teens inside. Williams is missing half his right arm and wears a prosthetic leg. 'What's up, nubs?' one teen said. They harassed Williams, punched him in the face several times, kicked him in the ribs and the face, and then, according to Williams, one of the attackers used the victim's own prosthetic leg as a weapon with which to beat him. Williams' lip, jaw and neck were injured. One of the perpetrators, Alexander S. Harris, was charged with felony third-degree assault. The charge was classified as a hate crime because the assault was motivated by Williams' disability. This meant that the crime was considered a felony rather than a misdemeanor. The other perpetrator was a 16-year-old boy who was cited into juvenile court for assault and curfew violation. Even though hate crime charges were laid in this case, the adult suspect struck a plea deal and was only found guilty of misdemeanor assault. This was not simply a back-down by prosecutors, however. Part of the reason for the dropped charges, according to *AAP* reports, was that there was a change in the victim's story. He originally said he was struck in the face and blacked out, only to awaken to find he was being beaten with the prosthetic leg. However, in a preliminary hearing, Williams remembered the prosthetic leg becoming dislodged but offered no testimony about being struck with it (Staff *Associated Press KAIT Jonesboro AR*, 2006).

One might hope that crimes where someone is beaten with a prosthetic leg would have never occurred before (or after) the attack on Williams. Sadly, this is not the case. There have been many, many crimes involving such attacks using prosthetics – and they are almost never considered hate crimes. For instance in 2006, four teenage boys in Chicago were arrested on misdemeanor battery charges after a young man's prosthetic was used against him as a weapon (Bowean, 2006). In Buffalo, New York, in 2007, a group of men attacked Richard Kelly, an amputee. They removed his prosthetic leg, beat him with it and then ran over him with a car while he lay on the ground, leading to a punctured lung, broken ribs, and skin abrasions (Staff *Associated Press*, 2007d). Similarly, in North Huntingdon, Pennsylvania, in January 2008, Donna Sturkie-Anthony, 41, was arrested for using her sister's prosthetic leg to beat her on the face and head (Dobranski, 2008).

Stealing the individualized prosthetic leg of a disabled person is another unique, and unfortunately common, aspect of disability hate crimes. Such crimes have occurred throughout the world, despite the fact that prosthetics can only be used by the individual for whom they were individually created. Some examples of this crime may indicate how it is a global phenomenon. In Australia in 2008, Brendan Burkett, a multiple Paralympic medalist, had his prosthetic leg stolen, costing him approximately $6,000 to replace (Elsworth, 2008; Ja, 2008). Another Australian case occurred in 2004, when a woman had both her prosthetic legs stolen while she was swimming at the Melbourne Sports and Aquatic Centre (Staff *The Age Newspaper*, 2004). In Canada in 2003, Paralympian Paul Rosen also had his prosthetic leg stolen (he later also had his Paralympic gold medal stolen, and then returned) (Teotonio, 2007). In Wales in 2006, John McFall, a disabled athlete, had his prosthetic leg stolen and eventually returned (Staff *BBC News*, 2006a). None of these crimes were regarded as a hate crime, however – underscoring the importance of knowing exactly what is, and what is not, a hate crime.

Many crimes against disabled people are senseless, horrific, and despicable acts. And it is tempting, but wrong, to assume that without any other apparent motive, a crime must have been motivated by disability bias or disability hatred – or at least a sense that the person was selected as the victim of a crime because their disability made them seem like an 'easy target'. This may, or may not, be the case. Criminals have many motivations. For instance, on January 9, 2007, in North Las Vegas, an elderly woman who used a motorized wheelchair was robbed. She was not physically harmed in the robbery, but it seems that the stress of the attack resulted in a fatal heart attack. No one has been charged with this crime, even though it has featured on the television show *America's Most Wanted* (*America's Most Wanted*, 2008). This was undoubtedly a tragic and despicable act – and as an elderly disabled woman, Josephine Muscolo would have appeared an easy target to many people. But that does not guarantee that her disability was the reason she was targeted.

The rate of crime against disabled people is much higher than for nondisabled people. A National Crime Victimization Study by the US Bureau of Justice Statistics published in October 2009 indicated that disabled people are 1.5 times more likely to experience nonfatal violent crimes and more than twice as likely to experience rape or sexual assault. People with cognitive impairments were more likely than other disabled people to be the victims of crime, and disabled women were more likely to be victimized than disabled men. People with more than one type of disability were especially vulnerable to violent attacks. They were the victims in 56% of all violent crime victimizations against disabled people (Rand and Harrell, 2009). In the UK, a report entitled *Promoting Safety and Security of Disabled People* by the Equality and Human Rights Commission reported that disabled people are four times more likely to be a victim of crime than nondisabled people (Equality and Human Rights Commission, 2009).

Hate Crimes or Bias Crimes?

The terminology chosen in this book is to refer to these crimes as 'hate crimes'. There is a specific political reason for this choice: most people refuse to believe that anyone could *hate* another human being because they are disabled. The term 'hate' evokes a visceral, venomous emotion, tainted with various negative emotions such as loathing, repulsion, and enmity. And yet the entire purpose of this book is to demonstrate that such animosity is indeed widespread. Additionally, this is the term by which such crimes are known in the community, and it is also the term used by disability organizations campaigning for recognition of such crimes. However, many governments have avoided the term 'hate crime' and have used the term 'bias crime' in their legislative responses. There is also some merit in the terminology 'bias crime'. The language of 'hate' captures a visceral, emotive dimension which is missing in the terminology of 'bias' – but the language of 'bias' captures additional elements about nonrandom selection of victims that may not be purely emotionally grounded. Levin suggests that people may actually engage in bias crimes and various forms of discriminatory behavior towards a particular group based on other motivations, and then develop significant emotional animus towards the victimized group after the commission of such crimes. Essentially, Levin suggests that behavior may precede emotions when it comes to the commission of bias crimes: 'Prejudices often develop or at least become strengthened to justify previous discriminatory behavior, including violence' (Levin, 2007).

All that is needed to prove that someone has committed a 'bias crime' is that they selected the victim *because of* the victim's identity characteristics. For instance, a perpetrator who selects a victim *because of* their disability identity is committing a bias crime, even if they do not (ostensibly) 'hate' disabled people. The mere fact that someone is targeted because of an identity is enough to prove that the perpetrator has committed a bias crime.

It is incredibly important to examine the particular language used in various state and national legislation when it comes to disability hate crimes, or disability bias crimes. For something to be a 'bias crime', all that is needed is for the selection of the victim to be wholly or partly motivated by the identity of the victim (i.e. they chose that victim – in part or in whole – because of the victim's identity). In other words, a bias crime means that the victim is not selected randomly; the identity characteristics of the victim are important in the perpetrator's choice of victim. A perpetrator need not choose a victim because they 'hate' disabled people, but if they choose a disabled victim thinking that he/she would be an 'easy target', that is sufficient evidence to demonstrate that the victim was not selected randomly; bias played a part in the decision. A disability hate crime or a disability bias crime, then, is a criminal act motivated by the victim's real or perceived disability status. The perpetrator must not select the victim randomly – the disability identity of the victim must be an important factor in why the perpetrator chose *that* victim.

It is essential that disability hate crimes be recognized as such – as a crime – and not as a form of 'abuse' (which is unfortunately used as a catch-all term for many types of crime that involve disabled people). Disabled people do not need a different vocabulary for criminal victimization; a crime is a crime. When someone steals from a nondisabled person, it is almost inevitably labeled a crime and called 'theft'. Unfortunately, there seems to be a completely different vocabulary when it comes to disability. Stealing money from a disabled person is often called 'financial abuse'. Likewise, hitting someone who is nondisabled is automatically called 'assault'; but hitting a disabled person is usually (often unconsciously) reframed as 'physical abuse'. The language of 'abuse' is incredibly problematic because it seems to decriminalize various acts against disabled people. But even studies written by scholars in the field of disability continue to use the 'abuse' discourse, seemingly without acknowledging the criminal nature of the acts being discussed. For instance, a study of men with physical disabilities recorded what would usually be called criminal acts – such as when a person 'hits, kicks, slaps or otherwise physically hurts' the disabled person, 'steals medication', or 'touches sexually or forces sexual activity in unwanted ways' – but the term 'crime' never occurs once in the whole article (Powers et al., 2008). That is typical of the entire 'disability and abuse' genre. 'Sexual abuse', 'financial abuse', 'steals medication' – these are common in the discourse of disability and victimization; but 'rape', 'molestation', 'robbery', 'larceny', 'assault', and other terms which are clearly related to crime seem eerily absent.

In order to be a disability hate crime, two requirements must be satisfied: first, it must be a criminal act (for instance, theft, murder, arson, vandalism, assault, robbery, intimidation); and second, it must be motivated in whole or in part by the victim's real or perceived disability status. (A person who is targeted for criminal victimization on a mistaken assumption that they are disabled is still covered under most hate crime laws.) Under most hate crime legislation, the disability identity of the victim need not be the only motivation – it simply has to be a major contributing factor in the choices of the perpetrator. A criminal act against a disabled person is not necessarily a disability hate crime – there needs to be evidence that the disability identity of the victim was a significant factor in the crime. Such evidence may be found in the confessions of perpetrators, comments made in the commission of the crime, repeated victimization of people with similar identities, the presence of hate group material, the destruction of symbols associated with disability, and so on. The presence of multiple perpetrators victimizing a single individual may also suggest a need to explore possible bias motivations for the crime.

Hate crimes tend to be associated with high levels of violence. Compared to other forms of crime, hate crimes are far more likely to involve physical threat and harm to individuals, rather than property. Victims of a hate crime are three times more likely to require hospitalization than victims of a nonbias assault (Bodinger-De Uriate and Sancho, 1990). In one study, half the victims of hate crimes were assaulted. This is a significantly higher rate than the national crime average, where only 7% of crimes involve assault (Levin and McDevitt, 2002). The psychological consequences of hate crimes also seem to be more significant than those for nonbias crimes, in terms of depression, anger, anxiety and post-traumatic stress (Herek et al., 1999; Herek et al., 1997). Many hate crimes involve multiple perpetrators (whereas most assaults usually involve two mutual combatants) and often the victims are unarmed while the perpetrators are armed (Bodinger-De Uriate and Sancho, 1990). Also, perpetrators of hate crimes often do not live in the area where they commit the crimes. They frequently spend time and money in travelling to unfamiliar areas in order to perpetrate the crime (Medoff, 1999). And in most property crimes, something of value is stolen, but hate crimes that involve property are more likely to entail the destruction rather than the theft of that property.

The following characteristics may indicate that a hate crime has occurred:

- symbols or words associated with hate;
- activities historically associated with threats to certain groups (e.g. burning crosses);
- comments, gestures or written statements that reflect bias;
- jokes which are demeaning and offensive;
- destroying or defacing group symbols;
- a history of crimes against other members of the group;
- crimes occurring shortly after group activities or conflicts involving the group;
- the belief of victims or witnesses that the action was motivated by bias;
- perpetrators demeaning the victim's group and exalting their own group;
- recent public or political exposure that may have highlighted the victim's identity;
- evidence on the offender's computer which may indicate membership of an organized hate group;
- comments by an offender that indicate the victim was a member of a 'target' group;

- the presence of hate group literature; or
- previous hate crimes in the community.

There are two victims with hate crimes – individuals and communities. Hate crimes not only represent an attack on the rights and freedoms of individuals, they indicate a lack of physical safety for many people in minority communities. Hate crimes are crimes against a community because the message of intolerance which they send can terrorize particular groups. As a result, penalty enhancement is a common response to hate crimes. In the literature on hate crimes, three reasons are generally given to explain why hate crimes deserve a different response from other crimes: first, hate crimes inflict more psychological harm than do nonbias crimes; second, hate crimes have negative impact upon communities by spreading fear and anger; and third, the bias which is expressed when the crime is committed has its own meaning which is separate from the actual crime (S.E. Martin, 1996). Hate crimes not only represent an attack on the rights and freedoms of individuals, they also flag that an area may be unsafe for other members of the targeted minority. Hate crimes are therefore sometimes considered crimes against a community because their message of intolerance can terrorize whole groups of people. For instance, a place where disabled people have been threatened or attacked may become informally regarded as a 'no go zone' which is avoided by many disabled people – not just the individual who has been personally victimized. Hate crimes also frequently involve multiple perpetrators – bullies, in effect. This is unlike nonbias crimes where assault cases usually involve only two combatants (Sherry, 2004). Some of the practical consequences of hate crimes are that other members of the targeted population may move away from or avoid the area, or may significantly alter their routines to enhance their safety (Craig, 2002).

One unique aspect of hate crimes is that they involve 'parallel crimes' (Jenness and Grattet, 2001). That is, there are two crimes embedded in a single act: a crime such as vandalism, theft, arson, murder, or assault, and another crime, a bias crime. In order to prove that any bias crime has occurred, it is necessary to demonstrate that the offender discriminates in the selection of his or her victim. In order to prove a *disability* hate crime exists, discrimination on the basis of real or perceived disability must be a substantial reason for inflicting a crime upon this particular individual. An example of a case where the perpetrator was alleged to have targeted a disabled person because of the disability is the (ongoing) case of James A. Gustafson, a 35-year-old man from Burlington, Wisconsin. Gustafson was charged with a hate crime after allegedly contacting a mentally disabled woman and scamming over $7,000 from her. He was charged with two counts of theft by false representation with a hate crime enhancement. Allegedly, Gustafson phoned the woman posing as a psychic and said that her deceased father wanted to speak to her. He later allegedly pretended to be her father and said, 'How are you doing? I see you ride your bike. I love you. If you wish to speak to me again, you need to go into the backyard and bury $430.00 and wait a couple of days and

I will call you'. The woman buried the money in the backyard and continued to do so until she had been scammed of over $7,000.

Hate crimes are not 'abuse', 'bullying' or 'antisocial behavior'. Abuse is often a catch-all term for negative experiences, and effectively becomes a synonym for crimes against disabled people. Bullying involves aggression and imbalances of power, but does not necessarily involve criminal acts. Conversely, when 'bullying' involves physical assault or vandalism, we should recognize it for what it is: a criminal act. When someone is a victim of crime, they have not just experienced 'abuse'. Unfortunately, in the field of disability, serious crimes (including rape, theft, assault, vandalism and so on) are frequently mislabeled as 'abuse'. Likewise, 'antisocial behavior' conjures up a set of legal and psychiatric definitions, which are not necessarily complimentary. Antisocial behavior can be anything that is likely to cause harassment, alarm or distress to another person. Crimes (such as rape, murder, theft) are in quite a different league. For instance, sexual harassment of Deaf people by nuisance callers sending obscene and malicious messages via text phones is also a unique form of disability hate crime which may be mislabeled as 'abuse' (Shakespeare et al., 1996). Likewise, it was not 'abuse' when the schoolmates of an 18-year-old North Carolina high school student with a developmental disability soaked his lunch in cleaning fluid and watched him eat it. He experienced life-threatening poisoning and had to be taken to intensive care (Consortium for Citizens with Disabilities, 1999). This was a violent and life-threatening crime; it was not 'abuse'. Such violent crimes need to be punished as such.

There is a great deal of evidence to suggest that disabled people are more likely than others to be victimized, and to be the victims of crime more generally. For instance, many studies from various countries indicate that people with mental illness experience much higher rates of both violent and nonviolent crimes than the general population (Fitzgerald et al., 2005; Hsu et al., 2009; Maniglio, 2009; Teplin et al., 2005). Likewise, studies consistently indicate much higher rates of sexual assault among disabled people than nondisabled people (Brownlie et al., 2007; Casteel et al., 2008; Grossman and Lundy, 2008; Martin et al., 2006; Powers et al., 2008; Saxton et al., 2006). Of course, there are different rates and different types of criminal victimization depending on a range of factors including the person's gender, age and the nature of the disability. But this book is not about crime victimization in general. It is about a specific form of criminal victimization – hate crime. Hate crimes are unlike many other crimes – both in terms of the motivation of the perpetrator and the impact on the victim. Demonstrating exactly how disability hate crimes are different from other crimes is one of the purposes of this book.

In the US, one publication from the Office of Justice Statistics compared official crime reports with victim reports and suggested that the actual number of hate crimes is 15 times the number reported by the FBI. Even the National Criminal Victimization Survey found that on average, 210,000 crimes are reported by victims every year but only 10,000 are included in FBI reports. Additionally, the survey suggests that less than half of the actual numbers of hate crimes are reported annually. Additionally, only half of complaints to police are actually reported. This report suggests that the actual number of hate crimes which occur annually in the US is closer to 400,000 (Bureau of Justice Statistics, 2005).

In many places, disability is not a category which is included in hate crime legislation. This means that some cases which may have been prosecuted as disability hate crimes (and therefore would have been subject to penalty enhancement) were not treated in this way. Many countries have hate crime statutes that prohibit and penalize hate crimes on the basis of race, religion, ethnicity, and other factors – but consistently fail to include disability in hate crime laws. This is somewhat odd, given that disability is frequently included in the antidiscrimination provisions of these countries.

Another problem which complicates the reporting of disability hate crimes is that many cases which might seem, *prima facie*, to be a disability hate crime are actually covered under other laws around abuse, maltreatment, or neglect of a disabled person (meaning that they are often not technically classified as a 'hate crime'). The case of Mark Reed Downs, a 27-year-old t-ball coach from Philadelphia, illustrates this problem. (t-ball is a children's version of baseball.) Downs was coaching a children's team in 2005 when he offered one of his players $25 to hit Harry Bowers Jr., an 11-year-old autistic boy on their own team, in the head with a baseball during warm-ups so that he would be unable to play that day. After speaking to the coach, the player threw a ball which bounced and then hit the disabled child in the groin with a pitch. Bowers ran off crying to his mother. She sent him back out to practice and the other child hit him again, this time in the ear. Bowers was unable to play in the game and was taken to The Uniontown Hospital. Bowers was targeted because his autism meant that he was not a great player, and every player is required to play three innings unless they are injured. The boy who threw the balls, Keith Reese Jr., was one of the better pitchers in their team and the team was in the play-offs (finals) that day. He testified in court that after he had struck Bowers on the first occasion, 'He (Downs) told me to go out there and hit him harder. So I went out there and hit him in the ear'. Reese Jr. testified that he did not receive the $25 from Downs. Interestingly, even though Bowers' disability seems central to the case, the charges brought against Downs did not include hate crime. He was convicted of criminal solicitation to commit simple assault and corruption of minors. Downs was found not guilty of the more serious charge of criminal solicitation to commit aggravated assault, and the jury could not reach agreement on whether his actions constituted reckless endangerment. Downs was sentenced to one to six years in prison but was granted bond while appealing to the state Superior Court (Ayad, 2006; Brittain, 2005; Foreman, 2005, 2007; Staff *Pittsburgh Post Gazette*, 2007).

Some people find it hard to understand why anyone would want to commit a crime against a disabled person. The UK disability movement has relied on the concept of 'disablism' to explain the widespread patterns of discrimination and prejudice which disabled people experience. Disablism is a term that is widely used, especially in the UK, to describe the social exclusion, marginalization, prejudice, and discrimination experienced by disabled people. Disablism has many dimensions – it occurs through stereotypical attitudes and prejudices and is reproduced in social institutions such as the media, the built environment, educational institutions, religions, and even in the family. Disablism occurs in a myriad of ways in everyday situations, but always diminishes the rights, freedoms and opportunities available to disabled people. Disability hate crimes are one manifestation of a much wider power dynamic that socially excludes, marginalizes, and discriminates against disabled people.

A Global Problem

Although some people continue to question whether disability hate crimes actually exist, awareness of disability hate crimes is rising globally. It is becoming widely recognized that disability hate crimes are a serious form of criminal activity which greatly affect the lives of victims and deserve greater recognition and more effective responses. Before 1997, the FBI did not even collect data on disability hate crimes. It was assumed that 'no one actually hates people with disabilities', so the problem was ignored. However, national and international awareness of disability hate crimes has been increasing in recent years and many legislatures have moved to include disability in hate crime legislation. The Local Law Enforcement Hate Crimes Prevention Act of 2007, otherwise known as the *Matthew Shepard Act*, is one such initiative in the US (though that law also covers other forms of hate crimes as well).

Many countries have included disability in hate crime legislation, including Canada, Brazil, Belgium, Northern Ireland, Spain, Wales, England, Scotland, Romania and Andorra. Since 1966 the Canadian Criminal Code has included a penalty-enhancement provision for crimes 'motivated by bias, prejudice or hate based on racial group, national or ethnic origin, language, colour, religion, sex, age, mental or physical disability, sexual orientation, or any other similar factor'. Civil remedies are also available in Canada for discriminatory acts. Penalty enhancement legislation for crimes motivated by antidisability bias also exists in Brazil. This is established in Article 140 of the Brazilian Penal Code, which established a harsher penalty (from a minimum of one year to a maximum of three years) for hate crimes motivated by prejudice against race, color, ethnicity, religion, nationality, disability and age. In Belgium, the Anti-Discrimination Act of February 25, 2003, specifically addresses hate crimes. Articles 7–14 of the Act provide that '… hatred against, contempt for, or hostility to a person on the grounds of his so-called race, color, descent, national or ethnic origin, sex, sexual orientation, marital status, birth, fortune, age, beliefs or philosophy of life, current and future state of health, a disability or physical characteristic' are aggravating circumstances in respect of a certain number of offences. In Northern Ireland, the Criminal Justice (No. 2) (NI) Order 2004 introduced a statutory requirement for judges to treat racial, religious, sexual, and disability hatred as an aggravating factor when sentencing. It also gave judges the power to increase maximum sentences when such hostility is proven. Maximum sentences were increased from five to seven years imprisonment for particular crimes, including grievous bodily harm, assault occasioning actual bodily harm and putting someone in fear of violence. Likewise, the sentence for criminal damage was increased from 10 to 14 years' imprisonment. A maximum penalty of two years' imprisonment, a fine, or both, was introduced for common assault.

The separate legislatures of Scotland, Wales and England have developed initiatives to include disabled people within the scope of pre-existing hate crimes legislation. In Wales, disability hate crimes are now recognized alongside hate crimes motivated by race, religion, sexual orientation, and transgender identity. Indeed, in 2008/2009 there were 166 disability hate crimes recognized by the Welsh Police force. (Statistics were not collected prior to 2008.) The Offences (Aggravation by Prejudice) (Scotland) Act 2009 was passed by the Scottish Parliament on June 3, 2009, and received Royal Assent on July 8, 2009. It added disability, sexual orientation and transgender identity to hate crime laws. Specifically, with regard to disability, it provides enhanced penalties for offences aggravated by prejudice relating to disability. Disability is defined in the Act as including a physical or mental impairment of any kind, including long-term, substantial or progressive medical conditions. Proof of disability bias is said to occur if the offender indicates malice and ill-will relating to the disability (or presumed disability) of the victim, or if the offence is motivated (in whole or in part) by prejudice against disabled people in general, or those with a particular impairment. It is immaterial whether or not the offender's malice and ill-will is also based on any other factor. The fact that the crime was a disability hate crime must be recorded on the conviction, and must also be taken into consideration in sentencing. The Scottish legislation was introduced after significant lobbying and testimonies from disability advocacy organizations. For instance representatives of the Royal National Institute for Deaf People testified that a survey of its members indicated that 14% of respondents in Scotland indicated that they had either been physically or verbally assaulted because of their Deafness. MP Bill Kidd made the following comments when the Bill was debated:

> The 2004 research by the Disability Rights Commission and Capability Scotland found that 47% of disabled people in Scotland reported experiencing hate crime. A third had to avoid certain places, and a quarter had moved home as a result of an attack. Disabled people are four times more likely to be violently assaulted than non-disabled people. Visually impaired people are four times more likely to be assaulted or attacked than their sighted neighbors. People with mental health issues are 11 times more likely to be victimized, and 90% of adults with a learning disability report being bullied (Kidd, 2009).

A submission from the Scottish Association for Mental Health, noted by MP Bill Butler, also indicated that among those who had experienced a hate crime, almost one-third indicated that they experienced verbal abuse, intimidation or physical attacks at least once a month. Another MP, Angela Constance, referred to a briefing by Leonard Cheshire Disability and suggested 'a disabled person is five to 10 times more likely to experience hate crime as a non-disabled person. Those with mental health issues are 11 times more likely to be victimised and ... 90% of people with a learning disability report experiences of being bullied'.

A number of European countries regard crime against a disabled person as an aggravating circumstance which can be taken into consideration in sentencing (European Blind Union, 2003). For instance, this principle is established in Andorra through Article 30.6 of the Criminal Code, which states that aggravating circumstances can include racist and xenophobic motives, or reasons related to ideology, religion, nationality, ethnic origin, sexual orientation, disease or the physical or mental disability of the victim. Similarly, Lithuania regards violence against disabled people as an aggravating circumstance which can be taken into consideration in sentencing (European Blind Union, 2003). In Romania, a new Criminal Code was adopted in 2005. It specifically includes disability, chronic disease and HIV/AIDS discrimination as aggravating circumstances which can be considered in sentencing. Disability occurs in this section of the Criminal Code alongside many other prejudices such as race, nationality, ethnicity, language, religion, sex, sexual orientation, opinion, political affiliations, wealth, social origin, and age. Likewise, in New Zealand, Section 9(1)(h) of the Sentencing Act 2002 introduced sentence enhancement where 'the offender committed the offence partly or wholly because of hostility towards a group of persons who have an enduring common characteristic such as race, colour, nationality, religion, gender identity, sexual orientation, age, or disability and the hostility is because of the common characteristic and the offender believed that the victim has that characteristic' (Coalition of Community Law Centers Aoteroa Inc., 2009).

Unfortunately, these countries seem to be the exception. Most countries seem to ignore the specifics of disability hate crimes and do not include sentence enhancement provisions, even when they recognize and incorporate other forms of bias. For instance, in most European countries other bias motivations such as race, national origin, religion or sexual orientation may be considered as aggravating factors in the commission of a crime – but not disability. According to Human Rights First, examples of countries which do recognize certain biases as aggravating circumstances (but do not recognize disability bias as one of them) include Armenia, Austria, Azerbaijan, Belarus, Bosnia and Herzegovina, Bulgaria, Croatia, the Czech Republic, Denmark, Finland, France, Georgia, Hungary, Italy, Kazakhstan, Kyrgyzstan, Latvia, Lithuania, Luxembourg, Malta, Moldova, Norway, Portugal, the Slovak Republic, Sweden, Tajikistan, Turkmenistan, and Uzbekistan (Human Rights First, 2008).

Chapter Outline

This introductory chapter has aimed to introduce the topic of disability hate crimes and to suggest that it is a serious problem, with global dimensions. It has shown that disability hate crimes may involve very serious incidents, such as torture. It has also suggested that it is important to recognize these events as crimes, and not simply as 'abuse'. The chapter suggests that there have been a number of positive legislative developments in recent years regarding disability hate crimes. Disability organizations have campaigned long and hard to place this issue on the public agenda. These organizations have been successful in having disability included as a protected category by many legislatures, both within Europe and North America. Disability hate crime is certainly an important social problem which needs to be acknowledged, reported, and investigated thoroughly, and victims need appropriate support.

The following chapters explore additional dimensions of disability hate crimes. Chapter 2 attempts to answer the question, 'Does anyone really hate disabled people?' In the course of researching this topic for over 10 years, this has been the most common response from audiences. This chapter attempts to answer that question with a definitive 'yes'. It provides evidence of disability hatred from a range of sources, but particularly the Internet. The Internet has provided a space where antidisability rhetoric has flourished; there are countless sites that contain various kinds of antidisability slurs. This chapter discusses some of the main kinds of antidisability statements that occur on the Internet. It also demonstrates that this pernicious hate does not simply apply to a particular form of disability; it is widespread.

Chapter 3 of the book examines hate crimes in the USA, and explores the first 10 years of FBI data on disability hate crimes in detail. It documents the most common, and the least common, reported hate crimes according to disability bias. In order to identify the unique characteristics of disability hate crimes, the chapter contains a detailed comparison of the statistical make-up of disability hate crimes, and contrasts them with other forms of hate crime. The findings are fascinating – not simply because they indicate that disabled people are more likely to be the victims of a hate crime in a home or residence, or that they are more likely to be the victims of rape, but because they demonstrate quite conclusively that disability hate crimes do have unique characteristics which distinguish them from other hate crimes. Even though hate crimes are a major social problem, this is the first book to carefully analyze the most recent FBI data on disability hate crimes and to explain how disability hate crimes are statistically different from other forms of hate crime. This chapter therefore is vital in outlining the ways in which disability hate crimes are unique forms of hate crime. This chapter also addresses the question, 'Why aren't more disability hate crimes reported?' Reasons for the failure to report a hate crime could include the victim's shame, fear of retaliation, fear of not being believed, and fear of being labeled 'disabled' in a context where such labels are regarded as stigmatizing.

Chapter 4 moves from the situation in the USA to the United Kingdom. One of the major differences between the US case and the UK is the activism of disability organizations. Although many disability organizations in the US did formally sign the petition to include disability in hate crime federal legislation in 2009, they have done far less campaigning than their UK counterparts. UK disability organizations have been relentless in their efforts to have this problem recognized and addressed. The fact that the BBC website has a section dedicated to the topic of disability hate crimes, for instance, is a direct result of the effectiveness of disability organizations in placing the issue on the public agenda. Such media coverage of disability hate crimes is also quite different from the North American situation.

Chapter 5 answers the question, 'What can be done?' in order to respond more effectively to disability hate crime. It summarizes recent initiatives and highlights positive measures that have been taken to raise awareness of the problem and to encourage more effective responses. The chapter suggests a number of possible avenues for responding to disability hate crimes, including legislative responses, improved reporting procedures, community interventions, and assistance for individual victims. One of the themes of this chapter – and the book more generally – is that disability hate crimes need to be acknowledged, reported, and investigated thoroughly, and victims need appropriate support. It is also necessary to provide more support for disabled victims of hate crimes, and encourage more people to recognize that some of their experiences of 'abuse' are actually 'hate crimes'. As well, there is a need to remove bureaucratic inefficiencies which impede the hate crime reporting process. Within law enforcement, there have been problems with departmental infrastructure, a lack of training and supervision, and communication breakdowns between line officers and those responsible for reporting the crimes which have impeded the effective investigation and reporting of disability hate crimes.

Chapter 2
Does Anyone *Really* Hate Disabled People?

One of the most common responses to this topic is to question whether disability hate crimes really exist. Usually, it is suggested that no one actually *hates* disabled people – victimization simply reflects the perception of disabled people as an 'easy target'. (This argument is itself based on a misperception of hate crime legislation – a person with a record of repeated crimes against disabled people is definitely demonstrating bias, if not hatred … and that is usually sufficient to be covered under bias legislation.) Nevertheless, there is significant evidence of disability hate. Throughout the Internet, there are hundreds of sites proclaiming hatred of 'retards', 'spastics', 'cripples' and so forth. (Despite the disturbing nature of these terms, it is important to record them in order to recognize the full extent of such hatred.) Documenting the widespread nature of disability hatred and its hyperviolent content is the purpose of this chapter.

Denying Disability Hatred

In November 2007, columnist Robert Shrimsley wrote about the inclusion of disability in hate crime legislation in the (British) *Financial Times*. He called it 'a mockery of the law and the disabled'. Shrimsley began by asking:

> Don't you just hate the disabled? You don't? That's odd; I was under the impression a lot of people must do. What other conclusion can one draw from the government's decision to create a new criminal offence of incitement to hate crime against the disabled? (Shrimsley, 2007).

Shrimsley's column is fairly representative of one school of thought which suggests that antidisability hate is quite rare. He further laughingly suggests that one 'criminal mastermind' must be orchestrating this hate. But one need not be so sarcastic to assume that antidisability hate is a marginal feature of contemporary social life. Even Tom Shakespeare, a well-known British disability studies scholar, is quoted in one report as saying that there was a danger of overstating the degree of disability hatred. 'I think there's a danger of exaggerating', he is quoted as saying on the BBC website. 'There's been a small number of truly appalling situations, but in the most part people don't hate disabled people' (Adams-Spink, 2008).

It is the purpose of this chapter to provide an alternative analysis. By examining the incidence of disability hatred on the Internet, this chapter demonstrates that antidisability hatred is widespread. Indeed, antidisability hatred takes many forms, and many impairments have been targeted. Many people contribute to a social climate in which disability hatred is a regular occurrence on the Internet. This chapter documents just a small portion of the antidisability hate which can be found on the Internet, but this small proportion is enough to cause alarm. It demonstrates the widespread nature of antidisability hate speech. But hate speech is different from a hate crime; this distinction is clarified in the next section of the chapter.

Hate Speech and Hate Crime

Hate crime laws typically emphasize their intent to punish conduct, not speech. In the US, the First Amendment guarantees the right to free speech; hate crime laws never can, and never intend to, override this Constitutional right. However, the right to free speech may protect the right to express offensive views but does not protect the right to behave criminally even if the crime consists solely of speech. That is, speech intended to seriously frighten someone is a verbal assault that may be punished (Lawrence, 1999). The 'hate crimes–hate speech paradox', as it has been labeled, involves simultaneously punishing the biased criminal and protecting the right of the bigot to free speech. Hate crime laws do not punish free speech – they simply increase penalties for acts that are already illegal. It must be recognized, however, that the line between speech and conduct is difficult in practice to establish. Whillock suggests that the function of hate speech is to create a 'symbolic code for violence' which inflames the emotions of followers, denigrates the out-class and inflicts harm on the victims (Whillock, 1995). Many victims of hate speech have very real fears that the speech will escalate into physical violence (Mallon, 2001).

Those who favor penalizing hate speech tend to take a more expansive definition of 'hate crimes' than those who strongly support free speech. That is, they do not conceive of hate speech or hate crimes as a series of discrete acts, but instead view them as part of a continuum of bigotry and prejudice. Bowling has highlighted some of the effects of regarding hate crimes as a process:

> Conceiving of violent racism (and other forms of crime) as processes implies an analysis which is dynamic; includes the social relationships between all the actors involved in the process; can capture the continuity between physical violence, threat and intimidation; can capture the dynamic of repeated or systematic victimization; incorporates historical context; and takes account of the social relationships which inform definitions of appropriate and inappropriate behavior (Bowling, 1998).

Perry also views hate crime as a process, which plays an important role in social power structures. Perry defines hate crimes as 'a mechanism of power intended to sustain somewhat precarious hierarchies, through violence and threats of violence (verbal or physical). It is generally directed toward those whom our society has traditionally stigmatized and marginalized' (Perry, 2001).

Examples of Disability Hatred on the Web

A Google search on the word 'retards' produced over 5 million results; 'cripples' produced over 1 million sites; and 'spastics' produced over 100,000 websites. There are almost 2 million images under the Google Image search 'retard' and another 4.9 million under the term 'retarded', many of which feature real people with developmental disabilities whose images have been 'Photoshopped' to include comments such as, 'Arguing on the internet is like running in the Special Olympics. Even if you win, you're still retarded'. These numbers speak volumes about the circulation of problematic language about disability, but many of these sites are obviously not disability hate sites. This chapter will highlight some of the sites which are obviously antidisability hate sites – but there were thousands of websites which could not be included in the chapter because of space constraints. The ones which are presented here are a fairly representative sample of the antidisability hate sites on the web, as of August 2009.

Many Internet blogs, authored by a single individual, proclaim loudly their hatred of disabled people. For instance, a web blog called 'My Hate Blog' contains the header, 'I hate … retards and autistic children' (Pirez, 2007). At the top of the website is a large photo of a person with Down's syndrome, wearing a Superman costume, flexing his arm muscles. He has Strabismus. The picture has been edited, and above the man's photo is the term 'STFU!' (short for 'Shut The Fuck Up!'). This 'hate blog' contains the following opening remarks: 'With its screwed up face and child-like mannerisms … What we have here is commonly referred to as a "retard" and I fucking hate them'. Having compared disabled people to animals, the author asks, 'Do you REALLY want to shake hands with someone whose idea of fun is to play with their own shit? Someone whose hand is likely to be so disgustingly dirty and sticky that you genuinely feel the need to either cut yours off afterwards, or dunk it in a vat of sulphuric acid. That's not my idea of fun'. The author, who identifies himself as 'Vince Pirez', likens disability support workers to a 'dog handler', 'horse handler' and a 'toilet handler'. (A central characteristic of this hate site is the constant dehumanization of disabled people, who are likened to animals.) And there is once again derision and secondary stigmatization of the carers who work or socialize with disabled people. He then proceeds to suggest that talking to a 'retard' about 'the shapes and sizes of poop and how when I was 3 years old, I tried to make a replica of the Eiffel Tower out of my own shit, I get chastised for talking to them in a demeaning manner, regardless of how much the retard finds it amusing and claps their hands like a fucking circus seal'. Vince often likens disabled people to animals, and at one stage asks, 'Do they even have names?'

Additionally, the reference to disabled people as 'disgustingly dirty and sticky' is designed to evoke a visceral discomfort among readers. The hostility towards disabled people is almost tangible. Elsewhere in the blog, the author often contrasts disabled people with a mythical 'normal person'. This is important because it highlights the connection between the ideas of people who engage in hate speech and many people's uncritical acceptance of dominant ideas about disability and (a lack of) normality. Disabled people are not 'normal', according to many people – highlighting the importance of challenging broader cultural ideas about disability and abnormality.

There is one more disgusting comment from Vince Pirez which deserves mention:

> If you're a woman and you're out alone one night, and a group of guys try to rape you – just pretend you're retarded. Start spitting on yourself and making retarded noises – see if they continue. Of course, you could very well be the unfortunate person who receives the rapist who's into retarded people. That would be seriously fucking unfortunate for you, and I'd suggest killing yourself that evening. Either that or buying a lottery ticket that night. One way or another the odds are either for or against you.

References to the rape of a woman likewise raise issues of sexual power, disrespect, and vulnerability – and are rhetorically linked to the author's underlying disgust, fear and loathing of disability. And the advice of telling a woman who has been raped to kill herself is not just misogynist and degrading, it is indeed sickening.

Respondents to the blog do include people objecting to the comments, but others restate the hate with remarks such as the following from a person whose nickname is 'Zibe': 'jesus, I just wish i could take a machete to those ugly useless fucks and do the world a favor ... but god damn our world for wanting to protect the weak and useless. I REALLY JUST WANT TO KILL THEM ALL'. (As with all the following quotations, the spelling and grammar mistakes were included for accuracy.) Another response to the blog is from 'Eviltreemonster', who comments: 'I'm ok with gays, blacks and muslims but I say FUCK retards, fuckers are an abomination to god and should be burnt, whipped, dragged or stoned to death'. Later, 'Eviltreemonster' elaborates: 'Retards are all devils. They fight, vandalize, rape, steal, molest children, and (somehow) get away with it. They must be the spawn of SATAN. These fuckers are not ill, or disabled, just possessed by demons'. Another poster, 'A Former Wrangler', comments: 'I use to be a retard "handler" as you put it, and man, your right, they do suck! Worst job ever! I hated them all with a fiery passion and still do. God must've had a serious hangover when he fucked up on those things. I consider myself as a "Retard Wrangler" instead of a "handler" though'. And a poster named 'E' comments that 're-Ts are a plague on humanity. A stain on society that should be wiped clean off this earth'. Another respondent, 'John Roberts', commented that 'I hate autistic creatures, I call them AUTARDED. Where is Adolf Hitler now, when we need him most?' Later, when

'Lori', the self-identified mother of an autistic boy, objects to the comments on the blog, Vince asks, 'Did you have to sleep with your brother in order to make him retarded? Isn't that how it works? Incestrious relations creates deformed fucked up children? Tell me, when you were fucking your brother did you call out his name?' Later, another poster identified as 'Liz' suggests, 'Retards need to be tortured in the most sadistic way possible'.

A final quote from this blog should suffice. It is from 'Mark':

> I hate tards i used to live with one … god this fat creature was simply awful to be around, it reeked of shit it had shit under it's nails and whatever it touched would automatically stink of shit. It would eat everything in sight and never stop eating until it needed it's sleep, it was a horrible creature indeed. What is the point of letting these creatures enter our world they should be terminated at birth they drag society down, no one wants to be in the presence of them, god they're so uncomfortable and embarrassing to be around aren't they? How are you suppose to act around them are you suppose to act like it's a human or an animal? I don't think the retard lovers on here quite know how awkward it is to be around one of these things, they hit you, moan at you and moan for everything. I've been so wound up I've had to insult the window licking freak but damn it felt good, sure did the trick i didn't see the goony fucker all day.

At the bottom of the page, after there had been 159 comments made, there is an 'Admin Edit' in bold typeface which states:

> The posting of comments is now DISABLED. I honestly don't give a fuck about any of you whiney, pussy retards or retard loving motherfuckers. I don't care that your "child has autism" or any of that bullshit. Here's the bottom line, folks: NOBODY CARES. You're living under the presumption that people care about your problems. You're living under the presumption that you can somehow tell me your heart-felt tale and I'll miraculously become a sensitive and caring person, and change my mind about the satirical blog post I'd written. You. Are. Living. In. Fucking. Delusion. Quite frankly you can all choke on a retard cock.

The vivid sexual imagery and hyperviolent tone of this post is not incidental. The violent imagery of choking on a 'retard cock' is an essential component of an attempt to convey disrespect and bodily domination. They also connect to longstanding images of the dangerous sexuality of people with intellectual disabilities. And the fact that a person who is 'choking' is silent symbolically underscores the intolerance of the author for alternative viewpoints.

It would be a welcome relief to assume that websites which contain this type of animosity towards disabled people are rare and hard to find. However, prior research demonstrates that there are many websites with such hateful comments on them throughout the Internet (Sherry, 2004). Indeed, there are far too many of these kinds of hate sites to simply dismiss this type of vitriol as an aberration. The rapid growth of disability hate sites on the Internet is an alarming feature of contemporary society which suggests that hatred of disabled people is not unusual, but is in fact quite widespread.

It is impossible to distinguish many of the slurs and insults used in these websites – words such as 'retard', 'cripple', or 'spastic' – and the terms historically used by the medical profession to describe disability. Medical terms about various impairments often slowly make their way into the wider social sphere as insults. Likewise, people who commit these crimes sometimes say that the person is 'useless' or 'a burden' – themes with a long and shameful social history in eugenics. It is tempting to view such comments as simple venting or offensive rhetoric, and to assume that there is little connection between this discourse of hate and the actual life experiences of disabled people. And it is certainly true that many of the people who express such hatred towards disabled people never actually commit crimes against them. Likewise, many criminal acts against disabled people do not contain any evidence of disability bias. However, in the commission of disability hate crimes, such vitriol commonly occurs.

One website expressed many of the common themes of disability hate, so I will quote it in its entirety. (This article is so popular it has been claimed by a number of authors as their own work. I will not enter into a debate about the original authorship. Instead, I will simply note the worrying fact that many people have rushed to claim it as their own.) The author of the webpage I have chosen to quote identifies himself as 'Jesus Christ' and has placed a picture of an American flag under the following article, entitled 'Cripples, Retards, and the Other Untouchables'. It is reproduced below:

> Useless self-pitying cripples and bothersome retarded fucks alike are all extraordinarily worthless. What is their purpose in society? Exhausting our precious resources while annoying the fuck out of us: the hard working American public. I hate crippled people, with their close up parking spots and their defective appendages. I especially hate lamenting cripples demanding compassion and consolation while being enormous assholes. The biggest assholes are those hopeless cripples new to the experience via some horrible accident or illness. These so called "new" cripples always demand solace while nostalgically remembering how they used to able to move without a machine to propel them. "I'm handy capable! I'm differently able!" No you aren't, fuck you. All cripples are just a waste of space and energy, expending costly resources while contributing virtually nothing at all. God damn it. I detest retards immensely. The babbling, drooling, flailing fuck ups irritate me to no end. When a one-year-old baby pisses itself and cries to be changed it's acceptable. However when a thirty-year-old balding fat man pisses himself and hollers incomprehensibly while violently thrashing about its just down right disturbing. Retards coast through life unknowing of the massive drain they put on society. These massive drains are nothing more then disgusting sub-human nuisances. The worst of

these untouchables is the combination of the two, the crippled retard. These sad sacs of human refuse have serious defects and don't deserve to live. What the hell is the point to keep these crack baby, drooling retard, wheelchair bound, disgusting fucks? There is none. I also loathe the "special" Olympics. What the shit is this sorry excuse for an athletic competition for? To try to make these undesirable worthless things feel wanted and cheerful through flailing about and falling over. Hell, these brain-dead fucks are content to flick water and blow bubbles of spit all day. Screw cripples, screw retards. I hate them all.

The theme of this webpage, in common with many other antidisability sites, is that disabled people are worthless and do not deserve to live. The venomous tone is clear; the hate and loathing palpable. The hate is directed at both people with physical impairments (who are labeled 'cripples') and those with cognitive impairments (who are labeled 'retards'). Likewise, the American flag and references to 'the hard working American public' are intended to suggest that disability is unpatriotic – a drain on the nation's resources and a burden on everyone else. This separation of disabled people from 'the nation' has been a mainstay of eugenic thought for generations (Sherry, 2007). Through the lens of eugenics, the murder and sterilization of hundreds of thousands of disabled people throughout the world was rationalized (Kerr and Shakespeare, 2002). One of the main themes of eugenics was that disabled people are worthless and a drain on society; this form of Social Darwinism remains alive on the web today in disability hate sites.

Disability is viewed completely negatively – there are no positive aspects of the experience, apparently, and no redeeming features of those who are disabled. They are called 'untouchable' and even 'sub-human', reduced to such slurs as 'useless self-pitying cripples and bothersome retarded fucks', 'brain-dead fucks' and 'babbling, drooling, flailing fuck ups'. Also, there is an attempt to paint the emotions of disabled people in a particularly negative way: they are labeled as 'self-pitying', 'lamenting', 'demanding compassion and consolation while being enormous assholes', 'hopeless', people who 'demand solace', people 'nostalgically remembering' being nondisabled. Any negative comments by disabled people are framed through a lens of disgust and animosity. On the other hand, any positive reframing of a disability experience (even through the very problematic phrases 'handy capable' or 'differently able') is met with immediate disdain, denial and hostility. 'No you aren't, fuck you' is the immediate, sworn reply.

One might expect that such hate against disabled people would elicit almost universal condemnation. Certainly, there are many people who respond to such websites with criticism and venom of their own. But more worrying is the number of people who respond positively to such comments. The site had 2,472 hits as of August 2009, but only 32 people had given it a ranking (which can range from –2 to +2 stars). On this webpage, 11 of the 32 responses had rated the post with the highest possible ranking, +2 out of 2 points. One person, who identified himself as Andy, continued the theme of hate. Andy's comments (and their spelling/grammar mistakes) are also revealing:

> Why bother with cripples as said they do nothing for society apart from sponge
> off it and mope and groan about how f**in hard theyve got it, if they dont like it
> pop themselves or ill gladly do it for them. As for the rest of you "its terrible to
> call a criple", "youre heartless" get real wait until one sues you for not providing
> disabled access or automatic doors. They always want more and are never
> gratefull for the lengths people have to go through just so they fit in.

Andy promotes suicide as a viable option for disabled people, or offers to 'pop'
them, presumably meaning to 'gladly' assist them commit suicide or perhaps even
to murder them (his meaning is not entirely clear). Among Andy's complaints are
that disabled people are not sufficiently 'gratefull' (sic) to others who enable them
to 'fit in'. But the reference to 'fitting in' is important. Indeed, it is inconsistent
with the rest of the comments. If it is possible for disabled people to be included
in society, and to 'fit in', then surely they can contribute and be valuable members
of society. Unfortunately, Andy does not even seem aware of this contradiction
in his argument. Andy is not alone in promoting death as an option for disabled
people. Another person, who uses the webname of 'Cripple', states, 'You speak
the truth, I hate fucking cripples. There is one in my office that comes and drools
at my desk. I am constructing a plan to throw him off the balcony, ensuring his
deserved death'.

Accessible parking spots and 'cripples' are actually a major focus of
antidisability hate sites. For instance, there is a Facebook group called 'I don't
care if your handicapped, its my spot now'. The spelling mistake in the group's
name has not stopped 42 people from joining the group. The description of the
group states 'You hate how all the people who are crippled get special spots to
park? fuck that. we're all a little ill in the brain so we might as well take the
spots we deserve'. Additionally, the location of the group is described as 'i cant
remember i have to park way down the fucking street and walk since all the good
spots are handicapped'. One of the members has written on the 'Wall' of the group,
'i believe in your philosophy sir, and will gladly follow you into battle against
the crippies'. Another member, who apparently attends 'Dunbar High School',
states, 'god i hate handicapped people'. Sixteen of the group members indicate
that they are attending Dunbar High School. The presence of so many spelling and
grammatical errors in these sites may reflect the young age of the members, as well
as their lack of formal education.

On angelfire.com, there is another website which also focuses on 'cripples'.
This self-described 'rant' is entitled 'Why we'll never cure the cripples'. It has
many themes in common with other hate sites, which will be explored shortly. The
main focus of the 'rant' is accessible parking spaces, but that seems like a vehicle
to allow the author (who goes by the web name of 'Slappy') to express a range
of disability prejudice. There is a picture of Slappy, apparently, on the webpage,
and a section dedicated to 'the college graduating class of 2000'. He is a young
white man wearing a formal outfit (white shirt, black bow tie). Slappy has other
'rants' on his webpage, indicates that he studies psychology, and 6,149 people had

accessed his webpage when I logged on. This is Slappy's antidisability 'rant', less a few sentences:

Why We'll Never Cure the Cripples

I hate handicapped parking spaces. I hate the idea of them. I see them as a punishment for being healthy ... every mall in America is expecting Cripple-Fest 2000 to visit them and they need to hold parking spots for all of the tour members. There are two types of drivers in "cripple cars" (those being cars sporting a little wheelchair on the plates). There are the cripples who spend lots of money so they can custom a car that still allows them to drive and those drivers that are taking care of their own personal cripple ... people who have pet cripples they fall into a few sub-types. There are those who cart cripples around and those who run out on behalf of the human pretzels. If you're bringing a mangle of flesh into a store with you I want to know why. What possible good could having a twisted bio-mass do you while buying food at the supermarket? You probably know what you're diaper wearing friend likes to eat so why hassle yourself?

I wouldn't want a tard or a cripple all my very own for the same reason I don't want a pony. It's a lot of free time I just don't have to spare.

Not to sound more crass than I already do but what ever happened to survival of the fittest? If you can't make it to the supermarket to buy pre-packaged food unless you're parked in the first two spots near the door maybe life really isn't worth it for you.

The parking at UMass – Lowell is horrid. I take all morning classes so I can work in the afternoon ... Have we really reached the point where a cripple (or gimp, if you prefer) has nothing better to worry about than parking? How about finding a cure for your injuries, buddy? All that wasted time and energy yelling when he could have been doing a telethon or something. For years and years the world has raised money to find cures for the cripples among us. In all those years we have two things to show for it. One, the wheelchair and two, a wheelchair with a joystick for those people too crippled and folded over to push their own ass around (Slappy, 2000).

Some of the themes from this 'rant' are common to so many hate sites: a direct statement linking hatred and disability; the use of insulting, demeaning and hateful language such as 'pet cripples', 'human pretzels', 'a mangle of flesh', 'a gimp' and 'tard and his owner' and a comparison of the person with a 'pony'; positioning caregivers as a disabled person's owners and the disabled person as a lifeless thing, or a piece of property; a recitation of Social Darwinist themes about 'survival of the fittest'; and an assumption that the 'quality of life' of all disabled people is so low that their lives are barely worth living.

Another common theme is that disabled people should not reproduce. The stereotype of the disabled person as unfit to breed is typified by the following comment:

> Retards. I hate them. I don't care how un-politically correct it is. I fucking hate retards. I watched something on Canadian television this weekend about a mother who had her mongoloid son chemically castrated. Thank GOD. He is twenty-four years old with the mind of a four year old, blind, and (obviously) not even capable of taking care of himself or others (d_i_s_s_i_d_e_n_t, 2003).

Another online essay entitled 'Retards in School' also promoted hate towards disabled people:

> So here is my plan, I think that we should take all the retarded people in the country, gather them at a big rally, then while they are having fun, if they even know why they are there or where they even are at, then the military should fence in to a big building that the construction companies want to blow up, you gather them in there lock them in then line the in and outside with the most powerful explosive you could find then blow the shit out of the building. And if there are any survivors, have guys with m-16 ready to shoot them down. Then you keep doing that until all of the retards in this country are gone. In my way you would kill two birds with one stone. All of the retards will be gone and you would remove the buildings that you want to get rid of. And then after they are all gone if a baby ever turns out retarded it should be a responsibility of all citizens of the united states to kill them if they cant do it they take the babies to a special are where one a week all the retarded people their will be killed for the good of the u.s. and for the good of humanity (Hellen C, 2004).

The essay may be error-ridden, but its theme is still evident: kill disabled people and it will be good for everyone. This message is eerily reminiscent of Nazi ideology.

Hate crimes often reflect the fears and anxieties of the haters. For instance, in a forum which was discussing how motorists hate cyclists, someone raised the topic of 'mongs' (a slur which is short for Mongoloid, itself an offensive word to describe people with intellectual disabilities and one with a long racist history that links Asian people to disability). Someone calling himself or herself 'Leonard Hatred' (apparently after the fictional British television character which appeared in the show *Look Around You*) commented, 'Yeah, i hate mongs too. if i have to walk past a retard in the street, i hold my breath incase i accidentally inhale some downs syndrome or something' (Hatred, 2007). The ridiculous idea that Down's syndrome is contagious shows the ignorance of the poster ... but it also reflects a great deal of fear about life with a disability.

Often the authors of hate sites vent about their personal desire to harm disabled people. Here is an example, from a website called www.angry.net. This webpage was eventually removed by the editor, but only after I publicized it throughout disability sites and many people protested about it. The initial reaction was to insert an editorial comment that 'it is unwise to hate what you are'. This pattern of using an insult – such as the term 'retard' – against someone who is disparaging disabled people is unfortunately common. It does not challenge the association of the term with insult; it simply recirculates it. And like 'Vince Perez', this (unnamed) author seeks to evoke a sensory disgust of disabled people:

> I hate those drooling fucking life less wall faced bastards all they do is shit themselves smell bad and try to wipe boogers and pass diseases to anyone and everyone around them. Sometimes I see them I want to take a hammer to their thick skulls. I get fed up with there stupidity and retarded blank stairs. They always smell bad and never make any sense. They have mush for brains, and not one has ever contributed anything useful for society! They have done nothing useful ever except for being a nuisance to everyone. And with brains like a 10 month old at age 16 it gets annoying real quick. I was fortunate not to go to a high school with these drooling vegetables. Every time I see them I want to puke! They disgust me and scare me. You never know when anyone of them will try and pull your hair or hit you. They have been known to attack people for no apparent reason. I just cannot stand them (Anger Central, 2002).

Once again, the post contains unchanged spelling mistakes, which seem to suggest a lack of formal education. But the tone of the piece – describing disabled people as useless, disease-spreading and drooling vegetables – has much in common with other sites that are more well written. By evoking an image of disabled people as dangerous and potentially violent at any time, the author connects to a long and much broader cultural history that denigrates and degrades all manifestations of disability.

The idea that disabled people smell, drool on others, and should be aborted *in vitro* is another common stereotype. It underpins a website entitled 'Retard Genocide':

> I fucking hate retarded people. I can't help it; they're personal space invaders. I am a person with an extremely large bubble. Not so with a retarded person. A retarded person will throw his big, meaty retarded arms around you in a hug that lasts longer than is appropriate. Sometimes while he's doing this, he'll rock excitedly back and forth and drool in your hair. Gross. Speaking of drool, there are also many other bodily fluids that retards are covered in on a daily basis. Simply put, they are goopy individuals. Often they have slime on their chins. Boogers under their fingernails. Stickiness on their arms. Unknown food particles spilled down the front of their shirts. Snot bubbles appearing every time they exhale. *This* is how they approach you for a hug. Oh God … Oh God … Oh

> God ... Speaking of raising an idiot, aren't there ways to determine if you have a retard baby *in the womb*? If so, why the hell don't you get that *shit scraped out of you*? I mean, do you *enjoy* polluting the gene pool? Are you *enamored* by the smell of body odor and juicy fruit bubblegum? Owning a gold fish wasn't *enough* for you? (Violent Acres, 2006).

Links between death and disability are common in hate sites. Indeed, the theme of killing disabled people is frighteningly common. A webzine entitled 'Colon D' published an article entitled 'Retarded People: A Blessing or a Crisis'. 'Colon D' was an e-magazine which began in 2001 and had 67 online editions until 2003. Its archives remain online to this day, although the front page of the website indicates that the magazine is no longer being produced due to 'financial reasons and the fact that most of the staff are in college or have full-time jobs now'. Emilenburg, who stated that he is 17 elsewhere in the magazine, wrote this in 2001 but it remains on the website in 2009:

> Well I will be blunt, I hate fucking retards. I dont see why they are let to live. All they are doing is continuing to supply the world with more retarded people. Im not saying they are evil or anything, Im just pointing out they are not helping the future of mankind. Now, I propose that all mentally challenged people be taken into the middle of nowhere and shot in the head and then burned in a giant hole that will be filled in with concrete ... (Emilienburg, 2001).

The violent nature of these comments, as well as the fact that it appeared in an online magazine (and was not simply in an individual's blog) is quite shocking. Indeed, it is surprising that an online magazine would print something that was riddled with so many grammatical errors – perhaps suggesting that the author, and the editors, lack formal educational qualifications. But that is beside the point. The author is clearly advocating death to disabled people en masse – which was basically the plan of the Nazis in World War II. And yet there is no connection between this group and Nazis, neo-Nazis, or white supremacist groups. It is essentially a fairly standard webzine, probably written by students, and contains discussions of television, selections of poetry, comics, reviews of products such as Canada Dry Ale and Polo Sport Cologne. Hatred of disabled people is indeed widespread – even in places where the whole topic of disability seems anomalous. Of course, it cannot be denied that Nazi and white supremacist groups do continue their campaigns of hate towards disabled people. An example can be found in the lyrics of the song 'Mongoloids' by Swedish white power music group Pluton Svea. Although the band stopped making music in 2001, its lyrics are still reproduced on many hate sites today and it is still possible to buy the song and use it as a ringtone on a phone as of 2009. Some of the lyrics to this song include: 'You're a drooling basketcase, With snot all over your face. Kick you to death is my aim'.

Despite the presence of such hate on Nazi wesbites, disability hate is perhaps more common on various blogs that are purportedly 'nonpolitical'. For example, there is a site called 'Is it normal?' (www.isitnormal.com) where people write about their feelings, dreams, aspirations and fears, and ask others to vote on whether this is a 'normal' feeling. One notable post, by someone calling himself 'Mysterious Rhinestone Cowboy' was called 'I really hate retards'. It begins with the comment 'Whenever I see a full-blown retard I get inexplicably angry. I want to kill them'. The response of people who voted on whether this is a 'normal' reaction to people with cognitive disabilities is very concerning: approximately 26% of the readers have indicated that 'yes', these feelings are 'normal' (Mysterious Rhinestone Cowboy, 2009a). Another comment by 'Mysterious Rhinestone Cowboy' states 'Retarded people piss me off'. In response to this comment, 37% of respondents (29 out of 79 people) had indicated by August 2009 that 'yes', these feelings are also 'normal' (Mysterious Rhinestone Cowboy, 2009b). In the 'I really hate retards' discussion, the author discusses his anger towards people with Down's syndrome: '... even if they're just walking by, when I see their faces, I get ANGRY!' He then states that he has 'strong' and 'persistent hatred of real Downies'. Again, there are some negative replies to this post – but the pattern of calling someone a 'retard' in response to someone saying they hate 'retards' is also present. Someone posted a reply about 'retards' and asked 'Any chance that you're in an institution with them?' This comment is meant to be critical of the author, but it falls into the trap of recirculating negative images about disability and using the word 'retards' as an object of derision, scorn and insult (Mysterious Rhinestone Cowboy, 2009b).

There is often an informal disability hierarchy underpinning antidisability websites. This hierarchy places people with cognitive impairments at a lower level than those with physical impairments. This theme underpinned a post entitled 'I hate retards' on a discussion board which is normally dominated by discussions of Internet gaming.

> I hate retards. I think that all cases of mental retardation should result in automatic abortion or simple infanticide without any input by the parents ... Producing a retarded child is about as horrible a crime as you can do ... I cannot find anyone more pathetic on this planet than a human being without a brain that'll never work right. I can sympathize with someone whose body is lovely like a Stephen Hawking. Who gives a poo poo if it takes a little extra effort for him to get around when his mind is as valuable as any other? But Trig Palin? Why the gently caress didn't we force the Palins to abort him and start over. It'd have been far less cruel because now we have something walking around pretending to be human that's no more than a loving mannequin; a facsimile of human life no more real than a dummy. Ugh. Severe autism is pretty lovely and the people who suffer it are pretty lovely people. I'd like to see them go, but they can sometimes be helped and sometimes are of use to the world. Schizophrenics really outta be killed ... they're horrid and need to be eliminated considering how much of a danger they are to society and how much rights we give them when they really don't deserve any with what they do with them. (going off their medication yields more craziness yields a danger to society WAY loving COOL THANKS

"RIGHTS OF THE INDIVIDUAL") Chronically depressed people are suffering their own hell, as are the paralyzed. I don't care about someone whose body is impaired when their mind is fine. That's why I hate and resent the retarded so much ... They don't have the capacity to understand what they're doing and will never be able to contribute intellectually to society. They can never do what a Stephen Hawking has done ... The entire purpose of breeding is that we might someday produce another Einstein, Hawking, Salk, et cetera. Where's the loving advancement of the human race in making retards, huh? Nope, just making fully dependent idiots who can't do anything, are a waste of life reliant on others for the entirety of theirs, will die early, can never intellectually advance beyond a very, very rudimentary level, and have health defects (Lil satre, 2009).

This website develops a clear hierarchy where people with cognitive impairments and psychiatric impairments are located at the bottom of humanity. People with cognitive impairments should be aborted, according to this hierarchy. And people with mental health problems, such as schizophrenia, 'should' also be killed, according to this form of hate. There are repeated personal attacks on Sarah Palin because she had a child with Down's Syndrome. Later in the thread, the author responds to some replies by positioning people with intellectual disabilities as a financial drain on society:

Retards are worthless wastes of flesh who need to be eliminated because they literally will never contribute anything to society and suck up hundreds of thousands of dollars of government support a year. Just dwell on that factoid: Palin herself gets MONEY because she shat out Trig. Yeah. And she'll continue to get money for that abomination for the rest of its life, all because she didn't abort him. Isn't grand? (Lil satre, 2009).

Other antidisability websites attempt to link intellectually disabled people and fatness (as if that is another reason to think less of them). The following website is a good example of this form of hatred.

Mentally handicapped individuals are bad enough, but what's worse is when they are also fat and ugly. The unsightly chunksters I'm referring to are people with Down Syndrome. A dumpy Down Syndrome baby is a huge drain on society and every parent's nightmare. These genetic screw-ups hog an extra chromosome, but they pay for it by being gruesome Quasimodoesque retards. Every goofy looking Down Syndrome fat-body wearing a bicycle helmet and running spastically at 2mi/hr should die an early death so they can be put out of their misery. And they do. However, I say before they die we should put the fatties to work. Here's the plan. Load them on a caravan of short buses and make them sweat off a few pounds picking lettuce or strawberries in a field. This guarantees the hideous chubbsters some good cardiovascular exercise, and if a few die in the process of manual labor, who cares? They were worthless anyway (Vicious Headbutt, 2004).

It should not be assumed, however, that people with physical impairments are not targeted in antidisability websites. One example of an antidisability webpage which particularly targets people with physical impairments is called 'I hate crippled people' and it contains a Social Darwinist fantasy of 'eliminating' all the disabled people in the world in the name of 'respectable' people (Spiral_Abraxis, 2004). This webpage states: 'Crippled people are a waste of time, and quite frankly, should be eliminated'. The rationale for this fantasy is two-fold: first, the author, who identified as 'Spiral_Abraxis', states that, 'They are annoying, disgusting, and just fucking eye sores to the normal, respectable, able to walk citizens. They drool, take up room in the halls, require a whole table in class instead of a regular desk, the list goes on an on'. Spiral also poses the question: 'Why do we allow crippled people to exist?' and then answers his or her own question by stating: 'I think the answer is obvious: We shouldn't ... We should have started the practice of killing off the weak long ago so the mindset of that being cruel would not exist now. Yes, it's wrong by today's standards to murder someone because they are crippled, but I think that's senseless logic'. Next Spiral offers a second rationale for the genocide which is proposed: it will save money. 'At our high school, I would say there is about 5–10 kids that are in wheelchairs. Each of those kids gets their own personal aide during the day to help them with their books, get them around to classes, wipe their asses and flick the piss off their dicks if need be. A personal aide for each kid?? That's hundreds of thousands of dollars for wasted on those aides to help a few kids that will never amount to anything in the world'.

Many websites seem to oppose inclusive schooling and propose death to people who are disabled. For instance, on www.ubersite.com, there is a post by 'murdergoround09' entitled 'I hate retarded people' (Murdergoround09, 2004). It is worth quoting the whole post, since it is fairly typical of the antidisability hate sites written by people in high schools:

> in my school there is this stupid class with stars who are people with disorders. most of the stars have down syndrom or someother disorder and most should be in college or something because it takes them five years to learn the alphibet. they can basicly do what every they want. like one time they were coming back from lunch and they all travel in one group like in third grade and while they passed me one of them kick me i was just about to beat the kid up when one of the bitch helpers stoped me. then one time i was opening a door and as i was stepping through it, one of the stars slamed it one my head i almost fated as soon as i got up i chased the retard down the hall ending in him running into a door and one of his stupid bitches sending me to the principle. i think they should just lets the frickin morons sit and die at home with there stupid mothers who created them instead of letting them make our lives worse. but i think the only reason

> why they have them is for them to do other peoples work. I see the stars cleaning the hall way and doing all this other shit that the staff should be doing but the staff is to lazy so they make the retards do it. they also have star bake sales where the star make these deformed food with there digusting hands were they have pick there noses with and shoved up there asses. then the most disgusting thing ever is if you ever go to the bathroom you see them taking shits in the stall with out closing the door because they are complete morons. i think they should all be shot before the start there misrable life. if one of the starrs hits me again i will fucking kill it.

What is typical about this post is that it dehumanizes the disabled students at this high school by referring to them as 'it'; it infantilizes them by comparing them to third-graders; it raises a threat of violence by disabled people (and counters that with a threat of violence to them); it portrays the bodies of disabled people as 'disgusting'; it proposes to kill disabled babies (presumably *in vitro*); and it makes an individual threat of murder to any disabled person who hits the author.

Another webpage worth mentioning is called 'How to kill a spastic' and it simply contains a drawing of someone holding a gun, pointing it straight at a person in a wheelchair (Lobo, 2006). There is a series of dots from the gun into the head of the wheelchair user. The person who is holding the gun and shooting the disabled person is smiling, with a grin from ear to ear. This webpage had 286 hits, but only 12 negative comments. This should not be surprising: using the word 'retard' as a derogatory term is so common, it is almost normative. Indeed, some of the Facebook groups which use the term include: 'There's a retard in my class that won't shut up!', 'No, it's not because your teacher hates you, it's because you are a retard', 'Does a cretin qualify as a retard?', 'People against retarded people', 'Fuck Retarded People', 'I hate retarded people', 'I hate Retards', 'National Hug a Stranger and Look Like a retard Day' and 'I hate midgets and like fisting the retarded ones'. What is particularly interesting about these sites is that disability activists have been joining the groups, and then using their privileges as a group member to change the names of the group, and delete all members except for the original administrator. As a result, there is a great deal of instability regarding sites which use the word 'retards'.

The hatred expressed towards 'midgets' in the last post is not unusual – little people are another group who experience a great deal of hostility and antipathy. There are a large number of groups on Facebook which specifically target 'midgets' for scorn and derision. Some of these groups are entitled 'National Kick A Midget Day', 'I secretly wanna kick a midget' (which was hacked and renamed 'Little People Are People Too!'), 'When I see a midget I want to kick it' (since removed by Facebook), 'Let's kick a midget in the balls!' (removed), 'I see a Midget and I want to see how far I can Kick them', 'People who hate the taco bell midget', 'To everyone who has ever just wanted to kick a midget in the face', 'I secretly want my own pet midget just so i can kick him in the head' and 'Secretly want to kick a midget in the back of the head, just cause i could', 'I Hate that MiDgET!!!', 'I hate Eric the Midget' and 'Midget Hate Group'. Again, because there are disability activists who search for these groups and report them (in particular the Facebook group 'Facebook: Stop allowing groups that mock special needs and disabilities'), they tend to have very short life spans … but new groups emerge all the time.

Another website contains a page called 'Looking out for the little guy … or why I hate midgets' (*The Ref*, 2004). It is (once again) riddled with spelling mistakes, which have been left unedited here. Like some other hate sites, this one tries to be amusing, apparently. But there is nothing truly funny about dehumanizing someone because of their height. This website has 1,577 hits as of August 19, 2009, and not a single negative comment. There are many websites that target little people, but this website is quite typical because of the way it compares them to animals, refers to 'midget' pornography, suggests that they can always be used for the entertainment of others, and finally (in common with many other antidisability hate sites) espouses the idea that they can always be killed:

I make it my daily mission to help those who need help. I have only one small (pun intended) exception to this rule: midgets … Midgets are like chihuahas. They might sound cute on paper but all they do is run around biting your ankles and shitting on the floor … In high school there was this midget on the varsity cheerleading squad … High school was years ago but I still find myself looking for reasons to hate midgets. Coutesy of google, I have found about 2 million. Midget porn is the new bane of my existence. During my studies I have found midgets fucking everything from other midgets (lord help us, they are reproducing) to midgets fucking horses. Bloody fucking horses! I don't know how that is possible but I have seen it happen. Goats, dogs, black people and even mexicans can be found having their way with midgets. Again, I do not know if they actually enjoy this or are doing it to make fun of them. i prefer the making fun of them line because there is o other way around it. If horses could laugh I'm sure these horses laughed their asses off everytime another garden gnome was brough before them.

Midgets have even starred in movies. The austin powers flics are a prime examples of midgets gone atray … this little bastard does nothing more than dance and bite people in the balls. How is that funny or cute? They should have played rugby with him. Now that would have been comedy.

I tend to think of midgets like I think of orphans. They are both no good for society and seem to be increasing in mumber. If only you could buy them. You know, go to an orphan/midget auction. You can raise them like dogs and kill them or sell them to slaughterhouses when they get too mouthy or outgrow their cages. You could feed them dog food and beat them and they will be happy for it because they know no other way of life. I see this as a viable solution for the midget problem. The main idea behind this post is that midgets are only here on this earth to be exploited. One way or another I want to help them achieve that.--see, i am a humanitarian!!

The reference to pornography is important: the commodification of sex enables 'midgets' to be exoticized and enfreaked and linked to 'Goats, dogs, black people and even Mexicans' through a mesh of prejudice. Both disabled people and people of color are 'othered' in this racist, disablist discourse. The comment that 'You can raise them like dogs and kill them or sell them to slaughterhouses' speaks volumes about fantasies of control, power and a desire to harm and kill others. The attempt to buffer this prejudice with humor ('I am a humanitarian!!') does not remove the violent fantasy of hate.

People with many different types of impairments are targeted by antidisability hate sites. For instance, the following quotes are from a page written by 'Brandon' and entitled 'You know who I hate: Deaf People'. The page has subsequently become password protected, but I retrieved a copy before this was done. On the top of the webpage, before the following description, is a Caucasian person wearing a sheep mask and carrying a gun, and underneath the photo is the comment 'I hate Deaf people'. Again, the threat of violence – indeed, extermination – lurks underneath the language of hate:

> Deaf People piss me off. I mean, they're basically retarded. And they act like you owe them something because their parent's genes sucked, or mommy beat 'em too hard, or the lead paint had just too much lead, or because daddy couldn't stop stabbing their eardrums. I'd rather talk with a can of beans freshly rolled across the rio grande than a deaf person. Learn English, you deaf motherfuckers. Another thing that pisses me off: Deaf Culture. Your culture is based on a lack. Some people might say that I'm being short-sighted, especially as someone who suffers from hearing loss. But when worst comes to worst, I'll just talk inappropriately loud … In English. Not some deaf person yelling-honking noise. In a perfect world, all infants would be administered a deaf-test. And then have their brains dashed out if they repeatedly failed it. That's how you handle deaf people. Coddling is not the answer – braining is.

The author leaves no doubt that this is a violent, threatening message by including images of a gun-toting and yet anonymous masked man who wishes deaf people had 'their brains bashed out' (and presumably shot, as well, since the image contains a gun). And the fact that the person is aware of the distinction between Deaf and hearing cultures suggests more than a casual familiarity with Deaf people and their lives, itself a concern considering the author's extreme views. Additionally, the equation of sensory disability with learning disability ('they're basically retarded') suggests a wider disdain and contempt for all disabled people. But 'Brandon' is not alone in holding such views alongside (at least) a minimal understanding of Deaf culture. Indeed, there was a t-shirt on sale in many places and over the Internet which says 'I hate Deaf people' in basic American Sign

Language but a campaign by Deaf activists led to the removal of this product from many stores.

Another anti-Deaf website, this time authored by 'Skanlyn', offers many reasons why it is important to hate Deaf people, calling them 'dregs' (Skanlyn, 2009). Such reasons purportedly include the cost of providing education in public schools, but many alleged personal characteristics of Deaf people as well, including 'They are lazy and shiftless', 'They are stupid', 'They talk funny', 'That annoying shit they do with their hands', 'They are dirty', 'They carry disease', 'They are often pedophiles' and 'They bring down housing values'. The author even claims that Deaf people 'killed our Lord'. And finally, Skanlyn concludes, 'In closing, if there are any parents of deaf children out there who have been offended by this blog, I would just like to say fuck you but more importantly, fuck your dreg child'.

It seems such hatred is more common than one might initially imagine. Another website has a poll entitled 'Do you hate Deaf people?' and although there have only been nine responses (four answering yes and five answering the other option, 'I can't hear you?'), the comments which people have added to the website are themselves revealing (CCC, 2009). Another person, who identified as 'Rew', comments, 'I hate deaf people. I wish they could hear just so I could yell at them'. One person discusses various inconveniences associated with being unable to hear and then concludes, 'I'm pretty sure I'd off myself if I couldn't hear'. This feeling that life with Deafness is not worth living is the starting assumption for many anti-Deaf hate sites. On another page, a person who identifies themselves as 'Cynical Bastard' has fantasies of control over Deaf people:

> i command the deaf, who read this page at this moment, to commit suicide. they make no contributions to make to society. music is the universal language. if you cannot partake in it, you are not part of the universe. beethoven was the only guy that pulled it off … otherwise … die (Cynical Bastard, 2004).

Disabled people have long criticized the concept of a 'supercrip', or someone who is held up as 'overcoming' their disability, against which all other people are judged. In this post, the remarkable achievements of one of the greatest composers in history are used as the litmus test for Deaf people's participation in music. If one is not able to match these (superhuman) levels of achievement, the 'command' from this author is suicide. On the other hand, 'black hunter', another contributor to this webpage, states, 'I hate deaf people, I fucking hate deaf people, Kill deaf people' (Black Hunter, 2008). The magnitude of this venom cannot be underestimated.

Blind people are also targeted. For instance, one webpage on 'BaneRants' is entitled 'Fuck, I Hate Blind People':

> Hey, if you don't read this to them, how are they gonna be offended? And so what if they are? I can kick some blind cocksuckers ass with one hand tied behind my back, and *fuck* alla their Blind-Fu.

The webpage contains a link to a 2006 Fox News story that a judge had ordered the US Treasury Department to make legal tender more accessible to blind people. The rant continues:

> This kinda shit just sets me off. Hey, blind-o! That's what coins are for! You assholes like to read faces, so just carry a sack of coins. Or a credit card, and get one of those credit card receipt reading dogs, you blind-ass fuck. Hey, shit happens. Deal. When are they gonna wanna set up SAT's for retards? Fuck, they already have their own Olympics. Needs more Javelin, if you ask me. Shit, I'm old and creaky, but I wanna play in the NFL. So it's only fair that I get to carry a handgun out on the field. You know, to make it fair. Oh c'mon, you know you'd buy that shit on Pay Per View. And I only wanna play against nigger retards. Midget retards. Muslim nigger midget retards. With big fat heads, cuz my vision ain't so good any more. Muslim nigger midget retards with no legs, on skateboards with oblong wheels. Blind Muslim nigger midget retards. Just to make it fair (Bane, 2006).

Once again, there seems to be an attempt at humor, but this cannot disguise the mix of antidisability, racist and Anit-Islamic religious hatred it contains. The rant clearly positions 'blind ass fuck', 'retards', 'nigger retards', 'midget retards', 'Muslim nigger retards', 'Muslim nigger midget retards' and 'Blind muslim nigger midget retards' as having unfair advantages over others. Of course, by linking these marginalized groups to a concept of 'fairness' and equal opportunity, this rant implicitly connects to a much wider discourse of opposition to affirmative action policies. So the language of disability hatred is a vehicle here for a much wider political agenda.

The issue of accessible money actually prompted the expression of a great deal of hatred towards blind people. On another Internet forum, Conquer Club, someone who is identified as 'heavycola' stated, 'I hate blind people and the way they never look at you when you're talking to them. It's just rude. I rip them off whenever i can. Why should the US taxpayer fork out for this bleeding heart nonsense when there are still people out there who haven't had a tax cut? Makes me sick' (Conquer Club, 2008). Often the hatred of blind people is posted on social networking sites. For instance, there are many brief updates on MySpace and Twitter which simply state 'I hate blind people'. A person who goes under the nickname 'Charlie Don't Surf' and identifies himself as a 46-year-old male from Glasgow, Scotland, gave a typical comment on a MySpace forum when he commented 'I hate blind people. THANK FUCK BLIND PEOPLE CAN'T READ OR I'D BE IN DEEP SHIT!!!' (Charlie Don't Surf, 2008). On another forum, a discussion about 'The best sign ever in America' became a vehicle for antidisability hatred. One poster (ironically named 'Happy Camper') commented, 'You guys know what I hate? BLIND PEOPLE! Frickin brail signs EVERYWHERE!' (Happy Camper, 2008). (Again, one notes the grammar/spelling mistakes – the word should be capitalized and should be spelled 'Braille'.) But more importantly, it is the visible sign of an accessible society which prompts the ire of the poster.

Unlike the hatred expressed towards other disabled people, those who tend to express animosity towards amputees tend to simply state their hatred, but not elaborate on their reasons for such hatred. For instance, there is a discussion on MySpace of a person's 'quotes from my life' where someone calling herself Cassandra Ambe simply states, 'You know I hate amputees' (Pagey/Bowser, 2008). Another website which is for computer game users contains a comment by 'KDS' dated May 21, 2009 stating, 'I hate amputees that still use computers' (KDS, 2009). Some people assume that being an amputee means that a person's life is condemned to misery – so much so that there have been long philosophical debates on the question 'Why does God hate amputees?' and various websites have been established to debate the merits of this question, including a Christian site aiming to reassure people that an all-loving God does not actually hate amputees (www. whydoesgodhateamputees.com). Of course, this is quite a different perspective from that given by many disabled people, who live rich, happy and productive lives and who make a genuine difference to society. But common assumptions about disability, and how dreadful it must be to be disabled, mean that these perspectives are rarely considered.

People with speech impairments have also been the victim of hatred. Often people express their hate for people who stutter quite straightforwardly, and do not elaborate on the reasons for these feelings. The following example, written by someone who calls themselves 'xxxotic' on an 'adult webmaster forum' called 'extreme bullshit' is typical of these comments: 'i hate people who stutter. spit it out prick' (xxxotic, 2005).

Those with psychiatric impairments are also hated. The Internet is littered with people asserting, 'I hate crazy people'. Like the word 'retard', the word 'crazy' is often used as a generic term of abuse and denigration, but it is also specifically targeted at people with psychiatric impairments. For instance, when Dave Chappelle was admitted to a psychiatric ward, Big Van Vader, a contributor to a web forum which was discussing his situation, commented:

> Fuck Chappelle. The guy is a millionaire, and im pretty sure hes got a attractive wife and a family. Hes got nothing to be complaining or sad about. I hate crazy people, dont have any respect for em, people with mental disorders just have weak minds. Screw Chappelle for not giving us another new season (Big Van Vader, 2005).

Another example comes from 'illuxtris', whose online journal states that her real name is Gemma and she lives in Quezon City, Philippines. She states that she is a psychiatric nurse, but hates 'crazy people':

> I hate crazy people. And I mean, pathologically crazy people who has some attention-seeking disorder. Freaking patient faux-fainted and faux-seizured

herself I wanted to slap her so bad. I don't care if this makes me sound like unfit
to be a psychiatric nurse because I know I am. I have no patience for those kind
of people. And our hospital doesn't have an area for psychiatric patients and
none of the medical personnel are trained to handle them, but the attendings like
to ignore this. Fuck these attendings too (illuxtris, 2009).

The fact that this person has such close contact with people who have psychiatric
illnesses is indeed concerning. One wonders what kind of 'care' they receive from
her! Another example of what has been called 'sanism' (prejudice against mentally
ill people) (Perlin, 2002) can be found on an online discussion of self-harm and
cutting. While some people shared their own experiences of such behavior, someone
with the screen name 'A.I._Obx' replied: 'You offend me. I hate schizophrenics,
psycho's and the chitter of the delusional. Self indulgent monkeys' (A.I._Obx,
2006). Likewise, when a man asked a question about his ex-girlfriend who had
bipolar disorder, one of the replies came from a person calling himself 'Chuck',
who said, 'I hate people with bipolar, they're just ridiculously crazy and nearly
impossible to deal with' (Chuck, 2008).

Is Every Famous Disabled Person Hated?

I first began to wonder whether every famous disabled person was hated when I read
the Internet posts of young people, some teenagers, who described their vehement
hatred of Helen Keller, a woman who died in 1968 – decades before many of them
were born. I read the hate sites about her, and then started brainstorming about
other famous disabled people. Christopher Reeve – yes, I found lots of hate sites
about him (though many were removed after his death) (Maddox, 2004). Steven
Hawking was hated too (Brigandi, 2008; HonestAbe, 2007). Gary Coleman as
well (Gauthier, 2008; D. Jones, 2008). Marlee Matlin (Rosindale, 2009). Stevie
Wonder (Jeff, 2003). There is even an 'I Hate Susan Boyle' group on Facebook
with almost 9,000 members as of September 2009. (Boyle was a contestant with a
cognitive disability from *Britain's Got Talent*.) Likewise, Scott Macintyre (a blind
contestant on *American Idol*) and Luke Adams (a Deaf contestant on *The Amazing
Race*). I was amazed. Anyone I thought of who was known to have a disability
– I found a hate site. It is virtually impossible to think of a well-known disabled
person in contemporary society who wasn't the target of disability hatred on the
web. It could be assumed that many stars would be hated by someone – but what
struck me in these posts was the way antidisability hatred blended with personal
attacks on the individuals. This section of the chapter documents some of these
hate sites.

There is a MySpace Group called 'helenkellersucks' which has a webpage
entitled 'I hate Helen Keller'. The group states that its address is 'SHITSVILLE,
Maryland, US'. The homepage for the group has a photo of a very young Keller
with a red line around her head and a line through it. There is a bulletin board

where someone called 'Sam' has posted. Sam's profile has a photo of him and four other young men wearing togas. His profile also indicates that he is 18 years old and lives in Elkton, Maryland. This is the only MySpace group to which Sam belongs. Sam's comment on the bulletin board was posted on February 9, 2008, and it is entitled 'most useless person ever', but it was subsequently made a private posting in August 2009. Before its removal, the post stated, 'god if i had a kid who couldnt see or hear i wouldve had them shot/put out of their misery' (Sam, 2008). Sam's comments are typical of many disability hate sites, and not just because his grammar is terrible. Like many people who post on disability hate sites, Sam's comments have two themes: first he insults the disabled person (in this case, by reducing Keller to 'the most useless person ever') and then he feigns a tone of concern or empathy that seems to rationalize killing the disabled person seemingly for their own benefit ('i wouldve had them shot/put out of their misery').

The MySpace group is far from alone in expressing hatred for Helen Keller. A blog at 'The Last Gaffe' written by 'Jeff Kelly' has two photos of an elderly Keller. Underneath one photo, where Keller is holding an award, Jeff has written, 'Just like this bitch. GOD. I hate her' (Kelly, 2009). Under the other photo, Jeff states, 'What I'm saying is that I would kick the SHIT out of Helen Keller (were she living today.) No joke, that bitch had it too good for too long'. There is also a Xanga group entitled 'I hate Helen Keller' (Madfreemindmuch, 2007). Its motto is, 'We will destroy that stupid idiot and send her back to her home on whore island!' (Again, the denigration of a disabled woman on the basis of her sexuality – she is reduced to the 'whore' slur – is common; there is both disability and gender bias in the slur.) There are also Facebook groups called 'I hate Helen Keller! Is that wrong?' and 'Helen Keller Would Suck Balls if She Knew Where to Find Them'. (The sexual denigration of Keller continues.) The latter group's description states 'helen keller was deaf, dumb and mute. she also sucks and i hate her. and she was a fraud. the miracle worker is the worst movie i've ever seen'. The hate site then continues with many Helen Keller jokes. Some people might think this takes the edge off some of the hateful comments on the site; but such a belief is mistaken. Demeaning jokes about a person, or about the group they identify with, are quite common in the commission of hate crimes. They are also present on hate sites. This is not a coincidence: mocking the person, and their disability, is part of the process of dehumanizing them.

In 2003, Alabama announced that Helen Keller had been chosen to be represented on the State Quarter. A likeness of Keller was on the coin, alongside her name in English, and in a reduced-size version of it in Braille. This was the subject of a blog entitled 'Nice State Quarter, Assholes' by a person who identified himself as 'Jayson Mattthews'. The author of the blog does not indicate any personal animosity towards Keller. He does suggest that all the credit for her achievements should go to Anne Sullivan, her teacher.

> Bullshit. Her movie isn't called "the Miracle Worker" because she taught herself to read. Anne Sullivan, her teacher, was the miracle worker. If anybody should

be on the fucking quarter it should be her. She taught a blind, deaf mute to read and write, for Christ's sake! Nobody fawns like an idiot over the people Jesus miraculously cured. They give props to the J-man himself. So why does Helen Keller get to hog Anne Sullivan's limelight? What a fucking sham! *"But what about all the books she wrote? That's pretty impressive!"* Big fucking deal. The only way she could communicate with the outside world was by writing things down. It's pretty easy to write a book when you have to write a paragraph every time you want to take a dump. It's like being impressed by a Polock who eats Pierogi or a crack head who's good with a lighter. It's what they do (Mattthews, 2005).

It was in the responses to this blog that more overt signs of hatred became present. The first respondent added, 'I wonder who the genius was that approved a raging socialist for a U.S. state quarter. I hate Helen Keller'. Another respondent, who identified himself as 'James', stated, 'I am an Alabama native and long time resident of the state. I have absolutely no recollection of ever being asked by anyone whether I wanted a deaf, dumb, blind, mute, and ugly woman on my state quarter'. A poster called 'Lil Bastard' introduced the topic of rape to the discussion, under the guise of humor. Such 'humor' had a nasty, violent, sexual edge. Lil Bastard commented, 'Why didn't Helen Keller scream when she was raped? Because the guy had her hands pinned down'. This hyperviolent, hypersexual image is seemingly humorous, but it actually contains many of the themes of disability hatred more generally.

Conclusion

Some people cannot believe that anyone actually hates disabled people. This flawed assumption is widespread. For instance, the Scottish Executive Working Group on Hate Crime produced a report on hate crime which seemed to indicate that the motive for crimes against disabled people was their 'vulnerability' rather than hate. One section of the report specifically addresses this topic. It states:

> It is important to note the distinction between vulnerability on the one hand and malice and ill-will towards a social group on the other. We were very aware that there can be a grey area where these overlap and that it should be an essential element of hate crime to prove that a crime has been motivated by malice and ill-will towards an individual *because of* a presumed membership of a social group rather than because of their vulnerability. For example, if someone is attacked, but because of their disability is unable to run away, the crime occurred because the individual was vulnerable and this would not constitute a hate crime. The individual has been targeted because of their vulnerability rather than because of their membership of a social group. [Emphasis in original] (Scottish Executive, 2004).

This comment is fascinating in two respects: first, it is impossible to imagine any group other than disabled people being considered innately vulnerable to attack. The reference to personal embodiment, rather than a social context is incredibly important here. The example does not refer to a person being in a vulnerable situational context – such as walking alone at night in a darkened alleyway. Instead, it places the onus for 'vulnerability' directly on the bodies of disabled people (itself an expression of disablist attitudes!). The second interesting aspect of this paragraph is that it involves a mistaken application of the concept of being targeted 'because of' a particular identity. If someone who is disabled is automatically assumed to be 'vulnerable' and this flawed and prejudicial conflation of disability and vulnerability is the motive behind a particular crime, the person has been victimized 'because of' their disability. And this is not a random crime – it is a bias crime. And bias crimes are hate crimes.

This chapter has demonstrated that disability hatred is actually widespread. It has documented many antidisability hate sites, but there were many more which were not discussed. The enormous number of antidisability hate sites made that task impossible. Newer forms of social networking, including Facebook and MySpace, have enabled people to express their hatred in new ways – and to join with others who share the same views. The chapter has also shown that some sites try to blend a mix of unadulterated hate, hyperviolent and hypersexual images, and attempted humor. However, this humor does not soften the blow when one considers that the authors often continue to advocate beating or killing disabled people.

This chapter has pointed towards an important conclusion: There are some unique characteristics of disability hate sites which may be different from other hate sites and other forms of cyberbullying. First, the language of insult is different. For instance, the terms used often stem directly from medical discourse. Words such as 'spastic', 'cripple', 'retard' and so on have a long history in medicine – raising the broader topic of the role of the medical model in creating a fault-finding and negative image of disability. This broader role of medicine is discussed later in the book, but it is important to flag it as a major cause for concern in the cultural construction of disability. A second feature of the websites which have been discussed in this chapter is that they are almost always dissociated from broader political groups. In essence, disability hatred is privatized. Rather than reflecting membership of larger political movements or particular hate groups, which is the case with a great deal of racially motivated hate sites, these websites tend to be created by lone individuals. But simply because they are run by individuals does not mean that they are not widespread. It may in fact mean that disability hatred is so broadly disseminated that thousands of people feel free to employ it without a second thought.

It might be possible to suggest that disability hate speech is not mainly aimed at disabled people, but rather terms such as 'retard' have become generic insults instead. Certainly, like the use of the phrase 'that's gay' as a generic insult, terms about disability have also moved into the realm of commonplace insults. But this chapter has suggested that these terms of hate and insult are still directed at disabled people, and often at specific disabled individuals.

The question then becomes: 'If hate speech about disability is so common, does that mean hate crimes against disabled people are also common?' The next chapter examines the FBI data on disability hate crimes. This data suggests certain unique features of disability hate crimes, but also suggests that disability hate crimes are fairly uncommon. The reliability of these statistics is also discussed in the next chapter.

Chapter 3

Disability Hate Crimes in the USA

Relative to other countries, the US is somewhat of an anomaly when it comes to disability hate crimes: the FBI has the world's longest running and largest dataset on such crimes and the US was the first country to successfully prosecute a disability hate crime – and yet disability organizations have largely been strangely silent on this issue. This stands in stark contrast to most other countries, where disability organizations have campaigned long and hard around the issue, and after years of struggle have been able to convince law enforcement and policymakers that this was a significant enough problem to collect data and develop appropriate responses. This chapter examines the FBI data on disability hate crimes in some detail, using this dataset to highlight the unique characteristics of these crimes. But it also points to the flaws in the database and highlights a number of cases where the system has failed to record these crimes.

FBI Data on Disability Hate Crimes

The FBI holds the largest international dataset on disability hate crimes. As a result of the Hate Crime Statistics Act of 1990, the FBI is required to collect data on hate-motivated crimes under its Uniform Crime Reporting Program and it publishes annual reports on hate crime in America. The FBI breaks antidisability hate crimes into two categories: those classified as 'anti-mental disability' and 'anti-physical disability'. This is the definition of 'physical' and 'mental' disability bias used in this context by the FBI: 'A performed negative opinion or attitude toward a group of persons based on physical or mental impediments/challenges, whether such disabilities are congenital or acquired by heredity, accident, injury, advanced age or illness' (Federal Bureau of Investigation, 1999). Of course, there are many other ways of categorizing disability, and this physical/mental disability binary is simplistic and deeply problematic. For instance, classifying people who have both 'physical' and 'mental' disabilities is problematic in this approach. Additionally, people whose impairments do not fit neatly into this divide (for instance, people with AIDS, or people with sensory impairments) are also prone to inconsistent classification. The recording process is also problematic, for reasons which will be elaborated later, but this database is still a very useful resource that can be used to analyze officially recognized disability hate crimes. The data hints at a much larger picture and suggests that there are some unique characteristics of disability hate crime, unlike other bias crimes.

From 1997 to 2007, the FBI recorded over 66,000 hate crimes of various motivations. However, it only recorded 520 disability hate crimes. Within the 520 antidisability hate crimes, 320 were classed as 'anti-mental disability' and 200 were classed as 'anti-physical disability'. The similarities and differences between disability hate crimes directed at these two groups will be outlined shortly, but it is first important to assess this data in aggregate, in order to see general patterns that distinguish disability hate crimes from other forms of bias crime. At face value, these numbers seem to suggest that a very small number of disabled people have experienced hate crimes. Such an impression would be understandable, but it is mistaken (for reasons that will be discussed later). The fact that disability hate crimes constitute less than 1% of the overall numbers of hate crimes recorded – when the disabled people are often estimated as constituting 20% of the overall population – is arguably more of a reflection of the failure of both victims and authorities to properly recognize and report such hate crimes, rather than a lower incidence of disability hate crime relative to other forms of hate crime (Sherry, 2003a). Nevertheless, the FBI data does indicate that disability hate crimes have unique characteristics, so it is worth analyzing in some detail in order to identify these characteristics.

Unfortunately, while there were attempts to analyze the first five years of this data (McMahon et al., 2004; Sherry, 2003b), no subsequent analysis of the next five years has been conducted. This is problematic because early efforts to record disability hate crimes focused on physical disability and paid limited attention to mental disability. The most recent FBI data on disability hate crimes, which has incorporated a larger focus on mental disability, has never been statistically analyzed to identify important trends and to enable researchers and policymakers to identify differences between disability hate crimes and other forms of hate crimes. This chapter is therefore the first attempt to analyze the FBI hate crime data from 1997 to 2007 – the first 10 years in which the FBI published data on disability hate crimes. (Disability hate crime data was not collected prior to 1997.) The increase in the proportion of disability hate crimes against people with 'mental disabilities' relative to 'physical disabilities' is presented in Table 3.1 and Graph 3.1.

Table 3.1 indicates that the number of anti-physical disability hate crimes in 1997 was three times higher than the number of anti-mental disability hate crimes. However, by 2007, hate crimes aimed at people with physical disabilities were far less common than those aimed at people with mental disabilities. Indeed, hate crimes aimed at people with mental disabilities were three times higher than anti-physical disability hate crimes by the end of this 10-year period. In other words, there had been a complete reversal in the ratio of reported disability hate crimes from 1997 to 2007.

Table 3.1 Increasing recognition of anti-mental disabilities in FBI statistics

Offences year	Anti-physical	Anti-mental
1997	9	3
1998	14	13
1999	11	10
2000	20	16
2001	12	25
2002	20	27
2003	30	10
2004	23	48
2005	21	32
2006	20	74
2007	20	62
Total	**200**	**320**

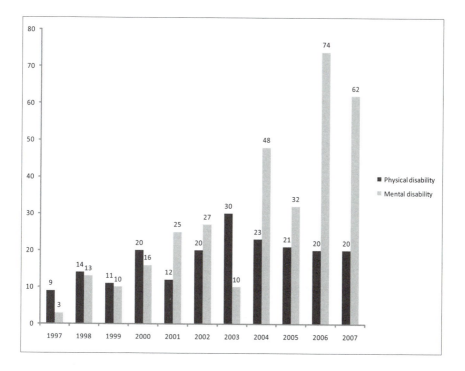

Graph 3.1 Total number of hate crimes 1997–2007:
       Mental and physical disability compared

Graph 3.1 is a visual representation of the raw data collected by the FBI on anti-mental and anti-physical disability hate crimes. It clearly records the massive increase in (officially recognized) disability hate crimes in this period and demonstrates that while the numbers are still relatively low, hate crimes motivated by prejudice against mental disability are far more likely to be recorded in 2007 than hate crimes motivated by prejudice against physical disability.

Differences in Hate Crimes aimed at Physical and Mental Disabilities

The first obvious difference between the reported incidence of hate crimes against physically and mentally disabled people is their magnitude: although the first five years of the FBI data suggests they occur in virtually the same numbers (the exact totals for the first five years were 66 anti-physical disability hate and 67 anti-mental disability hate crimes), the subsequent years have seen a great rise in the number of reported hate crimes motivated by anti-mental disability bias. This growth in the reported figures can be seen in Table 3.2. Not only are there more reported hate crimes directed at people with mental disabilities, there are other differences in the types of crime they experience as well. For these incidents, the FBI data on 'crimes against the person' shows important differences as well, which are recorded in the following tables and figures. The figures below demonstrate the following differences in bias crimes aimed at physically and mentally disabled people:

- The only officially recognized hate crime murder of a disabled person was directed at someone with a mental disability.
- Although the overall numbers are relatively low, there is a higher rate of rape among people with mental disabilities. (However, people with both physical and mental disabilities have a much higher rate of bias-motivated rape than nondisabled people.)
- There is a slightly higher rate of aggravated assault against people with physical disabilities.
- There is a slightly higher rate of simple assault among people with mental disabilities (though both are significantly higher than nondisabled people).
- There is a higher rate of intimidation against people with physical disabilities.

The FBI breaks down hate crimes into two categories – 'Crimes against the person' and 'Crimes against property'. Both of these categories are analyzed below. Crimes against the person are sorted into six categories: murder and nonnegligent manslaughter, forcible rape, aggravated assault, simple assault, intimidation, and 'other' crimes. 'Crimes against property' are divided into seven categories: robbery, burglary, larceny-theft, motor vehicle theft, arson, destruction/damage/vandalism, and 'other' crimes.

Table 3.2 Crimes against the person: Physically disabled persons

	2007	2006	2005	2004	2003	2002	2001	2000	1999	1998	1997	Total
Murder and nonnegligent manslaughter	0	0	0	0	0	0	0	0	0	0	0	**0**
Forcible rape	0	0	0	0	1	1	0	0	0	0	0	**2**
Aggravated assault	2	2	4	2	2	4	0	0	0	2	1	**19**
Simple assault	7	4	9	3	9	11	3	6	3	5	4	**64**
Intimidation	7	3	6	6	6	4	6	5	2	5	4	**54**
Other	0	2	0	0	0	0	0	2	0	0	0	**4**
Total	**16**	**11**	**19**	**11**	**18**	**20**	**9**	**13**	**5**	**12**	**9**	**143**

The first two categories in Table 3.2 indicate that the FBI has *never* recorded a single murder or nonnegligent manslaughter which was motivated by bias against a person with a physical disability; it has only recorded two 'forcible rapes' motivated by anti-physical disability bias. (One wonders what types of rape are not 'forcible rape'.) The largest number of hate crimes against someone with a physical disability involved simple assault (there were 64 of these crimes), followed by 54 cases of intimidation, and 19 cases of aggravated assault. Four cases were labeled an 'other' type of crime against the person.

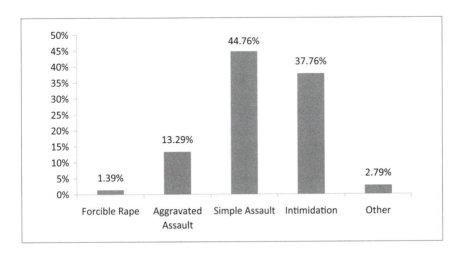

Graph 3.2 Percentage distribution of crimes against the person, motivated by disability bias, aimed at physically disabled people

Simple assault and intimidation are the most common hate crimes aimed at the person when it comes to hate crimes aimed at physically disabled people. Aggravated assault is another major aspect of hate crimes against the person for physically disabled people. Graph 3.2 shows that 44% of hate crimes aimed at physically disabled people involve simple assault, 37% of these crimes involve intimidation, 13% involve aggravated assault, 2% are classified as 'other' crimes against the person, and forcible rape occurs in 1% of this form of disability hate crime.

Table 3.3 provides data on antidisability hate crimes from 1997 to 2007 motivated by bias against mental disability.

Table 3.3 Crimes against the person: Mentally disabled persons

	2007	2006	2005	2004	2003	2002	2001	2000	1999	1998	1997	Total
Murder and nonnegligent manslaughter	0	0	0	0	1	0	0	0	0	0	0	**1**
Forcible rape	1	2	1	0	0	0	0	0	1	1	0	**6**
Aggravated assault	2	4	2	3	0	3	3	1	1	1	0	**20**
Simple assault	9	18	8	12	3	7	4	5	4	5	1	**76**
Intimidation	8	12	2	17	1	1	6	1	4	4	2	**58**
Other	2	0	1	0	0	0	2	0	0	0	0	**5**
Total	**22**	**36**	**14**	**32**	**5**	**11**	**15**	**7**	**10**	**11**	**3**	**166**

Table 3.3 details the raw figures for hate crimes aimed at mentally disabled persons for the years 1997–2007. This table includes the only murder or nonnegligent manslaughter ever formally recognized by the FBI as a disability hate crime. Additionally, only six rapes have been recognized by the FBI as motivated by anti-mental disability bias. The most common forms of hate crimes directed at mentally disabled people were aggravated assault (76 crimes), intimidation (58 crimes), and aggravated assault (20 crimes). There were five crimes designated as 'other' crimes against the person.

When this data is broken down into percentages, it becomes clear that approximately 80% of crimes against the person which are motivated by bias against people with mental disabilities are either simple assault or intimidation. Combined, simple assault, intimidation and aggravated assault comprise more than 90% of this type of bias crime. The percentage of hate crimes involving forcible rape (3.61%) may at first seem small, but it is considerably higher than the rate for any other form of bias crime.

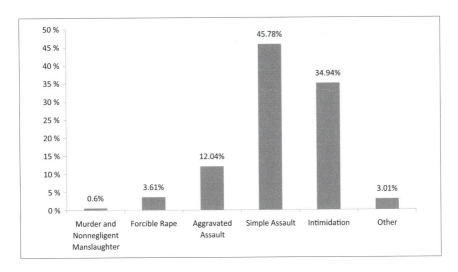

**Graph 3.3 Percentage distribution of crimes against the person, motivated
by disability bias, aimed at mentally disabled people**

Looking at the Data on Disability Hate Crimes in Aggregate

From 1997 to 2007, the most common antidisability hate crimes were simple
assault (133); intimidation (111); destruction/damage/vandalism (73); larceny/
theft (73); and aggravated assault (36). The tables and figures below record the
numbers of disability hate crimes in the FBI database, but also compare disability
hate crimes with hate crimes motivated by other forms of bias. The rationale for
comparing disability hate crimes to all other hate crimes is to identify the ways
in which disability hate crimes are a unique form of criminal victimization. For
instance, it will become clear that relative to other hate crime, disability hate crimes
are more likely to involve rape, larceny-theft, burglary, and simple assault; they
are also less likely to involve aggravated assault, intimidation and destruction/
damage/vandalism. Additionally, disability hate crimes are more likely to occur in
a residence or home. There are also higher rates of disability hate crimes in service
stations, restaurants and airline or bus terminals. On the other hand, disability hate
crimes are less likely to occur on a highway/road/alley/street, a place of worship,
in a bar/nightclub, or in a school or college.

Tables 3.4 and 3.5 record the exact numbers of 'crimes against the person'
motivated by antidisability bias and all other forms of bias. By providing the total
figures for disability and nondisability hate crimes, some of the unique features of
disability hate crimes become apparent.

Table 3.4 Crimes against the person: Disability bias

	2007	2006	2005	2004	2003	2002	2001	2000	1999	1998	1997	Total
Murder and nonnegligent manslaughter	0	0	0	0	1	0	0	0	0	0	0	**1**
Forcible rape	1	2	1	0	1	1	0	0	1	1	0	**8**
Aggravated assault	4	6	6	4	2	7	3	1	1	3	1	**38**
Simple assault	16	22	17	6	12	18	7	11	7	10	5	**131**
Intimidation	15	15	8	12	7	5	12	6	6	9	6	**101**
Other	2	2	1	0	0	0	2	2	0	0	0	**9**
Total	**38**	**47**	**33**	**22**	**23**	**31**	**24**	**20**	**15**	**23**	**12**	**288**

Table 3.5 Crimes against the person: All forms of bias excluding disability

	2007	2006	2005	2004	2003	2002	2001	2000	1999	1998	1997	Total
Murder and nonnegligent manslaughter	9	3	6	5	13	11	10	19	17	13	8	**114**
Forcible rape	1	4	2	4	4	7	4	4	5	10	9	**54**
Aggravated assault	1112	1172	1056	1035	918	1031	1238	1183	1119	1081	1236	**12181**
Simple assault	1668	1715	1549	1735	1797	1780	2147	1604	1759	1696	1795	**19245**
Intimidation	2550	2493	2531	2804	2737	3101	4327	3286	3262	3479	3808	**34378**
Other	30	15	13	16	25	10	18	14	12	3	5	**161**
Total	**5370**	**5402**	**5157**	**5599**	**5494**	**5940**	**7744**	**6110**	**6174**	**6282**	**6861**	**66133**

Tables 3.4 and 3.5 indicate that the most common crime against the person for a disability hate crime was simple assault, whereas intimidation was the most common crime for crimes against the person motivated by other forms of bias. When it came to the second most common crime against the person, these results were reversed: intimidation was second most common for disability hate crime and simple assault was second most common for other forms of bias crime. Aggravated assault was the third most common form of hate crime for both disability and other bias motivations, but occurred in significantly smaller numbers. Graph 3.4 details the exact percentage differences in these results.

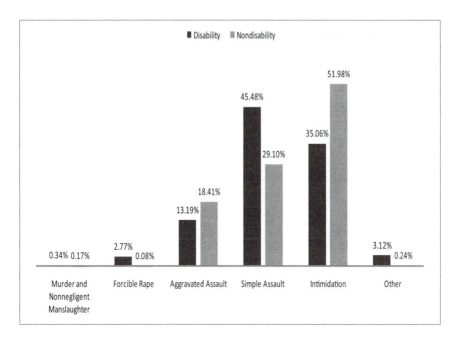

**Graph 3.4 Percentage distribution of crimes against the person:
Disability and nondisability hate crimes compared**

The key findings from this data comparison are highlighted below.

Much Higher Percentage of Rape for Disability Hate Crimes

Rape is 30 times more common in disability hate crimes than other hate crimes. While rape only amounts to 2.68% of all antidisability hate crimes, it only occurs in 0.08% of other types of hate crime. Additionally, while disability hate crimes amount to less than half of 1% of the overall number of hate crimes, they involve over 14.5% of all reported hate crimes involving rape.

Lower Rates of Aggravated Assault in Disability Hate Crimes

In contrast, FBI statistics suggest that disabled people are far less likely to experience a hate crime involving aggravated assault than nondisabled people. (The categories 'simple assault' and 'aggravated assault' are determined by various laws and then reported accordingly by the FBI.) Excluding disability hate crimes, there were 12,181 cases of hate crimes involving aggravated assault recorded by the FBI between 1997 and 2007 – which suggests that 18.41% of all hate crimes against the person involve aggravated assault. However, in this same time period, only 36 cases of antidisability hate crimes involving aggravated assault were recorded, amounting to 12.08% of all disability hate crimes against the person.

Much Higher Rates of Simple Assault in Disability Hate Crimes

Simple assault is an important factor in many hate crimes. Over 44% of all disability hate crimes against the person involved simple assault, which is much higher than the rate of simple assault associated with other forms of hate crime. For other forms of hate crime, 29% of crimes against the person involve simple assault. This difference may be important, in terms of crime and punishment, because simple assault is typically treated as a misdemeanor and not a felony in the US.

Lower Rates of Intimidation in Disability Hate Crimes

Another common feature of hate crime, intimidation, is also different for disability hate crimes relative to other hate crimes. In general, intimidation is the most common form of hate crime which people experience. Overall, there were more than 34,000 hate crimes involving intimidation (excluding disability hate crimes) – meaning that intimidation occurred in 52% of these crimes. However, the reported incidence of intimidation in disability hate crimes seems quite different. Intimidation is reported by the FBI in only 37.24% of crimes against the person motivated by antidisability bias.

Having outlined some of the major differences between crimes against the person motivated by disability bias and other forms of bias, it is now important to examine the FBI data on crimes against property.

Bias Crimes against Property

Crimes against property are allocated into seven categories within the FBI database: robbery, burglary, larceny-theft, motor vehicle theft, arson, destruction/damage/vandalism, and 'other' forms of property crime. By examining the data on these types of crimes as well, a more complete picture of the unique characteristics of disability hate crimes emerges.

Tables 3.6 and 3.7 demonstrate that destruction/damage/vandalism occurs more frequently than any crime against property which is motivated by bias – both for disability hate crimes and all other forms of hate crimes. However, simply stating this fact is insufficient: there were 76 disability hate crimes involving destruction/damage/vandalism, but there were 75 cases of larceny-theft motivated by disability bias. On the other hand, when it came to other forms of bias crime involving a crime against property, destruction/damage/vandalism was by far the most common property crime. There were over 30,000 bias crimes (excluding disability bias crimes) which involved destruction/damage/vandalism, and the highest figure of any other form of bias-related property crime in this timeframe was larceny-theft, with 1,718. This suggests a quite profound difference in the dynamics of property crimes motivated by disability bias compared to property crimes motivated by other forms of bias. These differences are even more evident in Graph 3.5.

Table 3.6 Crimes against property: Disability bias

	2007	2006	2005	2004	2003	2002	2001	2000	1999	1998	1997	Total
Robbery	3	1	1	1	0	0	2	1	0	1	0	**10**
Burglary	4	5	1	5	2	1	2	1	2	0	0	**23**
Larceny-theft	21	13	11	8	4	11	4	1	1	1	0	**75**
Motor vehicle theft	0	1	0	0	1	1	0	0	0	0	0	**3**
Arson	0	1	0	0	0	0	0	1	0	0	0	**2**
Destruction/damage/ vandalism	10	16	4	11	6	10	4	11	2	2	0	**76**
Other	6	4	3	2	1	2	0	0	1	0	0	**19**
Total	**44**	**41**	**20**	**27**	**14**	**25**	**12**	**15**	**6**	**4**	**0**	**208**

Table 3.7 Crimes against property: All forms of bias excluding disability

	2007	2006	2005	2004	2003	2002	2001	2000	1999	1998	1997	Total
Robbery	233	199	153	112	107	131	156	138	129	117	114	**1589**
Burglary	189	172	164	146	164	130	147	137	110	99	111	**1569**
Larceny-theft	209	270	221	169	173	140	146	113	102	80	95	**1718**
Motor vehicle theft	27	43	19	15	15	8	15	11	14	3	7	**177**
Arson	47	50	48	44	34	38	90	51	48	50	60	**560**
Destruction/ damage/vandalism	3318	3332	2865	2812	2618	2337	3014	2754	2652	2547	2549	**30798**
Other	41	58	40	35	28	14	27	22	21	5	7	**298**
Total	**4064**	**4124**	**3510**	**3333**	**3139**	**2798**	**3595**	**3226**	**3076**	**2901**	**2943**	**36709**

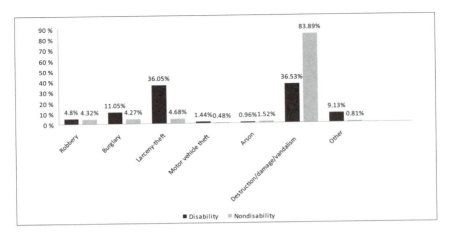

Graph 3.5 Comparing crimes against property: Disability and other biases

The most significant features of disability hate crimes (relative to other hate crimes) are summarized below.

Lower Rates of Destruction/Damage/Vandalism in Disability Hate Crimes

When people actively hate a particular group, and set out to commit a property crime against that group, they usually damage the group's property. Indeed, destroying symbols of the group which is being victimized is often regarded as central in establishing the bias motivation of the case. So it is not surprising that over 83% of all hate crimes (other than disability hate crimes) involve destruction/damage/vandalism. But this sort of bias-motivated property crime seems less common when it comes to disability hate crimes. Destruction/damage/vandalism only occurs in 36% of property crimes motivated by disability hatred. Unlike other forms of hate crime, destruction/damage/vandalism does not completely dominate the landscape of property crimes motivated by disability bias. Instead, larceny-theft is basically just as common as destruction, damage or vandalism in disability bias crimes involving property.

Much Higher Rates of Larceny-Theft in Disability Hate Crimes

Disability hate crimes involve much higher rates of larceny-theft than do other forms of hate crime. In hate crimes that do not involve disability, only 4.27% of hate crimes involve larceny-theft. In contrast, larceny-theft is almost (but not quite) the most common form of property hate crime involving disability bias; 36.05% of disability hate crimes involving property contain larceny-theft. This means larceny-theft is over eight times more common in disability hate crimes than in nondisability bias crimes involving property.

Higher Rates of Burglary in Disability Hate Crimes

Disability hate crimes which involve property crimes are almost three times more likely to involve burglary than nondisability hate crimes. Burglary occurs in over 11% of property crimes motivated by disability bias, whereas it only occurs in 4% of nondisability bias crimes.

Roughly Equivalent Rates of Robbery

The rate of robbery in disability hate crimes is only slightly higher than the rate of robbery in other bias crimes that involve property crimes. Robbery occurs in 4.8% of disability bias crimes, slightly higher than the 4.32% which occurs in nondisability bias crimes. This is a roughly equivalent percentage of robbery.

Higher Rates of Motor Vehicle Theft

Although the percentages are very small indeed, the likelihood of a disability bias-related property crime involving motor vehicle theft is significantly higher than other bias crimes involving property. Indeed, they are almost three times greater for disability bias than property crimes involving other forms of bias.

Higher Rates of 'Other' Property Crimes

Many more property crimes involving disability are likely to be classified as 'other' property crimes and not categorized within the regular FBI categories. For property crime motivated by other forms of hate, less than 1% of hate crimes.

Lower Rates of Arson

Disability hate crimes are less likely to involve arson. Though arson is a small proportion of every type of hate crime, it occurs in 1.52% of all nondisability hate crimes against property. On the other hand, it only occurs in 0.96% of disability hate crimes.

Tables 3.8 and 3.9 record the places where hate crimes occur in the community. By examining these figures in detail, it will be possible to ascertain whether the locations of disability hate crimes are any different from the locations of other hate crimes. Any difference may be significant in terms of law enforcement responses, prevention efforts, and community education.

Table 3.8 Location of disability hate crimes

	2007	2006	2005	2004	2003	2002	2001	2000	1999	1998	1997	Total
Air/bus/train terminal	2	2	1	0	0	2	1	0	0	0	0	**8**
Bank/savings and loan	0	1	0	1	0	0	0	0	1	0	0	**3**
Bar/night club	0	0	1	0	0	0	0	0	0	0	0	**1**
Church/synagogue/temple	0	0	1	0	0	1	1	0	0	0	0	**3**
Commercial office building	0	1	1	2	1	3	0	2	1	0	0	**11**
Construction site	0	0	0	0	0	0	0	0	0	0	0	**0**
Convenience store	0	1	1	3	0	1	1	1	0	1	0	**9**
Department/discount store	0	2	0	1	1	0	1	0	0	0	0	**5**
Drug store/doctor's office/hospital	0	0	0	0	0	0	0	0	0	2	0	**2**
Field/woods	1	2	0	0	0	0	0	0	0	0	0	**3**
Government/public building	0	1	0	0	0	1	2	0	0	0	1	**5**
Grocery/supermarket	0	0	0	1	0	0	0	0	0	0	1	**2**
Highway/road/alley/street	14	13	6	9	4	9	5	4	1	9	0	**74**
Hotel/motel/etc.	0	0	2	0	0	0	0	0	0	0	0	**2**
Jail/prison	0	0	0	0	0	0	0	0	0	0	1	**1**
Lake/waterway	0	1	0	0	0	0	0	0	0	0	0	**1**
Liquor store	0	0	0	0	0	0	0	0	0	0	0	**0**
Parking lot/garage	4	5	3	1	3	2	0	5	3	0	2	**28**
Rental storage facility	1	0	0	1	0	2	0	0	0	0	0	**4**
Residence/home	30	32	21	25	13	9	15	17	6	7	2	**177**
Restaurant	3	3	3	1	0	1	0	2	3	0	1	**17**
School/college	5	8	3	2	6	5	3	2	2	2	3	**41**
Service/gas station	4	2	2	0	1	1	0	0	0	1	0	**11**
Specialty store (TV, fur, etc.)	0	1	1	1	1	0	1	0	0	0	1	**6**
Other/unknown	15	4	7	9	3	8	5	3	2	3	0	**59**
Multiple locations	0	0	0	0	0	0	0	0	0	0	0	**0**
Total	**79**	**79**	**53**	**57**	**33**	**45**	**35**	**36**	**19**	**25**	**12**	**473**

The main features of Table 3.8 are that 177 cases of disability hate crime have occurred in a residence or home; 74 cases have occurred on a highway/road/alley/street; 59 cases occurred in other or unknown locations; 41 cases occurred in schools or colleges; 28 cases occurred in parking lots or garages; 17 cases occurred in restaurants; 11 cases occurred in commercial office buildings and in service/gas stations. No other locations contained more than 10 disability hate crimes.

Table 3.9 Location of non-disability hate crimes

	2007	2006	2005	2004	2003	2002	2001	2000	1999	1998	1997	Total
Air/bus/train terminal	78	78	54	72	55	61	80	85	84	68	80	**795**
Bank/savings and loan	13	12	23	20	14	19	17	12	13	8	8	**159**
Bar/night club	149	149	137	140	107	128	154	147	130	151	137	**1529**
Church/synagogue/temple	309	309	309	314	284	283	378	336	274	278	231	**3305**
Commercial office building	167	166	151	169	177	197	286	230	244	179	240	**2206**
Construction site	36	36	17	23	26	19	25	25	20	24	19	**270**
Convenience store	80	79	100	98	96	113	238	90	75	67	82	**1118**
Department/discount store	61	59	45	63	66	58	53	48	44	30	34	**561**
Drug store/doctor's office/hospital	57	57	52	59	39	51	52	58	48	49	31	**553**
Field/woods	109	107	72	70	80	69	111	77	62	95	90	**942**
Government/Public building	119	118	129	110	87	81	111	101	82	101	90	**1129**
Grocery/supermarket	57	57	62	49	57	51	129	42	54	63	57	**678**
Highway/road/alley/street	1424	1425	1308	1402	1312	1481	1779	1437	1457	1510	1685	**16220**
Hotel/motel/etc.	37	37	43	42	51	55	72	45	56	48	47	**533**
Jail/prison	50	50	48	54	38	42	46	58	55	41	42	**524**
Lake/waterway	11	10	21	13	11	12	19	20	16	10	24	**167**
Liquor store	17	17	18	9	14	14	49	8	8	7	12	**173**
Parking lot/garage	450	449	468	424	446	459	606	480	476	446	464	**5168**
Rental storage facility	4	5	7	12	9	7	13	4	8	11	4	**84**
Residence/home	2299	2297	2127	2423	2382	2189	2987	2573	2252	2370	2394	**26293**
Restaurant	158	158	107	147	118	165	224	189	155	145	140	**1706**
School/college	854	851	964	896	878	784	984	915	800	697	848	**9471**
Service/gas station	71	73	65	77	64	77	149	77	64	68	53	**838**
Specialty store (TV, fur, etc.)	67	66	77	109	105	93	200	125	97	126	120	**1185**
Other/unknown	860	871	692	840	936	907	926	837	1277	1131	1112	**10389**
Multiple locations	9	9	14	7	4	2	7	8	6	7	5	**78**
Total	**7545**	**7545**	**7110**	**7592**	**7456**	**7417**	**9660**	**8027**	**7857**	**7730**	**8049**	**85988**

The key figures in Table 3.9, which records statistics about the location of nondisability hate crimes, are that such crimes occurred in 26,293 cases at residences and homes; in 16,220 cases at a highway/road/alley/street; in 10,389 cases at other or unknown locations; in 9,471 cases at a school or college; in 5,168 cases in a parking lot/garage; in 3,305 cases at a church/synagogue/temple; in 2,206 cases at a commercial office building; in 1,706 cases at a restaurant; in

1,529 cases at a bar/nightclub; in 1,185 cases at a specialty store; in 1,129 cases at a government/public building; and in 1,118 cases at a convenience store. No other locations contained more than 1,000 nondisability hate crimes.

Simply presenting these statistics, without highlighting the ways certain locations are more or less likely to be the site of a hate crime – whether motivated by disability hate or another bias – would be inadequate. So Graph 3.6 visually represents the differences in the percentage distribution of locations that are the site of disability hate crimes and other bias crimes.

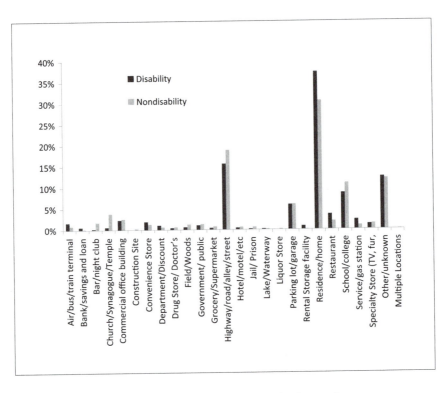

Graph 3.6 Location of disability and nondisability hate crimes

Graph 3.6 indicates that the most common places where disability hate crimes occur are residences or homes (37.42%) and highways/alleys/roads/streets (15.64%). Interestingly, although there are 26 possible locations in the FBI database, the third most common location was an 'other/unknown' location. These unknown locations contain over 12% of all disability hate crimes. The next most common locations for disability hate crimes are schools or colleges (8.66%); parking lots or garages (5.91%); restaurants (3.59%); commercial office buildings (2.32%); gas or service stations (2.32%); convenience stores (1.9%); air, bus or train terminals (1.69%); specialty stores such as TV stores (1.26%); department or discount stores (1.05%) and government or public buildings (1.05%). No other locations contained more than 1% of disability hate crimes. On the other hand, Table 3.9 identifies the locations where nondisability bias crimes occur most frequently. It indicates that residences are again the most common place where bias crimes occur, consisting of 30.57% of all crimes. Highways/alleys/roads/streets are again the second most common places where bias crimes occur – but in nondisability hate crimes, they comprise 18.86% of all cases. This is interesting because it indicates that these top two locations contain over 53% of all disability hate crimes, and 49.43% of all nondisability hate crimes. Other/unknown locations are again the third most common location for nondisability bias crimes – containing 12.08% of such crimes. Schools or colleges are the location of 11.01% of nondisability bias crimes; parking lots or garages 6.01%; churches/synagogues/temples 3.84%; commercial office buildings 2.56%; restaurants 1.98%; bars/nightclubs 1.77%; specialty stores 1.37%; government/public buildings 1.31%; convenience stores 1.3%; and fields or woods 1.27%. There are no other locations for nondisability bias crimes which occur in more than 1% of cases.

Table 3.10 Known offenders race, disability hate crimes, 1997–2007

	2007	2006	2005	2004	2003	2002	2001	2000	1999	1998	1997	Total
White	29	38	24	22	21	17	11	12	11	11	9	**205**
Black	13	20	8	27	8	9	8	11	2	4	1	**111**
American Indian/ Alaskan Native	2	0	2	1	0	0	0	0	0	0	0	**5**
Asian/Pacific Islander	0	2	1	0	0	0	0	0	0	0	0	**3**
Multiple races, group	1	0	3	1	1	3	4	1	1	2	1	**18**
Unknown race	4	9	6	1	2	5	3	8	7	10	1	**56**
Unknown offender	33	25	9	9	8	13	11	4	N/A	N/A	N/A	**112**

Table 3.10 contains the raw data on the races of offenders for disability hate crimes between 1997 and 2007. The figures indicate that whites are the leading offenders in disability hate crimes, with 205 offenders. There were also 112 unknown offenders – though the category 'unknown offender' was not present in the FBI tables on the race of known offenders in the years 1997 to 1999. The FBI database also indicates that there were 111 black offenders during this period. The races of 56 offenders was not known, 18 offenders from multiple races or who were involved in a group hate crime, 5 American Indian/Alaskan Native offenders, and 3 Asian/Pacific Islander offenders.

Table 3.11 Known offenders race, non-disability hate crimes, 1997–2007

	2007	2006	2005	2004	2003	2002	2001	2000	1999	1998	1997	Total
White	3773	3672	3561	3698	3649	3695	5138	4099	4081	4034	4514	**43914**
Black	1032	1006	925	1041	934	1073	1149	1010	945	954	1156	**11225**
American Indian/ Alaskan Native	73	66	66	40	56	46	44	43	40	67	55	**596**
Asian/ Pacific Islander	41	73	43	61	78	61	72	82	71	79	84	**745**
Multiple races, group	193	247	212	189	220	215	206	176	177	207	183	**2225**
Unknown race	596	882	745	851	660	646	716	649	3966	3867	3857	**17435**
Unknown offender	3216	3040	2775	3194	3078	3049	4189	3335	N/A	N/A	N/A	**25876**

Table 3.11 outlines the raw data for the 102,016 nondisability hate crimes which were recorded in the FBI database from 1997 to 2007. It indicates that there were 43,914 white offenders, 25,876 unknown offenders, 17,435 offenders whose race was unknown, 11,225 black offenders, 2,225 offenders who were from multiple races or who were members of a group, 745 offenders who were Asian/Pacific Islander, and 596 offenders who were American Indian/Alaskan Natives. (Again, the category 'unknown offender' was not present in the FBI tables on the race of known offenders in the years 1997 to 1999.)

Graph 3.7 documents the percentages of known offenders from various racial backgrounds. This indicates that there are differences in the racial backgrounds of offenders who commit disability hate crimes relative to the commission of other bias crimes.

Graph 3.7 indicates that there are differences in the known races of offenders who commit disability hate crimes compared to those who commit other types of hate crime. In particular, it indicates that offenders who commit disability hate crimes are slightly less likely to be white, more likely to be black, more likely to be of an unknown race or unknown offenders, and are more likely to be from multiple races or a group. Specifically in the case of disability hate crimes, 40.19% of known offenders were white (compared to 43.04% for nondisability hate crimes), 21.76% of known offenders in disability hate crimes were black (compared to 11% of nondisability hate crimes), 0.98% of disability hate crime offenders were American Indian/Alaskan Native (compared to 0.58% for nondisability hate crimes), 0.58% of disability hate crime offenders were Asian/Pacific Islander (compared to 0.73% for nondisability hate crimes), 3.52% of disability hate crime offenders were from multiple races or were involved in a group crime (compared to 2.18% of nondisability hate crimes), 10.98% of disability hate crimes were from offenders of an unknown race (compared to 17.09% for nondisability hate crimes), and 21.96% of disability hate crimes were committed by unknown offenders (compared to 25.36% of nondisability hate crimes).

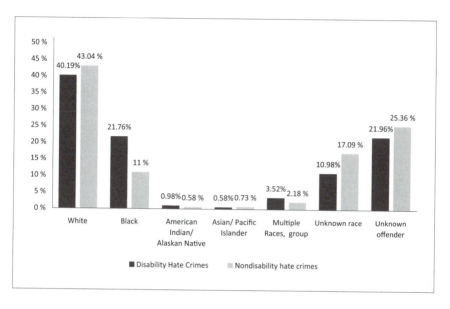

Graph 3.7 Known offenders race: Percentages of total offenders, disability and nondisability hate crimes compared, 1997–2007

Strengths and Limitations of the FBI Database

The main reason why the FBI database deserves so much attention is that it is the single largest statistical collection of data on disability hate crimes in the world. This database therefore can be useful in identifying patterns and trends in the commission of disability hate crimes. Additionally, as will become clear later in this discussion, these are typically cases where it is incredibly clear (virtually uncontestable) that the crime in question was motivated by disability hate. Another strength of the FBI database is that it is a widely recognized (and freely accessible) government source, with the credibility that comes with government documents. Results from this database often influence the allocation of federal funds (Maltz, 1999).

Unfortunately, the incredibly low numbers of disability hate crimes suggest that while the FBI database may be useful in acknowledging trends within officially recognized hate crimes, it has many serious limitations. It has been suggested that the following seven critical steps are necessary for hate crime data to be accurate:

1. The victim understands that a crime has been committed.
2. The victim recognizes the bias motivation of the crime.
3. Someone seeks law enforcement intervention.
4. Law enforcement officers are told of the bias motivation.
5. Law enforcement officers recognize the elements of bias crime.
6. Law enforcement officers document the bias element and file appropriate charges.
7. The incident is reported as a hate crime (Balboni and McDevitt, 2001).

Unfortunately, it seems that there are barriers, inefficiencies and inadequacies in each step which limit the numbers of disability hate crimes recorded in the FBI hate crimes database.

The first problem is that the vast majority of disability hate crimes are not reported to law enforcement agencies. A major element of this problem is that antidisability harassment and victimization is unfortunately assumed to be 'bullying', 'maltreatment' or 'abuse', but not criminal victimization and certainly not a hate crime. The lack of reporting of disability hate crime stands in stark contrast to the findings of hundreds of studies on 'abuse' and victimization which have been carried out over the last 20 years. In one study, a third of women with disabilities reported being assaulted, compared to one-fifth of nondisabled women (Nannini, 2006). Yet another study found that women with a severe disability were four times more likely to be sexually assaulted than nondisabled women (Casteel et al., 2008). Men and women with spinal cord injuries also experience higher rates of abuse than their nondisabled peers (Hassouneh et al., 2008). Such 'abuse' can include sexual and physical assault – unfortunately demonstrating the ways in which 'abuse' is often a synonym for crime victimization.

From childhood onward, people with speech/language impairments also experience higher rates of victimization and harassment. One study of 11-year-old children with speech/language impairments found that 36% were regularly victimized, compared to 12% of nondisabled children (Conti-Ramsden and Botting, 2004). Another study reported that approximately 45% of women and 4.9% of men with a language impairment had been sexually assaulted (Brownlie et al., 2007). Likewise, a study of people who use augmentative communication devices reported that 45% of respondents had experienced either crime or physical or sexual abuse (but of course, physical and sexual abuse are crimes – though they are often not recognized as such when they are inflicted on disabled people). Over 90% of these victims knew the perpetrator (which is similar to elder abuse and domestic violence), over 70% had been victimized on multiple occasions, and 66% had experienced multiple forms of victimization (Bryen et al., 2003). It has also been suggested that Deaf people are also at greatly increased risk of sexual abuse and physical abuse (Edwards et al., 2005; Obinna et al., 2006), as are people with intellectual and cognitive impairments (Martin et al., 2006; Reiter et al., 2007). Additionally, many studies indicate that there is a significantly increased risk of intimate partner violence in the long term amongst women with disabilities (Brownridge, 2006; Brownridge et al., 2008; Cohen et al., 2006; Tjaden and Thoennes, 1998). For instance, women with chronic pain and women with mental illness are at much higher risk of intimate partner violence (Coker et al., 2005).

The National Crime Victimization Survey, developed by the Bureau of Justice Statistics, found that people with serious mental illness were 11 times more likely than nondisabled people to be the victims of a violent crime in the past year. One-quarter of the respondents in this study who had serious mental illness had been crime victims in the past 12 months (Teplin et al., 2005). One study found that when people with a history of mental illness reported being abused or being the victim of crime, even to service workers who work with them, the chance of official action being taken in the court was only 13% (Williams and Keating, 1999). Instead, they often experienced a lack of help and sensitivity which left them feeling retraumatized. When such harmful experiences occur, the victim is often left feeling isolated, unseen, unheard, blamed, shamed, and betrayed (Copperman and McNamara, 1999).

It is tempting to provide a comprehensive review of all the literature on violence, abuse, harassment, bullying, and disability. If such a literature review highlighted the fact that many of these terms are actually misnomers that (consciously or unconsciously) make certain acts seem like they are not 'crimes', it might be a very useful contribution. But it is beyond the scope of this book. Nevertheless, the point must be made: virtually every study of disability and abuse in the last 30 years has found that disabled people are victimized and abused at much higher rates than nondisabled people. This is what the FBI database would say if it were accurate: that disabled people experience hate crimes, like other crimes, at much higher rates than nondisabled people.

For 20 years or more, studies have consistently shown that disabled people experience higher rates of 'abuse', 'maltreatment', 'bullying' and so on. And yet estimates of the prevalence of such acts vary greatly. So it would be a mistake to leave this topic without explaining why estimates of the prevalence of 'abuse' and crime victimization may vary significantly. These discrepancies can be explained as the result of definitional, design and methodological issues:

- Some studies are conducted at a population-level (Brownridge, 2006; Smith, 2007) or involve particular subsets of the population such as women with disabilities (Casteel et al., 2008), whereas others have utilized focus groups and individual interviews (Gilson et al., 2001; Saxon et al., 2001).
- Few studies have specifically used strategies to enhance accessibility and to improve participation by disabled people (Oschwald et al., 2009).

- Some studies have specifically targeted and included people from minority groups and have suggested that they have been inadequately included in previous research (Nosek et al., 2006).
- Studies typically focus on adults and rarely include disabled children.
- Some studies use a prospective methodology whereas others use retrospective analyses (Casteel et al., 2008).
- Some studies rely on secondary data analysis or crime reports whereas others rely on self-reported definitions of abuse (Barrett et al., 2009; Powers et al., 2009).
- A great deal of the literature on 'abuse' – even violent abuse – fails to cite or incorporate the literature on criminal victimization, and vice versa. Likewise, the connections between various forms of abuse are often underexplored – even though some reports indicate that some vulnerable groups of disabled people might be targeted more often for multiple forms of abuse (such as disabled people from poorer socioeconomic backgrounds).

All of these factors can explain differing estimates of the incidence of abuse, and crime victimization, but they may also contribute to the wider climate of underreporting disability hate crimes. Therefore, it should not be surprising that the Office for Victims of Crime has commented that 'many crime victims with disabilities have never participated in the criminal justice process, even those who have been repeatedly and brutally victimized' (Bureau of Justice Statistics, 2005).

Another aspect of the underreporting of disability hate crime may be the victim's shame and fear of retaliation. The underreporting of disability hate crimes has some similarities with the patterns of underreporting identified in cases of elder abuse and domestic violence: victims may be unwilling to report their experiences because of fears of retaliation. In the case of elder abuse (and of course there is a huge overlap between the elderly population and the disabled population), perhaps one-quarter, or maybe half, of elders experience elder abuse but only a small proportion are reported (Cooper et al., 2009; Cooper et al., 2008). And like victims of sexual assault and rape, other victims may not report being the victim of a disability hate crime because of a fear of not being believed. As well, many people do not want to be publicly identified as 'disabled' under any circumstances. To identify as disabled is to put oneself at risk of stigma, shame, exclusion, prejudice and often violence. Even people with serious illnesses, lifelong impairments and fatal diseases often refuse to be identified as disabled. As a result, some victims of disability hate crime refuse to testify against perpetrators because of the stigma of being publicly identified as disabled. In addition, the victim may not wish to believe that the victimization was motivated by bias, and may consciously or unconsciously ignore evidence to the contrary.

If the victim is a member of a group which has historically had a distrusting or antagonistic relationship with police, he or she may be even more reluctant to report the crime. Various groups have had longstanding problems with police forces, including some ethnic minorities and gay people. This dynamic may result in higher rates of underreporting from people in these groups compared to other disabled people.

A specific barrier for disabled people is the need to rely on caregivers to report the crimes, in some circumstances. This is particularly the case when the caregiver is committing the crime – a problem summarized in the journal article 'Bring my scooter so I can leave you' (Saxon et al., 2001). The vast majority of literature on disability and criminal victimization indicates that those most likely to commit crimes against them are people directly in their lives – such as family members, relatives, caregivers, or 'friends' (Coker et al., 2005; Grossman and Lundy, 2008; Hassouneh et al., 2008; Powers et al., 2002). Again, there are similarities between crime victimization aimed at disabled people and elder abuse (and also domestic violence): the perpetrator usually knows the victim. This is a somewhat different experience (at least the early representations of) hate crime in the literature. In that literature, it was often asserted – or at least assumed – that hate crimes were 'stranger crimes'. The victim was not expected to have any knowledge of, or pre-existing relationship with, the offender. This assumption has been summed up in the following comment, from an early book on hate crimes in the US: 'A second characteristic of hate crimes reported to the police is that they are often apparently senseless or irrational crimes perpetrated at random on total strangers' (Levin and McDevitt, 2002, p. 18). The unprovoked nature of the crime was further evidence that the act was simply motivated by bias or hate (McPhail, 2000). Of course, the lack of an existing relationship between a perpetrator and a victim makes bias easier to recognize, but that lack of connection is not typical of disability hate crimes or gender hate crimes.

Unfortunately, when law enforcement officers become aware that there is a pre-existing relationship between the victim and the offender, they are unlikely to believe that a particular criminal act involving these two parties could be motivated by hate. One crime that occurred at 1am on September 9, 2007, in Antioch, California, is a classic illustration of what happens when investigators become aware of a pre-existing relationship between the victim and the perpetrator. On that occasion, a group of Deaf people were having a birthday party. Police said that Phillip Hale, 18, and a 17-year-old boy were walking past the party and began taunting and mimicking them with exaggerated Sign Language gestures (Staff *Associated Press*, 2007a). One partygoer told them to leave, but they returned armed with a stick, a hoe and a concrete brick, ready to fight.

Initially, Antioch Police Corporal Michael Hulsey told the press that the 23-year-old victim was attacked because of his disability. The fact that the initial harassment was entirely enacted through aggressive mocking of Sign Language was seen as an indicator of hate. Hale was taken to the County Jail in Martinez, where he was held in lieu of bail of $135,000 on suspicion of assault with a deadly weapon and conspiracy to commit a misdemeanor, as well as the hate crime allegation. The 17-year-old was taken to Juvenile Hall. Within a week, the 17-year-old was charged with assaulting the Deaf victim, but the hate crime charges were dropped. 'It didn't appear to be a hate crime', Deputy District Attorney Daniel Cabral told the local press, because the two men had argued with the victim before. 'It appeared that there was a prior history between the two people and the victim', he said (Gerstman, 2007). Without going into the specifics of this case, it is essential to point out that the literature suggests that a disability hate crime is *more likely* to occur when the perpetrator knows the victim than vice versa. But police practice indicates the opposite: when a pre-existing relationship is confirmed, hate crime charges are almost always dropped. This can lead to many potentially unjust outcomes – but unfortunately, such injustice is characteristic of the entire justice system's response to disability hate crimes.

There is another obvious reason why many crime reports fail to acknowledge the disability identities of some victims: they are people whose impairments are invisible. Someone with an invisible impairment such as epilepsy may experience profound physical and social challenges in their life – but their disability status may be unknown to a law enforcement officer (even if it is known to the perpetrator). Crime reports, like many other records, commonly underestimate the numbers of people with invisible impairments. But knowledge of the person's disability status might nevertheless influence a perpetrator and could be a motivating factor in a crime. This is similar to the situation commonly experienced by victims of hate crimes who are HIV positive. Many people who have HIV are asymptomatic, but they may still be targeted for victimization because of ignorance, prejudice and hatred. And even when people have actually contracted the AIDS virus, their symptoms might not be immediately obvious to others. In 1999 a disability organization reported the case of a man living with AIDS who was attacked on a New York subway by a group of young men and women who screamed abuse at him, kicked him in the face, and left him with serious injuries (Consortium for Citizens with Disabilities, 1999). A law enforcement officer with limited disability awareness may not realize that both HIV and AIDS fit the legal definition of a disability, and may not report such a case as a disability hate crime. Perhaps it would be labeled a bias crime based on sexual orientation – but there is no necessary connection between having AIDS and a person's sexual orientation, so a disability categorization would be more accurate.

Even if a law enforcement officer did regard a case as an example of a hate crime, there is no guarantee that it would find itself into the FBI database. Submitting hate crimes reports is voluntary and not all jurisdictions within states submit reports. Some agencies only submit data for one quarter in a year, others may submit none, and others always enter the data. By the year 2000, fewer than 2,000 of the eligible 17,000 law enforcement agencies have ever filed a report of any sort of hate crime – whether by racial, religious, gender, sexuality, nationality, disability, or other bias (Sherry, 2003b). For a range of bureaucratic reasons, those agencies responsible for reporting hate crimes may not have reported all crimes in their jurisdictions. This is a problem generally with hate crime statistics, and not just disability hate crimes. Another administrative problem is that there is a great deal of inconsistency in the location of hate crime units, the nature and amount of training received by responsible officers, in procedures for screening and handling cases, and in record-keeping systems (Martin et al., 2006). This can lead to serious discrepancies in reporting. Also, lack of departmental infrastructure, lack of training and supervision, communication breakdowns between line officers and those responsible for reporting the crimes may inhibit accurate reporting of hate crimes (Balboni and McDevitt, 2001). Green et al. comment: 'One cannot compare jurisdictions that use different reporting standards or have different levels of commitment to the monitoring of hate crime' (Green et al., 2001, p. 295). Some authors have suggested the process is riddled with errors, failures to pass along information, misunderstanding of what constitutes a hate crime, and even falsification of data (Potok, 2001). Despite these misgivings, it should be acknowledged that many police departments are making significant efforts to implement hate crime policies and to monitor the incidence of hate crimes in their jurisdiction.

One major barrier in the identification of disability hate crimes is the mistaken belief that someone cannot share an identity with the victim and still commit a hate crime – a belief which seems to be quite common among many law enforcement officers. This is a particular concern when it comes to crimes against disabled people – studies demonstrate quite conclusively that other disabled people are one of the major groups who commit crimes against disabled victims. (This should not be surprising, really, because disabled people are often congregated *en masse* in group settings and other institutions with other disabled people, many of whom they do not know, and some of whom have long criminal histories (Gill, 2009).) And there is no logical reason to automatically assume that someone who has experienced one type of impairment (for instance, mental illness) may not possess hatred towards people with another form of impairment (such as mental retardation, cerebral palsy, blindness, or so on). Furthermore, Bell comments that 'the practice of dismissing cases when individuals had similar identities meant that detectives were often unable to appreciate the fact that victims and perpetrators had multiple identities and myriad perspectives on their identities' (Bell, 2002, p. 142).

Likewise, there is no definitive reason to suggest that a person with a particular impairment (for instance, mental health issues) cannot commit a hate crime against another person with the same impairment. One case where a person with a history of mental illness committed a violent sexual crime against another person with the same condition involved Steven Rodriguez, 19, and Michael Lunsford, 17, who committed a violent sexual attack on a developmentally disabled worker at a bowling alley. Rodriguez had known the victim for five years, having met at a children's psychiatric ward in Long Island in New York. He and Lunsford were not charged with a hate crime, even though Rodriguez had consistently bullied and victimized the man over a five-year period. In 2007, they forced a plumbing snake (used to unclog drains) into the man's rectum and spun it several times, causing him severe pain, internal injury and bleeding which necessitated a four-day hospitalization for the victim (D'Auria, 2007).

The intersection of disability with other identities such as race and ethnicity is not well understood in general, and it is particularly underexplored when it comes to disability hate crimes. Often times, people make simplistic connections – for instance, if they find out that a victim of a racial/sexual/religious or other hate crime has a medical condition (which may or may not be apparent to the perpetrator), they immediately suggest that an incident is therefore a disability hate crime as well. A typical example of this error can be found in the discussion of the brutal murder of James Byrd, Jr. by a leading disability studies scholar (Davis, 2002). This murder was committed in 1998 by three men, two of whom were members of a white supremacist gang. The victim was an African-American man. The perpetrators slashed Byrd's throat, stripped and beat him, and dragged his body for three miles, leading to his beheading. Byrd's remains were strewn over 75 places and the remainder of his body was dumped at the town's black cemetery. This crime was immediately recognized as a racial hate crime. Davis indicates that his own research indicated that Byrd was disabled, and seems to imply that the crime must have been a disability hate crime as well as a racially motivated hate crime. He said that 'when I called the sheriff's office, the local newspaper, the district attorney's office, Byrd's family and lawyers, no one could or would tell me' (the nature of his disability). Davis states that he eventually found out that Byrd was 'severely arthritic' and had seizures (2002, pp. 145–46). Whether the perpetrators could see these conditions, or whether they were even aware of Byrd's disability, is completely ignored by Davis.

Nevertheless Davis (2002, p. 145) states: 'Byrd was not only black and the victim of race hatred; he was also disabled'. He suggests that editors of progressive journals were wrong in characterizing this as a racially motivated hate crime; he believes they mistakenly 'saw race as the primary category and disability as a poor third cousin of race' (2002, p. 146). But Davis misses the most important point, as far as prosecutors (and indeed progressive editors) would have been concerned: there is no evidence to suggest any bias towards disability from the perpetrators. Such evidence may have included slurs made during or after the commission of the crime, hateful literature in the car which was used in the commission of the crime, or the connection of the location with a particular identity group. For instance, the cemetery where Byrd's body was dumped was known as a black cemetery – but there is no evidence to suggest any connection with disability. And the key issue here is that this was a crime – indeed, a capital offence – and Davis offers no evidence. Arguably, Davis's speculation diminishes and dishonors the very real evidence of racial hatred which was produced in the prosecution of this crime. Davis offers no evidence of disability hatred to either supplement or supplant this evidence of racial bias. Nevertheless, Davis's spurious claims have been repeated by other disability studies scholars. For instance, one author cites Davis and claims that 'reaction to disability may have played a role in the crime' (Weber, 2007).

What Davis does not recognize is that bias crimes are difficult to prosecute; they demand an explicit identification of motive. It is unacceptable, in a court case concerning hate crime, to speculate that a particular identity such as disability may have played a part in the motive of the perpetrators alongside another identity such as race. It is essential to have detailed evidence, preferably with admissions and corroboration, in order to prove that a crime is motivated by hate. Such racial animosity was clearly established in the Byrd case; Davis does not establish that the people involved in his murder had any history of bias against disability. One can imagine such a speculative argument being used by a defense counsel in a hate crimes case: 'The crime might have been motivated by racial hatred, it might have been motivated by disability hatred, it might have been motivated by something else … Who's to say? If you cannot clearly establish motive, then you must find my client not guilty of a hate crime'.

That does NOT mean that one cannot prosecute a hate crime case involving multiple biases. An example of a case where it may have been possible to provide such motivations (even though this approach was not attempted in the courts) occurred in California in 2007. This case involved assaults by a gang of six or seven people against four disabled people. The four victims were all disabled, and they were coming back from a Pizza Hut to the Bridges facility in Pomona, California, when they were attacked. They were simultaneously assaulted and subjected to racial slurs as well. Two of the victims, who were African-American, were stabbed. A third Hispanic victim was kicked and a Caucasian victim was beaten. There seemed to be a clear hate motivation on two counts: all of the victims were disabled, indicating a disability bias; and the stabbings (as well as the racist language) were particularly directed at the African-American victims. However, only the racist bias was emphasized in categorizing this crime as a hate crime. Two gang members, Bobby Perez, 22, and Jonathan Carrion, 21, were convicted of two counts of attempted premeditated murder with special gang and hate crime allegations. In addition to the attempted murder verdicts, Carrion and Perez were also convicted on one count each of assault with a deadly weapon with special gang and hate crime violations and one count each of felony battery also with special gang and hate crime allegations (Chatila, 2008; *City News Service*, 2008).

In his pioneering study of disability and abuse, Sobsey (1994) exposed the large number of caregivers who had criminal histories for sexual assault, molestation, child abuse, and so on. This is a particular concern because some recidivist criminals specifically look for work in the disability area so that they can have easier access to potential victims. For instance, in Billings, Montana, Floyd 'Todd' Tapson was a caregiver who was convicted of violent crimes towards one of the disabled people under his care. He abducted the woman, sexually assaulted her, drove her to a remote location, and shot her in the face. The woman survived the shooting and was able to identify her alleged attacker. It was subsequently revealed that he had worked in a number of group homes in North Dakota, Minnesota, and Maryland where disabled people have vanished. This case is an important reminder that a small minority of caregivers acquire positions of power and exploit this dynamic in order to perpetrate criminal behavior. There was some speculation by law enforcement officers that Tapson may have been a serial killer who targeted disabled women in particular – but even in the discussions of a potential serial murderer who focused specifically on disabled women, the term 'hate crime' was never mentioned (Staff *Associated Press*, 2003).

Even when disabled people are repeatedly victimized, there is often a reluctance on the part of law enforcement officers to label the act as a hate crime. And yet such characteristics as repeat offenses, the use of derogatory language, and a high level of violence (all commonly found in hate crimes) suggest a nonrandom pattern of victimization. The California Attorney General's Civil Rights Commission on Hate Crimes indicated that under-reporting often occurs because '… law enforcement is not adequately trained to make a determination whether these crimes should be charged as hate crimes' (Lockyer, 2001). This problem has also been identified in a Ph.D. study of disability hate crime awareness among 184 law enforcement officers from the Alachua County Sherriff's Department, where the attitudes of law enforcement officers towards disability, and their own personal experiences of disability, were recognized as major factors in determining whether they perceived particular crimes as disability hate crimes or not (Lane, 2006).

It would be a serious mistake to assume that perpetrators who specifically target disabled people are not currently being prosecuted. They are. But they are, in general, not recognized as hate crimes. They are classified differently, as the following cases illustrate. Marilea Mitchell and Danny Abegg were convicted of 'first degree criminal mistreatment', for which they each received an exceptional sentence of 96 months (*State of Washington, Respondent v. Marilea R. Mitchell*, 2009). This was considered a domestic violence crime against a victim who had a particular vulnerability – a disability which was considered a substantial factor in the commission of the crime. Mitchell and Abegg (the boy's father) were convicted of criminal mistreatment for starving Abegg's 4-year-old son. The boy was so severely malnourished that the body was beginning to consume itself. He was physically incapable of getting food for himself, because he was too weak to walk. The child's physical condition left him dependent on Mitchell and Abegg to provide him with the basic necessities of life. Mitchell appealed, arguing that no one used the word 'disability' when describing what was wrong with the boy and also suggesting that the child's food issues did not make him any more vulnerable to mistreatment that any other child. The court disagreed, finding that the child 'had a physical disability that a normal child of his age does not have' as a result of not being able to walk to get food. The court also emphasized that because of the child's eating disorder, he was particularly vulnerable to food deprivation. While the standard sentence for this type of crime would have been between 31 and 41 months, the court imposed an exceptional sentence of 96 months because the child's disability was considered to be a substantial factor in the commission of the crime.

While the exceptional sentence in this case directly related to the child's disability, it was never considered a hate crime (though many disability advocates would argue that specifically targeting someone's unique vulnerability associated with a particular physical or mental condition is, by definition, a disability hate crime). While the 'exceptional sentence' punishment may seem similar to the penalty enhancement provisions of hate crime legislation, the difference is that crimes such as this one are not formally recognized in the FBI database because they have never been labeled a hate crime. This underscores a wider point: where a person is targeted because of their disability identity, the courts have typically regarded this as an aggravating factor in sentencing, but almost never called it a hate crime and yet when an individual victim has experienced such a crime, they typically regard it as a hate crime and almost never consider it as simply an aggravating factor in the commission of a more general crime. Although the punishment for an individual offender may seem the same (if the offender receives extra punishment for exceptional circumstances against a vulnerable victim) the main difference is that a 'hate crime' is widely recognized as a crime against two communities – the individual victim(s) and the wider disability community – and there are no efforts to redress the harm done to the general disability community when a case is not recognized as a hate crime. Additionally, the level of terror and fear inflicted on the wider disability community by such actions is essentially ignored unless an offense is specifically recognized as a hate crime.

Three final cases, which again were not registered in the FBI database, will highlight the ways in which disability hate crimes are drastically under-recorded. The first concerns a case where disability bias was blended with racist bias; the second was simply a case of antidisability bias (indeed, it was the first disability hate crime ever to be prosecuted in the US). The last involved the torture of a disabled woman over an eight-hour period. But unfortunately, none of these cases were recorded on the FBI database as a disability hate crime.

The case of Billy Ray Johnson, an African-American man with developmental disabilities, contains some other horrific features which are quite common to many hate crimes (*Billy Ray Johnson v. Christopher Colt Amox*, 2006). One of their fundamental characteristics is excessive violence and a callous disregard for the victim – even if the person suffers death or serious injury. Johnson's case illustrates this pattern well. He was taken to a party in 2003 where he was ridiculed, harassed, called names such as 'crazy nigger', and was knocked unconscious. When Johnson was knocked to the ground, he began to vomit and make gurgling sounds. For an hour, he was left on the ground, despite being unconscious and in need of immediate medical attention. None of the partygoers used their mobile phones to call for emergency assistance. The partygoers debated what to do with him. One of them was concerned that he would lose his job as a jailer if they contacted the authorities. He discouraged another partygoer from taking Johnson to the hospital, arguing that his bloody body would stain her cloth car seats. They had three trucks available to them, but did not use them either.

Eventually Johnson's attackers decided to put him in the back of a pickup truck and to dump him on the side of a country road. They took him from the party (which was four miles from the local hospital) to a site a few miles further away from the hospital. There, they left him between five and eight feet away from the side of the road, where he remained for over two hours until one of them called the Sherriff's

Office and reported seeing him lying on the side of the road. As a result of the assault, Johnson sustained severe brain injuries and a subarachnoid hemorrhage, aspiration pneumonia from swallowing his own vomit, and a fractured clavicle. His injuries were so severe that he now lives in a nursing home, requiring constant care, and he will not live independently again. Contact with his family has been limited because the nursing home is over 50 miles from where his family lives. Even though one of the perpetrators, Colt Amox, was charged with three felony counts of injury to a disabled person, aggravated assault, and injury to a disabled person by omission, a jury found him not guilty on all felony counts, but convicted him of a misdemeanor assault and recommended probation.

Johnson's case involved racial vilification as well as disability bias – something which was not present in the case of Eric Krochmaluk. Krochmaluk is a cognitively disabled man from Middletown, New Jersey, who was the victim of a disability hate crime in 1999 (*The State of New Jersey v. Jennifer Dowell et al.*, 2000). He is also an exceptionally short person, is deaf in one ear, wears a hearing aid, has a speech impairment and has a heart condition. Between 16 January 1999 and 31 January 1999, Krochmaluk was brutalized by a large group of people in various New Jersey locations: Keansburg/Union Beach, Holmdel, and Middletown. (Nine people would subsequently be charged with this hate crime and eight were found guilty of charges including kidnapping in the first degree, conspiracy, aggravated assault – bias intimidation, terroristic threats, possessing a weapon for unlawful purpose, unlawful possession of a weapon and aggravated criminal sexual contact.) On the night of January 30, 1999, Krochmaluk was finishing his shift as a worker at a McDonald's restaurant when he was lured to a party by being told that a girl was there who wanted to meet him. He initially agreed to go to the party, but changed his mind on the way there. When he asked the driver to take him home, the driver simply ignored him. Then when Krochmaluk got to the apartment, he was forced to drink an iced tea/alcohol mixture – and told that if he did not drink it, he would be beaten. He spilled some of the mixture on the floor and was forced to lick it up off the floor. His backpack was taken, alongside two pagers, his wallet, $16 cash, a tape recorder, and various papers. Approximately 30 of his tapes were smashed with a mallet. Krochmaluk always carried a stuffed toy whale with him – it was taken from him, cut with a knife, and he was told that he was going to have to eat the stuffing. He was stripped of his clothing. Also, his necklace was ripped off. The necklace had a cross on it. One of the attackers said, 'You should not believe in God, you're White'.

The perpetrators took the tape from the broken cassette and wrapped it around his neck. He was strapped to a white plastic chair, with his feet, legs and mouth taped together. His head and eyebrows were shaved and then hot water was poured over his head. He was told that he would not be allowed to leave the toilet unless he put on women's clothing. Krochmaluk was given a skirt and jacket and a white bra. When he arrived at the party, he was wearing his McDonald's uniform, including the company tie. His tie was cut up by his attackers and used as bra stuffing.

Krochmaluk was then sexually assaulted with a string of wooden beads. The men and women in the room then attacked Krochmaluk with a brass metal rod, a toilet brush, and a towel rack. He was also kicked and slapped repeatedly. Next, his head was sprayed with hair spray and the vapors were lit on fire. Cigarette ashes were flicked into his mouth. After verbally abusing the victim, including calling him an 'asshole', one of the perpetrators said, 'Whose dick do you want to suck?' Krochmaluk was then threatened that if he told the police, his house would be burned down while his parents were inside. The perpetrators allowed Krochmaluk to put on his own clothes and he was ushered into a Dodge Caravan. A pillowcase was tightly held around his head while Krochmaluk was transported for approximately 10 minutes into a woody area. When the driving stopped, the pillowcase remained on his head and he was walked into trees and branches. Both the male and female perpetrators punched their victim. After a short time, Krochmaluk ran away and found people who would help him.

Monmouth County Prosecutor John Kaye said at the time, 'They tormented this mentally disabled man because of his disability ... They did it to him because they could – because they could manipulate him, and because they believed he could not tell on them, which was almost true' (Sherry, 2003a). Krochmaluk's case was the first US case where charges were laid and the perpetrators were sentenced to detention – thus becoming a model for further prosecution of disability hate crimes. Like many other victims of disability hate crimes, Krochmaluk knew (at least some of) his attackers. A pre-existing relationship with the perpetrator is unusual in some hate crimes (for instance, racist hate crimes) but it is relatively common in disability hate crimes. Also, the victim was sexually assaulted. Violent sexual humiliation seems to happen frequently as well.

There is no legitimate reason why Krochmaluk's case should not have been on the FBI database. It was officially recognized as a disability hate crime and it received media publicity because it was the first disability hate crime ever to be prosecuted in the US. And yet, for whatever reason, it does not appear in the database. When a case which is so high profile cannot make it into the FBI database, the official figures clearly underestimate the real number of such crimes, and the reporting procedures deserve closer scrutiny.

The final example of a crime which did not make it into the FBI database involved the violent victimization of Ashley Clark, an 18-year-old girl who was viciously beaten and tortured by 16-year-old Joseph Nagle and 17-year-old Cheyenne Blanton. They had broken into Clark's home hoping to steal a car, but missed their chance. So they turned on Clark and viciously attacked her for roughly eight hours. Clark was the victim of a hyperviolent assault: she was tied up, gagged, punched, kicked, and struck with a baseball bat. Also, her head was shaved, and she was forced to walk barefoot in the snow. Nagle and Blanton both pleaded guilty and received lengthy sentences – but their actions were not considered a disability hate crime. Nagle was sentenced to 39 years' imprisonment and Blanton 44 years for aggravated burglary, aggravated robbery, complicity to aggravated robbery, felonious assault, two counts of kidnapping and vandalism.

Unless official crime data acknowledges that these types of crime are disability hate crimes, it will be possible for some people to suggest that disability hate crimes don't really exist – that they are simply a figment of the imagination, or a ridiculous creation of political correctness. And legislators will not provide enough resources for hate crime prevention (such as educational resources, victim advocate training, self-defense classes for disabled people, and so on) if they do not believe the issue is a significant problem. That would be a tragedy – not just because the figures would continue to be so inaccurate, and the resources for addressing them so inadequate, but even more importantly, there is a real need to be honest about the experiences of these victims. People's lives have been forever altered by these crimes; they deserve to have the crimes which have been inflicted upon them named accurately. It's a matter of respect for victims.

Conclusion

This chapter has carefully examined the FBI database on disability hate crimes because it is the largest single database in the world on such crimes. The FBI database is useful because it can outline the main trends in those disability hate crimes which are officially recorded. It demonstrates that the characteristics of disability hate crimes are different from other hate crimes. Specifically, disability hate crimes are more likely to involve rape, larceny, burglary, and simple assault but they are less likely to involve aggravated assault, intimidation and vandalism. A disabled person is also more likely to be the victim of a hate crime inside their own home than nondisabled people. However, the chapter has also suggested that the FBI database does not, by any means, provide a comprehensive coverage of disability hate crimes. It is significantly flawed and vastly underestimates the level of such crimes.

The next chapter examines the situation in the United Kingdom. While the UK has developed its hate crime legislation much later than the US, disability organizations there have been far more effective at raising the profile of the issue. As a result, there is a much higher level of awareness of the issue, much greater levels of media reporting of these crimes, and much greater recognition of the problem by law enforcement than in the US. The next chapter highlights the seriousness of the problem of disability hate crimes in the UK, which prompted such responses.

Chapter 4
The United Kingdom Experience

Disability hate crimes in the United Kingdom have some similar features to those in the US (for instance, although they are typically hyperviolent, they are almost never officially recognized), but the primary difference has been the effectiveness of disability organizations in publicizing such crimes and demanding more effective responses. Campaigns by disability organizations – especially through the disability magazine *Disability Now*, and in particular the publication 'Getting Away with Murder', written by Katherine Quarmby, a comprehensive report about the failure of authorities to respond appropriately to many disability hate crimes – raised community awareness of the problem and increased the pressure on authorities to respond appropriately (*Disability Now* et al., 2008). *Disability Now* published an in-depth investigation into the deaths of five disabled people in 2009: Steven Hoskin, Barrier-John Horrell, Rikii Judkins, Raymond Atherton, and Kevin Davies. This report was so groundbreaking, so influential, that it deserves detailed attention. It basically put disability hate crimes on the forefront of the disability movement's political agenda in the UK – and resulted in changes in policy and practice from the Government, the Crown Prosecution Service, police, disability organizations, and many other agencies. *Disability Now* also published an analysis of 51 crimes which were identified as 'potential disability hate crimes'. Also written by Katherine Quarmby, the 'Hate Crime Dossier' compiled by *Disability Now* is incredibly powerful reading – containing cases of murder, torture, assault, grievous bodily harm, theft and arson. These two documents will be used as an entrée to discussing hate crimes in the United Kingdom.

'Getting Away with Murder' and the 'Hate Crimes Dossier'

The 'Getting Away with Murder' report had enormous impact because it demonstrated that the murder of disabled people may not simply be a 'motiveless' crime; it often stems from deep-seated animosity and prejudice which feeds off the wider cultural devaluation and social exclusion of disabled people. The murders mentioned in the report are the cases of Albert Adams, Raymond Atherton, Kevin Davies, Christopher Foulkes, Steven Gale, Colin Greenwood, Frankie Hardwick, Shaowei He, Barrie-John Horrell, Steven Hoskin, Rikki Judkins, Christine Lakinski, Brent Martin, Sean Miles, Laura Milne, Keith Philpott, Fiona Pilkington, and William Ripsher.

Most of these cases involved a direct physical assault upon the disabled person which caused death. They are not just violent – they are shockingly brutal …

hyperviolent. For instance, Brent Martin was repeatedly punched, kicked, stamped on, and head-butted and died one day later. Rikki Judkins was also punched, kicked, stamped on – but the murderers also dropped an 11-kilogram (24 pounds) stone on his head. Sean Miles was knifed, hit with a golf club and drowned. Stephen Hoskin begged for help as he was drugged, tortured, humiliated and abused for hours. He was then taken to a viaduct and forced to hang from the railings, before one of his torturers stamped on his feet, causing him to fall 100 feet to his death. Barrie-John Horrell was beaten, hit with a house brick, kicked, stamped on, and strangled. His body was then set on fire and hidden in a wooded area, where it decomposed for 11 days before being found. Colin Greenwood was punched to the ground and kicked in the forehead as he waited at a tram stop in Sheffield. He died from a build-up of blood on his brain the next day. Keith Philpott was bound and gagged, tortured for four hours, and then stabbed in his own home, before he was disemboweled. His murderer, Sean Swindon, sawed his stomach with a knife until his insides fell out. Philpott was still alive, but probably unconscious from all the bleeding, after being disemboweled. Jennifer Henry repeatedly stabbed Albert Adams. Ryan Palin and Craig Dodd, the teenagers responsible for Raymond Atherton's death, terrorized him for months, beating him, setting his hair ablaze, urinating in his drinks, pouring bleach over him, daubing make-up on his face, and regularly breaking into his apartment and writing graffiti on his walls. The initials of a gang, LBA (the Longford Balmy Army) had been etched into his wall. Also, a number of names had been burned into the ceiling of the flat or smeared on with blood. The night he was killed, Atherton's killers beat him with planks of wood on the head until he bled and then threw him into the Mersey River, where he drowned. Shaowei He was subjected to what a judge called a campaign of 'sustained physical cruelty' which included being attacked with various weapons ranging from copper piping to wood embedded with nails. She was also hit so hard with a broom handle that it snapped in half. Shaowei He died after being locked outside in freezing temperatures.

Kevin Davies was kept as a prisoner in a garden shed, fed on potato peelings (leading him to lose three stone in weight), poisoned with weed killer, branded and cut in the backside with a knife leaving a cross-shaped scar, and he was beaten to the point where he had fractures to the ribs and larynx, a large burn caused by a chemical agent being thrown on him, and cuts and bruises all over his body. He was tortured for four months, until he died. Christopher Foulkes was battered around the head and chest until he died of blunt trauma to the head and abdomen. Steven Gale was the victim of such physical and mental torture that he has been compared to a victim of a Nazi concentration camp. He was beaten and tortured for two years. He suffered a brain hemorrhage, three of his ribs had been fractured, and his legs, thighs and groin were bruised, consistent with stamping and kicking. He had facial injuries as well. He had also been starved – weighing less than six stone (less than half the normal weight for his 5ft 11in stature). Laura Milne's throat was slashed with a knife, but she was also punched and kicked on her head and body, and repeatedly stamped on when she fell to the floor. She experienced repeated blows to the head and body with a knife. One of her killers tried to dismember the body and he made a video where he boasted that he was glad she was dead. He danced next to the mutilated body of his victim. William Ripsher was repeatedly harassed by his murderer, with his stereo being smashed, his apartment being broken into, and his medication stolen. He died after being battered over the head, strangled with an electric cord, having his head stamped on, and being stabbed in the abdomen. His sadistic killer is said to have tortured Ripsher to death for his own entertainment. The night he died, his attackers also tried to set fire to Ripsher's furniture. Ripsher had cuts and bruises to his neck, eyebrow, ear, chin, eyes, lips, shoulder, chest, forearm, hand, fingers and knees.

The case of Christine Lakinski is somewhat different. She was not directly killed by her attacker. She was actively dying beforehand. She had fallen as she went home, and was carrying a box of laminate at the time. Her attacker, Anthony Anderson, initially tried to rouse her by kicking her, but then tipped a bucket of water over her. To degrade her, he urinated on her, and one of his friends filmed him screaming 'This is YouTube material' as he did it. He also got a tin of shaving foam and covered her from head to toe in it. He then left her lying motionless in a doorway as she took her dying breaths. A crowd of people stood around, watching and laughing as Anderson behaved this way. Because of Lakinski's underlying medical condition (she was actively experiencing pancreatic failure), it was not believed that Anderson's actions contributed to her death, so he was simply charged with 'outraging public decency'. In many ways, this makes this case somewhat different from the violent deaths of these other victims at the direct hands of a killer. (Although of course, this does not excuse his actions, or make them any less reprehensible.)

Another case which is somewhat different from the others involved Fiona Pilkington and Francesca (Frankie) Hardwick. Pilkington was Hardwick's mother and they were both cognitively disabled. Pilkington took both of their lives after they had experienced seven years of harassment and intimidation. She had contacted police and social services on at least 33 occasions. A gang terrorized the family – damaging their property, throwing eggs, stones and flour at her house, smashing windows, kicking on their door, urinating in their back garden, and putting live fireworks in their letterbox. On one occasion, a gang of 16 yelled at Frankie to lift up her nightdress. Not only had Fiona and Frankie been victimized, Fiona's son Anthony had also been attacked because of his disability. (He has dyslexia.) A gang beat him with a metal bar and locked him in a garden shed at knifepoint. However, without any relief to the constant abuse and intimidation, Pilkington set their car alight, killing both her daughter and herself.

The reason for discussing these deaths before going into wider data on disability hate crimes in the UK is because it is essential to recognize the hyperviolent nature of disability hate crime. It is common to hear objections to the inclusion of disability in hate crime legislation on the grounds that 'no one hates disabled people'. Hopefully, these shocking stories have debunked this myth. The violent underpinnings of these crimes, which occur in a context of sustained harassment, demonstrate clearly the malice which is directed at some disabled people.

It is commonly assumed that offenders are young people. However, only 35.14% were under the age of 18; the remaining 64.86% were legally adults. That is, almost two-thirds of these perpetrators were over the age of 18. This data suggests that killings of disabled people may be more likely to be committed by adults than young people. The youngest (convicted) offender in these cases was 14 and the oldest offender was 42. Offenders under the age of 20 represented 43.24% of the total, those between 20 and 29 constituted 37.83% of the total, and offenders 30 years and over represented 18.91% of the total. On average, victims were 14 years older than perpetrators. The average age of perpetrators in these deaths was 23 years while the average age of victims was 37. While over 80% of perpetrators were under 30, only 31% of the victims were under 30. Likewise, while only 5.4% of perpetrators were over 40, 37.5% of victims were over 40. Only 6% of victims were under 20, 25% between 20 and 29, 31.25% were between 30 and 39, 12.5% were between 40 and 49, and 25% were over 50 years of age.

The 'Getting Away with Murder' report was a watershed in UK responses to disability hate crimes not just because of the harrowing crimes which it documented, but also because it was endorsed at a very high level politically. Indeed, the endorsements read as a virtual 'Who's Who' in criminal justice in the UK. The Minister for Crime, Vernon Coaker MP, wrote an endorsement, as did Sir Ken Macdonald QC, Director of Public Prosecutions, and Alfred Hitchcock, Deputy Assistant Commissioner, who leads on hate crime for the Metropolitan Police Service. Scott Westbrook, the Chair of the National Disabled Police Association, also wrote an endorsement. Additionally, there were endorsements from Brendan Barber, the Trades Union Congress (TUC) General Secretary, and Stephen Brookes MBE, Chair of the Disability Members' Council, National Union of Journalists.

Following this report (and the wider campaigns of disability organizations) which publicized the frequency and severity of disability hate crimes, as well as the inadequate response of the criminal justice system, the Director of Public Prosecutions, Sir Ken Macdonald QC, said that disability hate crimes are 'very widespread' and the justice system was 'letting disabled people down'. He added, 'At the lower end of the scale there is a vast amount not being picked up. The more serious offences are not always being prosecuted as they should be. This is a scar on the conscience of criminal justice'. He also said that regarding disabled people as 'easy targets' was actually the biggest barrier to effective prosecution because it marginalized the issue of hostility and prejudice. 'A mistaken focus on vulnerability risks enhancing an already negative image of disabled people as inherently weak, easy targets and dependent. This approach is wrong. It means that the opportunity to condemn the prejudice and hostility of the offender is missed' (Macdonald, 2008).

**Table 4.1 Homicides discussed in the 'Getting Away with Murder' report:
Victims, perpetrators, ages of perpetrators, and sentences**

Victim	Perpetrators	Age	Minimum sentence (years)
Brent Martin, age 23	William Hughes	22	22
	Marcus Miller	16	15
	Stephen Bonallie	17	18
Rikki Judkins, age 51	Simon Unsworth	20	18
	Arron Singh[1]	17	15
Sean Miles, age 37	Edward Doyle[2]	34	17
	Terry McMaster	24	15
	Karen Feathers	35	14
Stephen Hoskin, age 38	Sarah Bullock	16	10
	Darren Stewart	29	25
	Martin Pollard	21	8[4]
	Unnamed juvenile[3]	17	Unknown
	Unnamed juvenile	16	Unknown
Barrie-John Horrell, age 31	Lee Davies	28	18½
	Brett Davies	23	17
Colin Greenwood, age 45	Lewis Barlow	15	2[5]
	Leon Gray	14	2
Keith Philpott, age 36	Sean Swindon	25	20[6]
	Michael Peart	22	15[7]
Albert Adams, age 56	Jeniffer Henry	36	14
Raymond Atherton, age 40	Craig Dodd	14	6[8]
	Ryan Palin	16	7
Christine Lakinski, age 50	Anthony Anderson	27	3[9]
Shaowei He, age 25	Su Hua Liu	29	9[10]
	Lun Xi Tan	42	6

Note: [1] The judge lifted reporting restrictions on Singh despite his young age because of the brutality of the murder. Singh is 'detained at her Majesty's pleasure' but the minimum time he must serve is 15 years; [2] A fourth defendant, Tracey Feathers, was cleared of the charge; [3] Both unnamed juveniles were charged with assault and false imprisonment; [4] Pollard was found guilty of manslaughter, not murder; [5] Both Barlow and Gray were initially found guilty of murder and sentenced to 12½ years. But on appeal their murder convictions were quashed and they were found guilty of manslaughter, with 4-year sentences, including a minimum of 2 years; [6] Minimum term increased to 28 years on appeal; [7] Increased to 22 years on appeal; [8] Life sentences (with minimum of 6 years for Dodd and 7 years for Palin) reduced to minimum of 3 years for Palin and 3½ years for Dodd; [9] Anderson was not guilty of murder, but found guilty of 'outraging public decency'; [10] Liu pleaded guilty to manslaughter and inflicting grievous bodily harm as an alternative to a murder charge, and Tan pleaded guilty to causing or allowing the death of a vulnerable person and the judge directed that he be found not guilty on a manslaughter charge.

A classic illustration of the failure of the criminal justice system to appropriately punish those responsible for the deaths of disabled people can be found in the case of Christopher Foulkes, a wheelchair user from Rhyl, North Wales. His case was not discussed very much in the 'Getting Away with Murder' report, except for the following three sentences, one of which is inaccurate:

> A teenager, who had been regularly visiting him and stealing his money, viciously attacked Christopher Foulkes, of Rhyl, Wales. Mr Foulkes died. The teenager was originally charged with murder, but the charge was dropped, and the youth pleaded guilty to wounding with intent (*Disability Now* et al., 2008, p. 21).

In fact, the teenager responsible for this crime did not plead guilty to wounding with intent; he was found guilty of assault occasioning actual bodily harm. Christopher Foulkes' death was caused by blunt trauma to the head and abdomen. His mother, Valerie Foulkes, issued a statement through the police which said: 'Christopher was a kind and loving son who was popular amongst family and friends. He enjoyed socializing and listening to music and it's been a great shock to the family. He will be sadly missed by all of his family and friends' (Staff *eNews Park Forest*, 2007). A 16-year-old boy was responsible for his death. Although the name of the juvenile offender is protected, the author submitted a Freedom of Information Request to the North Wales Police about the case, which received the following reply:

> On the 10th August 2007, the youth involved in the circumstances surrounding the death of Christopher Foulkes appeared before Caernarfon Crown Court for the following alleged offences;
>
> 1. *Murder*. For that offence, proceedings were stayed and the indictment quashed;
>
> 2. *Causing grievous bodily harm with intent to do grievous bodily harm*. The offence was allowed to lie on file and not to be proceeded without the leave of the court or the court of appeal.
>
> 3. *Assault occasioning actual bodily harm*. He was found guilty of this offence and given a detention and training order of 18 months (North Wales Police Heddlu Gogledd Cymru Freedom of Information Team, 2009).

Usually, juveniles on detention and training orders are released after serving half their term and are placed under supervision for 18 months. The courts effectively ruled that the life of Christopher Foulkes warranted a jail sentence of a year and a half – perhaps nine months. (It is impossible to find out if the jail sentence was reduced because of privacy rules for juvenile offenders.) Either way, the process of legal injustice for disabled victims of crime was never more evident.

Despite the criticisms of disability agencies that these original sentences were too lenient, many of the perpetrators of crimes discussed in the 'Getting Away with Murder' report were successful in appealing against the severity of sentences. It was not possible to confirm whether appeals were actually lodged in each of these cases; however, it was possible to find details of appeals for people involved in eight of the deaths discussed in the report. In total, it was possible to find information about the appeals of 13 of the perpetrators. Eight of the 13 perpetrators (61.53%) were successful in having their sentences reduced; on average, successful appeals reduced a perpetrator's sentence by five years, three months. People who were convicted in the deaths of Steven Gale, Colin Greenwood, Raymond Atherton and Brent Martin all had their sentences reduced as a result of court appeals. In the case of Steven Gale, Lisa Smith was found guilty of perverting the course of justice, but had her sentence reduced from 27 years to 20 years on appeal.

The two murderers of Colin Greenwood also had their sentences reduced: originally convicted with murder, they were sentenced to a minimum of 12 and a half years each, but their murder convictions were overturned and instead they were found guilty of manslaughter with a minimum of two years and a maximum of four years. Raymond Atherton's killers, Craig Dodd and Ryan Palin, were initially sentenced to life (with a minimum of six years for Dodd and seven for Palin) but their sentences were reduced on appeal to three years for Palin and three and a half years for Dodd. Brent Martin's murderers, Stephen Bonallie, William Hughes and Marcus Miller, all had their sentences reduced too. Bonallie was originally sentenced to 18 years, reduced to 15 years on appeal; Hughes was sentenced to 22 years, reduced to 19 years on appeal; and Miller was sentenced to 15 years, reduced to 13 years on appeal.

Three appeals were denied and the original sentences remained intact; these cases involved the deaths of Christine Lakinski, Shaowei He, and Rikki Judkins. It is interesting that in the case of Lakinski and He, the perpetrators had received quite lenient sentences already: one was for three years, another for six years, and a third was for nine years. The perpetrator in Christine Lakinski's case, who urinated on her dying body, was unsuccessful in his appeal to reduce his three-year sentence for 'outraging public decency'. Shaowei He's murderers were also unsuccessful in reducing their six- and nine-year sentences. The appeal court stressed that they had not received the maximum sentences for their crimes: Lui had received only nine years for manslaughter and Tan had received only six years (when the maximum was 14 years). Lord Justice Laws at London's Court of Appeal said that the case 'must turn the stomach of any humane person' and both murderers 'richly deserved' their sentences (*R. v. Liu (Su Hua) and Tan (Lun Xi)*, 2006; Staff *BBC News*, 2006c). Rikki Judkins' murderers, who savagely beat him, robbed him, dropped an 11kg stone on his head, and then boasted of their actions, were unsuccessful in their appeals for a reduction in their 18-year and 15-year sentences.

Only one of the cases discussed in the 'Getting Away with Murder' report actually led to an increased sentence on appeal – the case of Keith Philpott. Sean

Swindon and Michael Peart, both convicted of Philpott's murder, were originally sentenced to 20 years and 15 years respectively, but their sentences were increased on appeal to 28 years and 22 years respectively. Their sentences were increased only after an intervention by the Attorney General, Lord Goldsmith QC, who stated that their punishment was 'unduly lenient' because the murder involved 'sadistic conduct' as defined by the Criminal Justice Act 2003 ('2 Cr. App. R. (S.) 80', 2006). The Court of Appeal found that the judge in the lower court had erred in believing that a crime had to contain sexual behaviors in order for it to be defined as 'sadistic' – the conduct of the perpetrators in this case met the definition of 'sadistic' behavior. Philpott's murder was never considered a hate crime by the courts – though it was labeled one by disability advocacy groups. It was the 'sadistic' nature of the murder that led to the increased sentences for Swindon and Peart and the lower court judge's legal error in misunderstanding the nature of 'sadistic' conduct which led to the increased sentences.

Some of the details of this case demonstrate the premeditated and hyperviolent nature of Keith Philpott's murder. On March 21 (two days before his attackers began their murderous rampage), Philpott received a threatening text message which stated 'You perv. We're going to break your legs. Watch your back. Watch your flat'. Keith Philpott spoke to a neighbor, Mr. Marron, about the message, but didn't want to report it to the police. On March 23, 2005, Philpott had visited Mr. Marron to show his new bicycle. But when Philpott returned to his own house around 10pm, Swindon and Peart were waiting for him. They knocked on the door, entered his house and locked the door using the security chain. Then they bound Philpott's ankles and wrists, gagged him, and assaulted him for several hours. Swindon and Peart kicked Philpott repeatedly and stamped on his face until it was unrecognizable. Then, while he was still alive, Swindon disemboweled Philpott. After trying to remove their fingerprints from the premises, the murderers stole Philpott's new bicycle (which they subsequently discarded), cash, a mobile telephone, and Philpott's gold ring, which Swindon tried to sell. The pathologist who examined Philpott's body said that it was impossible to estimate how many blows he had received, but the external evidence of injury was 'spectacular'. Additionally, Philpott's disembowelment was particularly gruesome – he had a single gash running from one side of his abdomen to the other, created through a series of stab wounds that were drawn across the abdomen with a knife, using a sawing action. Such forensic evidence was a significant factor in convincing the court that Swindon and Peart had engaged in 'sadistic' behavior.

Unfortunately, the 'Getting Away with Murder' report may have conveyed an inaccurate impression about the nature of hate crimes against disabled people, because of its failure to include sufficient examples of crimes against disabled women. There are some general statements about disabled women experiencing sexual abuse, domestic violence and rape, but the 'Getting Away with Murder' report does not provide details and cases to back up these assertions. This lack of specificity stands in stark contrast to the report's approach towards other crimes – where the horrific details of these crimes are often spelled out in gruesome detail. The victims whose stories are discussed at length in the 'Getting Away with Murder' report are largely men. More than three-quarters of the homicides discussed in the report, for instance, involve male victims. The report discusses 13 homicides involving disabled men (Brent Martin, Rikki Judkins, Sean Miles, Stephen Hoskin, Barrie-John Horrell, Colin Greenwood, Keith Philpott, Albert Adams, Raymond Atherton, Kevin Davies, Christopher Foulkes, Steven Gale, and William Ripsher), but only three homicides involving disabled women (Christine Lakinski, Shaowei He and Laura Milne). To be fair, these three homicide victims are not the only female victims of disability hate crime whose cases are discussed in the report; there is also a two-sentence discussion of vandalism involving an unnamed woman with a learning disability in Warrington in November 2007. But the overall gender bias of the cases recorded in the report remains overwhelmingly male. The failure to include sufficient stories of crime involving disabled women, I believe, is a major flaw in the report.

A lack of primary sources or original research, particularly when it comes to the issue of sex crimes, is also a significant evidentiary problem in the 'Getting Away with Murder' report. In general, the report only discusses sex crimes when it refers to the results of other studies. Also, it does not contain detailed case reports for sex crimes, in contrast to the way such information is provided for the cases of homicide discussed above. Passing mentions of sex crimes in the 'Getting Away with Murder' report occur in three places in its literature review: in its discussion of the British Crime Survey (but it uses the term 'more serious personal crimes', rather than hate crimes, to discuss them); in discussing a joint research program from the Universities of Bristol and Warwick (again, a case where the terminology 'hate crime' is never used – 'domestic violence', 'abuse' and 'sexual assault' are adopted instead); and its discussion of a report by The Mental Welfare Commission for Scotland, involving the case of 'Ms A'. In that case, 'Ms A' had made multiple reports about being raped and sexually assaulted, but her case was not pursued by authorities because they thought she would not be considered a reliable witness (Mental Welfare Commission for Scotland, 2008).

Disability Now also published a 'Hate Crime Dossier', again written by Katherine Quarmby, which discussed 50 disability hate crimes, and the lack of appropriate responses to them. In the vast majority of cases, the 'Hate Crime Dossier' suggested that prosecutors had ignored or overlooked evidence which suggested the person was targeted because they were disabled. Additionally, the notion of antidisability bias (let alone hatred) seemed so unimaginable to many judges that they could only conclude that the person was attacked because they appeared 'vulnerable'. The 'Hate Crime Dossier' suggests that the notion of vulnerability is deeply problematic: first, they believe that the emphasis on the 'vulnerability' of disabled people suggests that there is something inherent in disabled people's bodies or minds (and not in the social environment) that made them vulnerable; and second, by immediately assuming that the person was simply considered 'vulnerable' by the perpetrators of crimes, they argue that the legal system was completely ignoring the possibility of antidisability hatred.

Additionally, if antidisability bias is not explored (let alone prosecuted) then an offender will automatically escape any enhanced penalties which accompany hate crime legislation.

However, there is another side to the 'vulnerability' issue which needs to be recognized. Courts are commonly required to consider a number of 'mitigating' and 'aggravating' factors associated with particular crimes. One of the 'aggravating' factors was the 'vulnerability' of the victim. 'Vulnerability' is a term which has often been applied by the courts to disabled people, elderly people and children. That cannot be denied. But what the *Disability Now* campaign failed to acknowledge is that the courts have also emphasized that 'vulnerability' is contextual – the 'vulnerability' of victims has been recognized as an aggravating factor for an incredibly wide range of people, groups and situations. For instance, the 'vulnerability' of victims has been considered as an aggravating factor in crimes against people working in small grocery stores and service stations late at night (Agombar, 2009; Staff *Braintree and Witham Times*, 2009), passengers arriving from international flights (*R. v. Frith (Helen)*, 2008a) and travelers with shoulder bags (*R. v De Weever (Rawle)*, 2009), individuals in changing rooms or shower rooms in community centers (*R. v Healy (Joseph)*, 2009), women who are lost at night (Raynes et al., 2009) and lone women under the influence of alcohol (*R. v Morgan (Nicholas)*, 2009), and even security guards who transport large amounts of money for the post office (*R. v Grocock (Sharon Lesley)*, 2008). So perhaps the criticism of *Disability Now* is somewhat misplaced. The courts are required to assess the social and physical vulnerability of all crime victims, disabled or not, because it is always a potential aggravating factor to be considered in sentencing. Rather than discouraging the courts from assessing the physical or social vulnerability of disabled victims, it might be more effective if disability organizations simply highlighted the hateful motivations of the offender, in order to ensure that hate crime laws are applied in particular cases.

The campaign by *Disability Now*, including the publication of the 'Hate Crime Dossier', played a key role in keeping the issue of disability hate crimes in the public spotlight. The 'Hate Crime Dossier' included the stories of 12 hate crimes against people with learning difficulties, 28 against people with physical impairments, six against people with sensory impairments, one against a person with autism, and three against people with unnamed impairments. (Unfortunately, the discussion of hate crimes against people with learning disabilities does not count Fiona Pilkington and her daughter Frankie Harwick as separate cases of hate crime. It counts their case as one experience of hate crime, not two, even though they were both targeted – as was Fiona's son, whose own disability hate crime is not counted either.)

In terms of the 12 distinct cases mentioned in the 'Hate Crime Dossier', 10 involved men with learning difficulties and two involved women with learning difficulties. Of the 28 cases where victims with physical impairments were identified, 20 involved disabled men, seven involved disabled women and one case involved both a disabled man and a woman. When it came to people with sensory impairments, seven disabled men were identified as being the victims of disability hate crimes and no disabled women were. The one case of a person with autism identified in the 'Hate Crime Dossier' was also a male victim. Among the three victims with unnamed impairments, two were male and one was female. In total, then, the 'Hate Crime Dossier' identified 52 victims in the 50 cases of disability hate crimes, with 41 victims (79%) being male and only 11 (21%) being female. This gender difference demands further investigation.

Sex Crimes

It would be easy to assume that these figures accurately represent the total number of disability hate crimes, and that there is an overall gender bias in victimization rates that means disabled men are targeted far more often than disabled women. But that suggestion is not consistent with a great deal of literature about crime victimization and disability which shows that disabled women experience much higher rates of some crimes than disabled men (such as sexual crimes and domestic violence). It could be argued that there may be an implicit gender bias in the approach of the 'Hate Crime Dossier', and further that 'disability hate crimes' may have been defined largely in masculinist terms – evidenced through such crimes as assault or robbery, but not in sexual crimes such as rape, sexual assault or domestic violence. Unfortunately, by failing to include these crimes in the 'Hate Crime Dossier', readers might mistakenly be given the impression that disability hate crimes are largely asexual, and sexual crimes against disabled people are not disability hate crimes. This is a problematic approach since disabled women (in particular) experience a virtual epidemic of sex crimes, abuse and neglect, as well as domestic violence, and it cannot be automatically assumed that these crimes are not motivated by antidisability bias or hate. Many of these crimes, on further inspection, involve the deliberate targeting of disabled women because of their disability – in other words, they are not random sex crimes; they may indeed be disability hate crimes with a particular gendered connotation.

At the same time as the 'Hate Crime Dossier' was recording certain types of crimes as disability hate crimes, there were many stories in the UK courts, and in the press, about rapes and sexual abuse (mostly of disabled women) which were not included in the *Hate Crime Report*. That is not to suggest that every form of sexual violence which is directed at disabled people is necessarily a hate crime. Of course not. But the opposite cannot be automatically assumed either: such crimes cannot automatically be assumed to NOT contain elements of hate and disability bias. Indeed, the nexus of antidisability and antifemale bias which manifests itself in disabled women's experiences of domestic violence, abuse, sexual assault, rape and other sex crimes is an important reminder that hate is not one-dimensional. Hate is multidimensional (much like other forms of power) and people can be targeted because of one or more of their identities.

The failure to recognize that rapes can be a form of disability hate crime – and to recognize the importance of sexual violence in crimes against disabled people more generally – is one of the most significant limitations of the 'Hate Crime Dossier' and the 'Getting Away with Murder' report. Some of the crimes which were NOT reported in the publications of *Disability Now* include a January 2006 attack on a 48-year-old woman who had kidney problems, a communication impairment and who was a wheelchair user (Horne, 2007); another 2006 attack involving attempted rape on a 48-year-old Edinburgh woman with a hearing and sight impairment (Staff *Edinburgh Evening News*, 2007); two 2008 rapes of a 46-year-old Bradford woman with Huntington's chorea, a brain disorder which affects her speech and movement (Wright, 2009); and the rape of a middle-aged woman with multiple sclerosis in Croydon, London, by three men in September 2007 (Moody, 2007). Another disabled woman, who could not walk or talk, was found to have been raped while she was in a nursing home – a crime which was only discovered when doctors realized she was six months pregnant (Narain, 2006).

Both male and female disabled people have been subjected to sex crimes, though the number of female victims far outweighs males. Many of the disabled women who are subjected to sex crimes are elderly. The following example illustrates the ways in which some predators take advantage of their power positions to inflict sex crimes on elderly disabled victims. In 2004, a 74-year-old woman with both a cognitive impairment and physical disabilities was indecently assaulted by her physician in Darlington (Attorney-General's Reference No. 79 of 2004 sub nom *R. v. Husain (Syed)*, 2004). The physician, Dr. Syed Husain, was a 30-year-old man who pled guilty to indecently assaulting five of his patients, including the 74-year-old disabled woman. He filmed some of his indecent assaults on patients and kept copies of the files on his home computer. One of his computer files shows Husain examining the woman at her home, without wearing gloves. He fondled her breasts, removed her pants (exposing her genitals), rubbed her clitoris and digitally penetrated her. He deliberately played to the camera for some of the time. Also, he massaged her buttocks and placed his penis against her buttocks. Then he told her to kneel down on the bed and, having exposed her vaginal area, filmed her from behind. Husain was originally sentenced to three and a half years in prison for the five indecent assaults on his patients, but this sentence was increased on appeal from the Attorney General to four and a half years of imprisonment.

Sex crimes are often inflicted upon people with impaired cognition. Two examples may illustrate: one of a woman with learning disabilities, and one of a woman with severe dementia. The first example involves Hugh Kunz, a 57-year-old man who raped and indecently assaulted a 46-year-old woman with learning difficulties in September 2005 (*R. v. Kunz (Hugh)*, 2008). Kunz has a long criminal record of 62 offences including convictions for rape and indecent assault. Initially engaging the woman in a pleasant conversation about her dog, he invited her to his nearby flat where his demeanor changed dramatically. He began drinking large amounts of vodka, became aggressive, and grabbed a hammer. He told the victim that he hated women, especially those who 'led him on' and that his victim was going to 'get it tonight'. (This comment raises an important issue: the role of gender hatred in sex crimes, and the intersection of gender and disability in this situation.) He assaulted her, and raped her vaginally and anally. He also put his penis in her mouth. Kunz was convicted on two counts of rape against this woman, and was sentenced to a minimum of 16 years.

Another sex crime against a disabled woman occurred at the Glenmoor House Residential Home, Northamptonshire, a nursing home which caters to people with Alzheimer's disease, dementia, physical disability, and also serves frail and elderly people. A 72-year-old resident of the nursing home, who has advanced severe dementia, was the victim of various sexual acts by Norman Edward Clements, a 59-year-old man, in March and April 2008 (*R. v. Clements (Norman Edward)*, 2009). The woman's dementia was so severe she could not have given evidence in any court case – and she certainly could not be considered to have the cognitive capacity to consent to sex. In this case, the perpetrator was able to give uncontested accounts of their sexual contact – and he blamed her for instigating the sexual activities. He said that she asked him to digitally penetrate her, she placed his penis in her mouth, and he said he had ejaculated, but not in her mouth. He also admitted to attempting to have full penetrative sex, and admitted to touching the woman's breasts, but he said it stopped because she complained about discomfort. The vulnerability of the victim was emphasized in the court's decisions: she was not able to give evidence, she was not able to consent, and his actions were done secretly, when others had gone on walks, or were away from her room. The sex crimes only stopped when someone from the home walked in on Clements in her room, and he was reported to police. Clements was convicted of two counts of sexual activity with a person with a mental disorder impeding her choice and was sentenced to eight years' imprisonment for these sex crimes. Clements' case is a reminder that the residential institutions in which many disabled people live may be very unsafe places.

Because of the impaired cognition of some disabled people, perpetrators sometimes make quite erroneous assumptions about their age. This was the case for Peter Chenery, a pedophile who committed a variety of sexual offences against two Asian women: one girl under the age of 16, and one disabled woman who was 27, but who had the mental age of 13, and whom Chenery believed was only 14. He randomly telephoned the houses of Asian people looking for young female victims. Again, the intersection of various forms of power is evident: Chenery targeted his victims according to their age, and ethnicity, as well as their gender. He also targeted young women who were suggestible; this was part of the reason he victimized his disabled victim. She resided at a home for vulnerable adults, and in December 2004, Chenery told this woman, who was very suggestible, to masturbate herself and to perform sexual activity both vaginally and anally with a banana or a carrot. He also told her to urinate and defecate while he listened. He used degrading language and asked the girl to repeat to him that she was a 14-year-old whore. He called from a particular telephone box, and police videoed him masturbating there while he spoke to her. Chenery was convicted for his sex crimes against both of these women. For his crimes against the girl under the age of 16, Chenery was convicted of buggery, rape, indecency with a child, making indecent photographs of children, and possession of indecent photographs of children. For the crimes against the disabled woman, he was convicted of attempting to incite a child to engage in sexual activity. Chenery was sentenced to 15 years of imprisonment.

One of the most horrifying sex crimes ever inflicted upon a disabled person involved the violent sex victimization of a 16-year-old girl in London in January 2008. The hyperviolent, hypersexual nature of this crime has much in common with other hate crimes discussed in the 'Getting Away with Murder' report. Unfortunately, the report only mentioned one case of rape in its discussion of disability hate crime – in the literature review section of the report, discussing the findings of a report by The Mental Welfare Commission for Scotland. (And even then, that particular rape was never labeled a 'hate crime'; it was given as an example of the problems that disabled people experienced being believed in the judicial system.) This failure to include sex crimes and rape in the narratives of disability hate crime is, I believe, a serious deficiency. One particular case involved the pack rape of a 16-year-old girl with learning difficulties by a group of assailants – perhaps 10 men. Only three of the men involved in the rape were charged – Rogel McMorris, Jason Brew and Hector Muaimba. McMorris, 18, was jailed for nine years for rape and grievous bodily harm; Brew was jailed for six years; and Muaimba was sentenced to eight years for rape and robbery (Moore-Bridger, 2009). (Another alleged perpetrator, Stephen Bigby, was charged with rape but was killed in a gang fight before he could face trial.) One of the most obscene and brutal elements of this crime was that after the perpetrators finished raping the victim, they doused her body in caustic soda in an effort to remove traces of their DNA in her body. They then poured water over her, intensifying the burning, and as skin peeled off her face, chest and genital area, the perpetrators laughed and filmed her suffering on their mobile phones (Staff *Associated Newspapers*, 2008).

Young disabled males have also been targeted by the perpetrators of sex crimes. A 13-year-old boy who attended a special school was subjected to sex crimes by David Redhead, a 67-year-old man, between January 2006 and March 2006 (*R. v. Redhead (David)*, 2006). Redhead was convicted of 10 offences against this disabled child. Redhead committed various sex crimes, including showing the boy videotapes of hardcore pornography, masturbating in the boy's presence, inciting the boy to masturbate himself, masturbating the boy, sucking the boy's penis and touching the boy's anus with his penis. Another disabled male teenager was the victim of a sex crime perpetrated by Stephan Paul Walsh in Doncaster in May 2006. The victim was a 19-year-old man with learning difficulties. Walsh, aged 53, approached the young man and asked him for directions to the bus station. The teenage man took him there and Walsh offered to buy him a coffee. As they left the bus station and walked towards the train station, Walsh took the young man's hand. This upset the teenager, and he unsuccessfully tried to phone his mother. When they got to the train station, the young man tried to get away from Walsh. He went to one of the toilets on the railway platform, but Walsh followed him in and entered the same cubicle and locked the door behind them. The youth urinated. And Walsh grabbed him and kissed him on the lips, but the young man resisted and pushed Walsh away. After leaving the toilet, Walsh hugged and kissed the young man on the railway platform. He then asked the young man for his address. Although the young man gave his correct name, he lied about his address and caught a train. He reported the offense to the station manager, and Walsh was convicted of sexual assault on a male.

There are many more sex crimes which could have been discussed, but this brief summary of sex crimes directed towards disabled people has shown that these crimes are a very serious aspect of the criminal victimization of disabled people in the UK. The publications from *Disability Now* – both the 'Getting Away with Murder' report and the 'Hate Crimes Dossier' – may have implicitly adopted a masculinist approach by failing to recognize such crimes and by instead focusing on violent crimes associated with murder, assault and robbery. Examining sex crimes is one way to overcome this unconscious masculinist bias. The vast majority of victims of sex crimes are women, and disabled women's experiences of sex crimes should be examined within an overall examination of disability hate crimes.

Crimes by Family Members

It would be tempting to think that the 'Getting Away with Murder' report and the 'Hate Crime Dossier' would have outlined the major forms of disability hate crime. And it cannot be denied that they are incredibly important in identifying and naming certain types of disability hate crimes … but they do seem to have some limitations. In general, they implicitly accept the public/private divide. That is, in general they do not recognize that hate crimes can occur within the home – or within the family – of disabled people. They tend to project an image of crimes occurring 'out there' – somewhere out in the community, but not in the homes of disabled people themselves. And yet the literature on abuse, on domestic violence, and even on murder consistently suggests that the home – the primary site of love and intimate relationships – can also be a place of violence, fear, criminal victimization. Indeed, *many* crimes against disabled people, including hate crimes, are committed by family members or carers of the disabled person. Unfortunately, these crimes are underreported even more often than other disability hate crimes. This is a particular concern because one early study indicated that two of the groups most likely to offend against a disabled person were family members (including natural family members, foster families, step-families and other relatives) and disability service providers (both paid and unpaid carers) (Sobsey, 1994, p. 75). And yet there have been many cases in the UK where the courts have recognized that a victim was deliberately targeted by a family member for crime victimization due to their disability.

Heston Rayan Cuffie pleaded guilty to a 2006 burglary against his step-sister, who is a woman with a very severe visual impairment. Heston Cuffie stole the computer which his step-sister had received through a disability grant. On the computer were accessible programs which enabled her to access various print materials and have a better quality of life. The computer was worth about £1,000 and the programs were worth several hundred pounds. After he was arrested, Cuffie admitted stealing the computer and promised to return it, but he did not keep this promise. As a result, his legally blind step-sister remained without an important connection to everyday life. The court found that Cuffie had deliberately targeted her because of her disability, but considered this as a 'serious aggravating feature' in determining punishment for the crime, rather than a disability hate crime *per se.* (Of course, the danger with this approach is not just that it exacerbates the underreporting of disability hate crimes, but it also impedes the accurate identification of perpetrators of such crimes.)

Another example of a crime against a disabled woman committed by a family member occurred on June 27, 2007. This case involved a sex crime inflicted upon a 22-year-old woman by her *de facto* stepfather (*R. v. W (Andrew S)*, 2009). The young disabled woman was visiting her mother. She was living in Peterborough at a center for vulnerable people at the time. She had significant learning disabilities which affected both her intelligence and her social interactions. Also, she had a physical impairment. On the day when she was victimized, her *de facto* stepfather made a number of sexual comments to her, and then took her to a wooded area away from her mother where he undressed her, sucked her breasts, digitally penetrated her vagina, and had vaginal sex with her. He told her not to tell the police and that the police would not believe her. After she had said that she did not want vaginal sex, he withdrew his penis, ejaculated on the ground, and she sucked his penis. He walked her to a bus stop, and when she got off the bus, staff at the bus stop saw her sobbing and after speaking with her, they called police. When questioned, he described her as 'cuckoo', claimed that she had previously made false allegations about him, and labeled her as 'mentally impaired' and a 'walking prostitute'. A pre-sentence report stated that he did not display any regret or remorse, was not motivated or committed to address his offending, claimed that everything was consensual, and minimized his own role. Initially, the Crown argued that there had been a rape, but he pleaded guilty to sexual activity with someone suffering from a mental disorder and was initially sentenced to nine years' incarceration. This sentence was reduced on appeal to seven years.

Another case which garnered a great deal of media attention involved Gareth Gunning, a 31-year-old man who stole the entire contents of his Deaf parents' bank accounts. Gunning acted as a carer and interpreter for his Deaf parents, and was responsible for managing their financial affairs as well. He transferred all their money to his own bank account. Sentencing him to 14 months in jail, Judge Christopher Llewellen-Jones QC said, 'I regard you as being despicable. You plundered the accounts of your vulnerable, elderly parents, removing the entire sums from the two accounts, to a total of more than £8,000, knowing they were vulnerable, Deaf, and totally reliant upon you and others. I cannot think of anything at the moment more horrendous than that' (Staff *Echo Reporter*, 2008; Turner, 2008).

Another case where a family member committed a financial crime against a disabled person occurred in Braintree, Essex. This time, the crime was committed over an extended period – five years. One of the victims, Marjorie Talmadge, was a 77-year-old disabled woman with both vision and hearing impairments. The other victim was Talmadge's next door neighbor – 86-year-old Beatrice Flynn. Talmadge's daughter, 51-year-old Denise Adley, defrauded her of over £17,000 and also stole 10 checks worth £6,700 from Flynn. Talmadge commented at the time, 'I don't think I will ever get over it'. She disowned her daughter and said she does not want to have anything to do with her. Adley escaped incarceration. She was given a nine-month suspended jail sentence, suspended for two years – a lenient punishment which outraged her victims (Agombar, 2009; Staff *Braintree and Witham Times*, 2009).

There is a strong correlation between age and disability: the older a person becomes, the more likely it is that they will develop an impairment. And yet the connections between disability hate crimes, hate crimes against older people, and various forms of elder abuse are often neglected. The role of family members, and also carers, in these crimes is also commonly underestimated. And yet a report by the National Centre for Social Research and Kings College, London, suggested that an alarmingly high number of elderly people experience abuse, neglect, assault, theft, robbery, sex crimes and other forms of criminal victimization. This study estimated that 350,000 elderly people in Britain were neglected, robbed and sexually harassed in 2006 (Staff *Daily Mail*, 2007a). This included thousands of people who were abused in their own homes. And the authors acknowledged that this estimate was probably lower than the actual number, because people with dementia and people who were seriously ill were not included in the report. The report indicated that 35% of these crimes were committed by partners, 33% were other family members, and care workers were responsible for 9% of the total. (However, the percentage of carers responsible for robbery was much higher – 20%.) Such crimes by carers also deserve further attention.

When a crime is committed against a disabled person, and their disability is specifically mentioned by the perpetrator as a motivating factor in the crime, UK disability organizations have (in the last two years at least) a fairly good record for recognizing that crime was probably a hate crime. But there is an exception to this rule: when the crime is committed by a family member. Nowhere is this dynamic more evident than in the case of Joanna Hill, who drowned and murdered her 4-year-old daughter Naomi in 2008 because she was 'embarrassed' about her child's cerebral palsy (Staff *Sky News*, 2008). This case also evoked mixed reactions because the murderer was herself disabled: A 'Serious Case Review' conducted after this murder found that Joanna Hill had experienced mental health problems (in particular depression) since she was 17 and experienced a serious relapse in January 2007, which was so serious she was allocated to the Crisis Resolution and Home Treatment Team (a mental health service which aims to keep people out of hospital) and was visited twice a day (Raynes et al., 2009). While Naomi's father responded with anger, labeling Joanna 'evil', and many mainstream press organizations emphasized her antidisability attitudes, organizations such as *Disability Now* never labeled the case a disability hate crime.

Sometimes, as in this case, there seems to be a degree of ambivalence in the response of the disability movement to crimes committed by family members. That is not to say that the disability movement does not care about situations where the rights of a disabled person are reduced because of the actions of a family member – of course not. But what it does indicate is that there is less of a 'rush to judgment' in cases where crimes against disabled people are committed by family members who claim to have reached their breaking point (particularly when the perpetrator has a long history of mental health issues). This ambivalence reflects the unique dynamics which family members of disabled people experience. They have a duty to care after their disabled family member, particularly if the person relies on others for assistance with activities of daily living, but they often feel overwhelmed and undersupported. Likewise, family members may feel compelled to take on caregiver responsibilities due to funding and other difficulties in the disability service system. Feeling frustrated by (at least potentially) dealing with many different systems (educational systems, health systems, disability systems, and so on) and straddling the ambiguous line between the formal and informal care systems can leave family members feeling both included, and excluded, when it comes to decisions about a vulnerable loved one. Longstanding family dynamics, jealousies and resentments can manifest themselves in abusive relationships and even crimes against vulnerable members of the family, such as disabled people. And yet it cannot be said that the murder of Naomi Hill was simply a random act, or that she was not targeted because of her disability identity. Far from it. The undisputed facts of the case were that this was a murder motivated by Joanna Hill's reactions to her daughter's disability. *That means it is a disability hate crime.* And yet even organizations such as *Disability Now*, which has mounted such a tremendous campaign on the issue, did not label it as a disability hate crime. This reluctance to identify parental crimes – particularly when the parent is disabled – is deeply disturbing.

Perhaps some of the reticence to label this case a disability hate crime stems from the fact that the perpetrator and the victim shared an identity: disability. This is a mistaken approach to hate crime. It is absolutely possible – indeed, it is fairly common – for people who purportedly share an identity with the victim to commit hate crimes around that identity. 'Disability' is an enormously wide, contested, and often ambiguous category, and it is very common for someone who commits a disability hate crime to suggest that they are themselves disabled. It is only a fantasy of identity politics to assume that because someone has one impairment (for instance, a mental health issue) that they will feel a sense of commonality or community with another person's experience of any condition that might range from blindness to spinal cord injury, autism to dwarfism, cancer to breathing problems, and AIDS to cerebral palsy. It is far more common for the reverse to happen: that people do not feel a sense of community with others that have quite different sensory, cognitive, neurological, psychiatric or physical conditions. Even if they have the same impairment, it should not be assumed that a perpetrator cannot hate others with the same impairment. One study of 38 physical assaults against people with learning disabilities found that 12 assaults were committed by other disabled people, 15 by carers and staff, and 11 times by family members (Brown, 1999).

Simply having a familial connection to someone who is disabled is no guarantee that a person will not have a range of biases, prejudices, and stereotypes about disability. Far from it. Indeed, it could be argued that disablism (a range of negative attitudes and social practices concerning disability which isolate, exclude, marginalize and disrespect disabled people) is so widespread in the community that it could be expected to exist in some families where there is a disabled member. Additionally, most disabled people are the only ones in their family who are disabled – much the same as most homosexuals are the only ones in their family with that sexual orientation. (The case of genetically inherited impairments is somewhat different.) So it cannot be expected that another family member will necessarily understand or empathize with the range of formal and informal social practices which deny disabled people a chance to fully participate in society.

It is therefore a serious failure by many disability organizations to ignore disability hate crimes committed by people who themselves may be identified as disabled, and/or may be family members.

Crimes by Carers

There have also been many times where carers have been convicted of crimes against disabled people – and the courts have found that they targeted the person because of their disability – but again, these are almost never recognized as disability hate crimes. A classic example of this situation occurred in the case of Helen Frith, who pleaded guilty to six offences of theft that had occurred in Nottingham in 2007 (*R. v. Frith (Helen)*, 2008b). Frith was employed as an administrator at the Aspley Euro Disability Unit in Nottingham, an organization which serves clients aged from 18 to 65 years with neurological impairments, such as multiple sclerosis, brain injury and post stroke syndrome. Frith had control over the residents' money and had access to the accounts of some residents. Frith had a key to the organization's safe where the residents' checks were kept. Money in the safe was intended to be used for pocket money for personal items such as toiletries. However, over a nine-month period, Frith stole over £16,000. She targeted three disabled people in particular – all who had Court of Protection orders. She stole the cash card of one resident, Miss McGillon, a quadriplegic woman in her twenties. Between October 2006 and March 2007, Frith took £1,925 – emptying McGillon's account. Frith also emptied the account of another resident, Mr Skelton, a man in his fifties with multiple disabilities. She took his bank card and between November 2006 and

March 2007, took over £4,500. Frith also took his weekly disability allowance, approximately £42 or £43 per week, amounting to almost £700. Miss Scamans, a woman in her fifties with multiple sclerosis, was a third victim of Frith. Frith stole Scamans' bank card and her PIN number, and stole approximately £4,319 from Scamans' account. Frith also stole from the Disability Unit where she worked, taking money that had been raised at charitable events, money intended for staff uniforms, and money from the organization's taxi account. She used the money on nights out with friends, clothing, tickets for concerts and sporting events, and gifts for friends and their children. The victims of her crimes reported feeling angry, stressed, not being able to sleep, and so on. Frith was sentenced to 21 months' imprisonment for theft; this case was not regarded by the courts as a disability hate crime, even though she had repeatedly targeted disabled people in order to commit her crimes.

Another person employed as a disability carer who stole considerable amounts of money from a disabled client was Sharon Lesley Grocock (*R. v Grocock (Sharon Lesley)*, 2008). Grocock was employed by the housing charity Shelter and used her position to steal approximately £16,000 from the bank account of Doreen Saville, a 77-year-old vision-impaired woman from Heeley, Sheffield. The thefts occurred over a six-month period ending in April 2005. The victim reported to social services in July 2005 that Grocock had been taking her property and stealing her savings, and they interviewed Grocock. However, Grocock told social services that she was merely a friend of the complainant, who was simply confused. Social services dropped the case (unfortunately, a common response when disabled people make complaints). It was not until October 2005, when Grocock left Shelter, that the full extent of her crimes became apparent (to people other than the disabled victim). Grocock continued to steal from Saville after she left Shelter, telling her that she was still working voluntarily. But Saville's complaints about the thefts were finally addressed. Grocock denied the crimes until the day of her trial, when she changed her plea to guilty. Eventually, it was revealed that Grocock had used the money to buy carpets and blinds for her home, to pay a debt, to pay her rent, to buy her partner a motorbike, and to pay off some of her partner's drug debts. Grocock was initially sentenced to 30 months' imprisonment and to pay £10,000 compensation within a limited period. She paid the £10,000 compensation money and on appeal her sentence was reduced to 18 months' imprisonment.

Many carers have their sentence reduced on appeal when they have committed financial crimes against disabled people. Such was the case for Theresa Irene Twinn, who was initially sentenced to 12 months' imprisonment for stealing £1,400 from Miss Selfe, a woman in her sixties with a learning disability. Twinn, aged 48, was convicted of four counts of theft, occurring between November 2003 and January 2004. The sentencing judge said that people who break the trust placed in them when they are employed as a carer must expect to go to jail. However, her defence presented the following mitigating factors: she had paid back the money in full by the time of her appeal in March 2006; she had been dealing with various psychiatric issues in her own life; and she probably was experiencing depression herself as a result of a recent episode where she was assaulted at work. These factors were considered by the court when she appealed her sentence. She had served two months of imprisonment at that time, and the Court of Appeal gave her an immediate release as 'an act of mercy'.

Another carer who was convicted of stealing money from a disabled person was Caroline Laura Irvine (*R. v Irvine (Caroline Laura)*, 2008; Robinson, 2007). Irvine (also known as Maddison) was a 47-year-old care worker who was convicted of theft from Thelma Hall, an 83-year-old woman with learning difficulties. Hall's ATM card had been used on 24 occasions, for withdrawals of amounts up to £1,400 – far more than would be spent on Hall's modest and meager lifestyle. (Hall was known to shop at charity stores and survived on yoghurt and mashed potatoes.) Irvine claimed that Hall's disability was not as severe as the prosecution suggested, and that Hall regularly spent a great deal of money on herself, for instance, dancing or drinking. However, three other carers denied that Hall ever spent anywhere near the amount of money that Irvine suggested. The jury did not believe Irvine and she was convicted of stealing £3,650 from her victim and was sentenced to six months' imprisonment. Irvine appealed against the sentence but her appeal was denied.

Another carer who was convicted of financial misconduct towards a disabled client was Collette Francess Marshall, a 24-year-old woman who was convicted of fraud in 2009 (The National Autistic Society, 2009). Marshall was the joint manager of a residential care home in Rotherham called Orchard House, which her parents owned. Four disabled people lived in this home. One disabled woman in the house was not considered legally competent to manage her own financial affairs. There were strict rules over the management of her funds – for instance, money should only have been withdrawn in her presence and all the money should have been used entirely for her benefit. However, Marshall wrongly withdrew over £7,600 from this disabled woman's account. This amounted to virtually all of her client's financial resources. Her parents loaned her the sum of £3,500 to repay some of the stolen money. She was sentenced to 12 months' imprisonment for this profound breach of trust, a sentence which was upheld on appeal.

Some carers steal relatively small amounts of money from numerous disabled people. One such carer was Shirley Cutts, who pleaded guilty to stealing from three different elderly and disabled women in 2005 (*R. v. Cutts (Shirley)*, 2006). Her victims were aged 87, 69 and 85 and she was employed as a carer for all of them. She stole £20 on September 23, 2005, from one victim, and then while she was on bail for that offence she stole £90 from another victim on November 29 and (while still on bail for the first offence) stole £40 from a third victim on December 4. Because of this pattern of repeatedly victimizing people in her care, she was sentenced to three consecutive terms of three months' imprisonment (nine months total). Again, despite a pattern of repeat offending against the same type of victims over a period of time, this was not seen as a hate crime. The fact that the victims were all elderly and disabled was simply regarded by the court as evidence of their 'vulnerability' – and therefore considered as an aggravating factor in determining the sentence.

Other Reports

The 'Getting Away with Murder' report and the 'Hate Crime Dossier' published by *Disability Now* were not, however, the first documentation of the serious nature of disability hate crime in the UK. Far from it, in fact. In 2004, Capability Scotland and the Disability Rights Commission published 'Hate Crime Against Disabled People in Scotland: A Survey Report' (Capability Scotland and the Disability Rights Commission, 2004). The survey contained responses from 158 people in Scotland (approximately 70% of these people were disabled). Respondents came from the north, south, east and west of Scotland, and included a diversity of locations (urban, semi-rural and rural). It found that 47% had experienced a hate crime because of their disability. The results from the survey suggested that people with different impairments experienced quite different degrees of harassment. When asked about their experiences of being frightened/attacked, the responses were uneven. Eighty-two percent of people with a mental health problem reported such experiences, compared to 63% of people with a learning difficulty/disability, 57% of people with a visual impairment, 49% of people with a mobility problem who did not use a wheelchair, 45% of people with a hidden disability, 41% of people with a hearing disability, and 38% of wheelchair users. Fifty-five percent of carers also responded that they knew someone who had been the victim of a hate crime because of their disability identity (Capability Scotland and the Disability Rights Commission, 2004, p. 14).

The *Hate Crime Against Disabled People in Scotland* report did not distinguish between hate incidents (which might include verbal abuse) and hate crimes which specifically involve the violation of criminal law. Hate incidents are often a precursor to hate crimes, though they may not themselves contain criminal behavior. Nevertheless, many law enforcement agencies have found it useful to collect data on hate incidents because they can be used as a preventative measure to address community problems before something escalates into a hate crime. The *Hate Crime Against Disabled People in Scotland* report simply lumps all these behaviors into the categories of 'attacks' on disabled people. Likewise, this report also asked people if they had been 'frightened' or attacked and lumped these responses together. This is quite a serious error – there is no *necessary* connection between simply being frightened and experiencing crime victimization. More information is needed about the nature of the incidents which led to such fears or safety concerns. Having said that, an indication of the severity of the attacks to which disabled people were referring can be found in the following statistic: one-third of the victims had moved house as a result of an attack.

Nevertheless, read in conjunction with the other data, *Hate Crime Against Disabled People in Scotland* does provide some additional information, specifically in a Scottish context. It indicated that of the 82 disabled people who indicated they had been frightened or attacked, 73% had been verbally attacked, 35% had been physically attacked, 35% had been harassed in the street, 18% had something stolen or taken away, 15% had been spat at, and 12% had experienced damage to property. (Presumably, most respondents indicated that they had experienced more than one form of harassment, since these numbers add up to far more than 100% in total.) A respondent with mobility problems commented:

> I had to move because the upstairs neighbor was spitting on the door, kicking the door and throwing eggs at the window. He used to phone me and I had to go ex-directory. My dad had to stay over at my bedsit (Capability Scotland and the Disability Rights Commission, 2004, p. 18).

The frequency of these attacks also varied. Twenty-one percent of disabled people who had been frightened or attacked had such experiences once a week or more, 10% experienced them once or twice a month, 14% experienced them every two to three months, 23% experienced them once or twice a year (or less often), and 27% had experienced them once or twice in their lives (Capability Scotland and the Disability Rights Commission, 2004, p. 16). Another important finding was that although 40% of the victims had told police about the attacks, they felt that police in general were unable to help.

The *Hate Crimes Against Disabled People in Scotland* report was also consistent with earlier studies. The report cited a Disability Rights Commission Awareness Survey in 2003 that indicated one in five disabled Scots experienced harassment because of their disability identity, and one-third of people who knew a disabled person had witnessed that person being harassed. Almost 90% of respondents believed that disability-based harassment should be an offense. Likewise, the Highland Wellbeing Alliance (which brings together public agencies such as health, police and social work) conducted a small survey (100 people) and found that 23% had experienced bullying because of their disability, with 16% indicating that they had been physically attacked (Ross, 2008). Women were more likely than men to have experienced bullying. Only half of disabled victims of physical attacks had reported these incidents to police, with many indicating that they were worried that it might 'make things worse'.

The disability charity Mencap, which advocates for people with learning disabilities, has published many reports that have highlighted the victimization of people with learning disabilities. One report entitled 'Living in Fear' was published in 1999 (Alcock, 1999). Although it nominally focused on 'bullying', much of the evidence is mislabeled 'bullying' when it should in fact be identified as criminal behavior. Indeed, the report states that the following forms of victimization were most common:

> Kicking, biting, name-calling, teasing, stealing, pushing, threatening, having things thrown at you, being told to leave a building, hitting, being shouted at, swearing, demanding money, hair-pulling, throwing stones, spitting, poking, being punched, being beaten up, having one's head banged against the wall (Alcock, 1999, p. 2).

Many of these forms of 'bullying' are actually crimes, crimes that might include assault, theft, grievous bodily harm, intimidation, demanding money with menaces, vandalism, breach of the peace, antisocial behavior, and other crimes. Nevertheless, the language of 'bullying' was used throughout the report. The report was based on 5,000 questionnaires which were sent to group homes, leisure clubs, disability employment services and self-advocacy groups in England, Wales, Scotland and Northern Ireland. Its key findings were: 88% of interviewees had been bullied in the previous year; 66% had been bullied regularly; and 32% reported being bullied on a daily or weekly basis. Two of the main types of bullying were verbal and physical abuse: 47% reported name calling or verbal abuse as the kind of harassment they experienced and 23% reported physical assault. Seventy-three percent had been bullied in public places and 26% had been bullied at home. Robbery was also noted as a common experience, but the report did not list what percentage of respondents experienced this crime.

Some of the quotes from people with learning disabilities in the 'Living in Fear' report clearly fit into the category of disability hate crimes. A woman in Yorkshire said:

> We had stones thrown at our windows and yoghurts and bad eggs. They used to put fishing wire across the gate so when we went out we fell over the line. After a period things got even worse. They threatened that they would burn our house down and we had dog shit through the letter box. They said people like you should be put down at birth (Alcock, 1999, p. 5).

Clearly, this woman's victimization stemmed directly from her disability – the comment about 'people like you' being 'put down at birth' makes that abundantly clear. But awareness of disability hate crimes as that – as crimes motivated by bias – was not widespread at that time. Experiences such as these were often mislabeled as 'bullying' or 'abuse'. Another example of a disability hate crime is the comment from a 28-year-old male from Bishops Stortford who said: 'A group of school boys call me names and spit at me. Once they threw a coke bottle at me, then they forced my hand into a letter box and forced the skin off my knuckle'. Another man commented:

> I live in a council estate, kids, a group of four or five children abuse me all the time. One of them has threatened to beat me up when I leave the home to visit my sister. I fancy moving as I can't go on. I cry about it. They make fun of me, they throw stones, they smash my windows. Last year, our gate was broken, and somebody smashed all the glass windows in our greenhouse. The police won't do anything about it (Alcock, 1999, p. 8).

A woman from North Wales also indicated that she and her property had been attacked:

> We used to have a lot of trouble. People threw stones and eggs at our windows, I tried to ignore it but one lad followed me as I was going to work and chucked a stone at me … eventually we had to ask the housing association for a move (Alcock, 1999, p. 10).

Another man's story highlights the connection between verbal and physical abuse. This 30-year-old from Hertfordshire commented that 'I was in a pub, a man came up to me, called me a name, hit me on the head, and then walked off'. Finally, a 52-year-old male from London discussed his own experiences as a victim of a violent crime:

> I was walking along the road, after getting money from the post office. I was pushed to the floor and knocked in the face. One of the people put a knife to my ribs, pushed me about and stole money from me. I felt very unwell, scared and frightened (Alcock, 1999, p. 5).

The reporting of disability harassment by Mencap did not end with the publication of 'Living in Fear', however.

Mencap also published 'Don't Stick It, Stop It!' in 2007, which focused specifically on the experiences of children with learning disabilities (Mencap, 2007). The 'Don't Stick It' report was the result of workshops Mencap carried out with 46 schools across England, Wales and Northern Ireland, to explore experiences of 'bullying' at school. Over 500 children and young people between the ages of eight and 19 participated in these workshops. The report indicated 82% of children with a learning disability had been bullied (twice the level of other children); 60% of children with a learning disability had been physically hurt by bullies; 80% of children with a learning disability were scared to go out (particularly to school, the park, or to go out on the street); and 77% of the children with a learning disability had been verbally abused. Also, for 40% of the children, bullying did not stop when they told someone. Half of the children had been bullied in more than one place. Thirty percent of them had been bullied on the street, 30% at the park, 30% on the bus. Other places where bullying occurred included youth clubs and leisure centers.

Again, quotes from the victims give some indication of the level of violence and intimidation, which is often mislabeled as 'bullying' instead of criminal victimization. For instance, one child named Ciara stated:

> I was bullied when I was younger because of my learning disability. They said I was ugly and they banged my head so badly that I had to go to the hospital to have 18 stitches in my forehead. The bullying made me feel so unhappy and scared and I would make myself ill every day. It still affects me now even though it happened years ago. It will always stay with me because of how bad it was (Mencap, 2007, p. 3).

This vignette clearly communicates the pain and hurt, as well as the fear that accompanies hate-based violence. Another girl, Ashley, commented that she was 'spat on, sweared at and kicked' by two boys and a girl on her first day at school (Mencap, 2007, p. 5). The mother of one child, Ben, indicated that he had also been spat upon, and the tires on his bike were also deflated. 'Ben was bullied wherever he went. He would return from the park with bruises and torn clothes. As far as the local kids were concerned, Ben was there for entertainment. He was the butt of their jokes, an object of ridicule' (Mencap, 2007, p. 8).

People with learning disabilities, and the advocacy groups which support them, seem to regard hate crimes as a much more important issue than some of the broader (nondisability) organizations established by the Government to address crimes in the local area. A study entitled *Learning Disability Hate Crime: Identifying Barriers to Addressing Crime* indicated that more than 80% of disability advocacy groups and 75% of Learning Disability Partnership Boards reported that hate crime was a problem. These groups are much closer to people with learning disabilities than many other (nondisability) organizations charged with responding to crime in the community. The authors of this report suggested that the closer one gets to people with learning disabilities, the more aware one becomes of this issue – or conversely, the further away someone is from disabled people, the less aware they are. To highlight this finding, they pointed out that only 43% of Crime and Disorder Reduction Partnerships (also known as Community Safety Partnerships), which are not disability-specific organizations, regarded disability hate crimes as a problem (Lamb and Redmond, 2007). This obviously has flow-on effects: one could expect little or no effort being directed towards an issue which is not regarded as a problem.

People with learning disabilities are not the only ones who experience high rates of bullying and intimidation, of course. For instance, the National Autistic Society has reported that 56% of people with Autistic Spectrum Disorder have been bullied or harassed as adults, a figure which rises to 70% for those people with Autistic Spectrum Disorder who live alone (Rosenblatt, 2008). Their response to the Government's 'Anti-social behavior: policy and procedure' document contained one story about a person who was given the pseudonym of Matthew. The document explained that Matthew had experienced verbal abuse, graffiti on his home, and was hospitalized after being physically assaulted within his own home. Matthew's Autistic Spectrum Disorder made it harder to communicate effectively with police. He lacked support workers or family who could help him in lodging such criminal complaints (The National Autistic Society, 2009). This problem raises another issue: the importance of support programs that assist disabled people in accessing the criminal justice system. And there is obviously a need to raise awareness of the problems that such barriers exist in the first place.

One of the major barriers in the legal system for disabled people is that many cases of victimization of disabled people are not classified as disability hate crimes, even when there is evidence that the person's disability identity is being targeted. For instance, the *South Wales Echo* newspaper reported on the case of a severely disabled woman with cerebral palsy, Rachel Thomas, who experienced a two-and-a-half-year campaign of harassment from her neighbor, Michael David Haywood. Thomas requires 24-hour care. On one occasion, Haywood angled his lawnmower so that he sprayed her with dirt as she sat in her wheelchair. On other occasions, Haywood threw dirt, stones and food at their house while Rachel Thomas was there; obstructed the dropped curb she used to exit a vehicle; blocked the entrance to their house with a wheelie bin; called Rachel a 'Mongol child'; and poured slurry from a cement mixer over their garden. There were 153 incidents reported by Rachel's family over this time; magistrates found against Haywood in all but three of these cases. Unfortunately, however, this intimidation was not considered a disability hate crime. Instead, it was logged under the category of 'anti-social behavior' and Hayward was simply given a five-year antisocial behavior order with 13 conditions banning him from causing harassment to anyone, especially the Thomas family (Horton, 2007, p. 9).

It is important to stress that while people with learning disabilities certainly experience crime victimization at much higher rates than members of the general community, other groups of disabled people also are victimized at alarming rates. People with psychiatric impairments, for instance, are frequently the victims of crime. In 2007, Mind (a leading mental health charity for England and Wales) published a report entitled *Another Assault*, which exposed the shocking level of victimization and harassment that people with psychiatric impairments face in the community. The report was based on responses from 304 people with direct experience of mental distress and 86 support workers. One of the key findings was that 71% of respondents with mental health problems living in the community had been the victim of a crime in the previous two years. (This compares to the general rate of 24.4% reported in the British Crime Survey.) People with mental health problems were more than six times more likely to have been physically assaulted in the past two years than other members of the community (22% compared to 3.4%). Additionally, 27% of people with mental health problems had been sexually harassed and 10% had been sexually assaulted in the previous two years. Forty-one percent were the victims of ongoing bullying and 26% reported that their homes had been targeted. Nearly 90% of people living in local authority housing had been victimized. Not surprisingly, perhaps, considering these figures, only 19% of people with mental health problems reported feeling safe in their own homes.

Another Assault also chronicled other crimes which people with mental health problems experience. For instance, it reported that 34% of people with mental health problems had been the victim of theft of their money or valuables, either from their person or from their bank account. Also, 62% had been called names or insulted and 29% had been followed, pestered or chased, or had things thrown at them. Seventeen percent had received hate mail or prank calls. Thirteen percent had been spat at. Equally importantly, many people who had experienced these crimes did not feel empowered to report these crimes, or did not feel that their experiences of victimization were taken seriously. Indeed, 60% of those who reported their victimization to the police felt that their case was not taken seriously and 36% of the people who did not report an incident said that they did not think they would be believed if they went to authorities. A little over a quarter of respondents said that they believed that their experiences would not be considered a priority for police officers, and another 23% did not report the incident because they did not believe anything would be done and there was no point. Other respondents felt that 'being a victim was part of living in the community with mental distress' (Mind, 2007).

While the *Another Assault* report focused on the experiences of people with mental health problems in the community, another Mind publication entitled *Ward Watch* highlighted the experiences of victimization of people with mental health problems in inpatient settings. More than one-quarter of people who were mental health inpatients reported that they rarely felt safe in the hospital. Over half of recent or current inpatients reported being verbally or physically threatened during their stay and 20% reported experiencing physical assault. One in five respondents indicated that they had experienced sexual harassment and 5% reported sexual assault while an inpatient. Seven percent indicated that they had been harassed because of their race and 3% indicated that they had been the victim of a racially motivated assault. Ten percent reported being harassed because of their sexuality, and 5% reported being assaulted because of their sexuality. The majority (56%) of the harassments or assaults were perpetrated by other patients, but 31% were perpetrated by a staff member of the inpatient wards. Almost a quarter of the respondents reported being either physically or verbally threatened while they were an inpatient in hospital. Twenty percent reported being the victim of physical assault in hospital. This report is important, because it highlights the need for independent disability advocacy in psychiatric settings, which may be able to connect disabled victims of crime to appropriate authorities. There have been cases in other countries of recidivist criminals working in such settings in order to commit offences against people who they feel may not be believed, or may not be able to respond/resist effectively. Existing reporting mechanisms within the hospitals do not seem to be working: only 37% of people who had been threatened, harassed, abused or assaulted reported their experiences to a staff member in the hospital. They often said that they were afraid of reprisals and that they lacked confidence that staff would do anything to improve the situation. Of those who did report their experiences, only 30% were satisfied with the response from hospital staff.

Official Disability Hate Crime Statistics, 2007–2008

While the US has been collecting disability hate crime data for many years (as discussed in Chapter 3), the Crown Prosecution Service in the UK published its first disability hate crime data in December 2008 (Crown Prosecution Service, 2008). In the year ending March 2008, 183 defendants were prosecuted for disability incidents. (In the 'key finding' section of the report and elsewhere, 183 is the figure most often presented. However, page 36 of the report indicates that 187 people were charged, there was a request for further evidence in two cases, 75 cases were not prosecuted and seven cases involved 'another decision'. The discrepancy between the numbers reportedly charged is not explained.) In other words, in 69% of cases which were reported to police as disability hate crimes, charges were laid. Although the number of people charged with disability hate crimes in the UK is larger than the US (even in its first year), this number is still relatively small compared to the overall number of hate crimes which are prosecuted yearly in the UK. Indeed, disability hate crime prosecutions represented only 0.2% of the total number of hate crime prosecutions. Over 78,000 people were prosecuted for hate crimes in the UK in 2007–2008, and only 187 of these people were charged with disability hate crimes. Many disability advocacy groups consider this low rate of prosecution an outrage.

The most common disability hate crimes in 2007–2008 were offenses against the person, burglary, theft and handling; 150 (82%) of the defendants who were prosecuted were men and 33 (18%) were women. The Crown Prosecution Service did not keep good records on the gender of victims. Its report states that 30 (20.8%) of the victims were women, 33 (22.9%) were men, and the gender of the victim was 'unknown' in 81 cases (56.3% of the total). (This is particularly disappointing given the consistent findings of gender differences in crime victimization rates and in the types of crime experienced.) Likewise, the failure to record the ethnicity, age and location of victims and perpetrators is another missed opportunity – one which might have been particularly useful for prevention efforts. And the failure to identify which impairments are targeted for particular types of crimes is another serious flaw in the report. There are studies which seem to suggest that people with different impairments experience different rates of sexual assault, assault, and so on – but the opportunity to report these differences (and to begin to respond to them effectively) has so far been missed.

Unfortunately, the Crown Prosecution Service report demonstrates that unless they plead guilty, those that are charged with disability hate crimes have minimal chances of being found not guilty. In the UK in 2007–2008, the defendant had entered a guilty plea in 131 cases (72% of the total number of disability hate crime cases). The Crown Prosecution Service seemed pleased that the overall conviction rate for people charged with disability hate crimes was 77% (higher than the average for all other hate crimes). But beneath these statistics lies another, less positive picture. There were 52 other cases where the defendant did not plead guilty. In these cases, for various reasons (including 27 cases where prosecutors dropped the charges and 9 cases where the victim either retracted, failed to attend the hearing, or did not provide evidence which supported the case) only 10 of the 52 cases resulted in successful prosecution. *In other words, a defendant who decided to go to trial for committing a disability hate crime had a less than 20% chance of being convicted in the UK in the year 2007–2008.* This limited likelihood of success may well be one of the reasons why disabled victims do not bother to report hate crimes in the first place.

Conclusion

The legal system consistently fails disabled victims of hate crimes. It is not just that the vast majority of disability hate crimes are not reported at all. Those that are reported are often not recognized as hate crimes by police or prosecutors – or by victims, either. As well, many crimes which are reported to social services authorities are 'handled internally' – meaning that police are not contacted, so perpetrators are not prosecuted (Lewin, 2007). Should they decide to pursue legal avenues, disabled victims cannot be automatically guaranteed of getting the disability accommodations they require. Also, many prosecutors are wary of putting a disabled witness or victim on the stand, for fear of them being considered an unreliable witness. But disabled people's testimonies are not necessarily any less reliable than any other witnesses and there are recognized strategies to improve accessibility to justice for disabled people. For instance, specific programs have been developed to enhance the accessibility of the legal system to people with learning disabilities, mental illness, and most other disabilities (Marinos et al., 2009; Perlin, 2000; Stefan, 2001; Willott et al., 2004). Often, improvements can come from simply identifying and challenging discriminatory stereotypes about disabled crime victims. The widespread cultural stereotype about disabled people being unreliable witnesses in court limits their access to justice. Furthermore, even if charges are brought against a defendant, lesser charges (rather than the penalty enhancements associated with hate crime laws) are likely to be pursued. If charges are brought against a defendant for a disability hate crime, in one-third of the cases they will be dropped by the prosecution before going to trial. Equally concerning, unless the offender pleads guilty, there is a strong possibility that the disabled person will not be believed and that the defendant will be found not guilty.

The cycle of injustice surrounding disability hate crimes does not have to continue, however. There are many practical things which can be done to address this problem. Identifying areas for improvement – and steps to achieve them – is the goal of the next chapter.

Chapter 5
Responding to Disability Hate Crimes

Studying disability hate crimes is not an easy task. The crimes are often so appalling, so hyperviolent, so hypersexual, or so cruel that they leave observers stunned and shocked, wondering how such injustice can occur and what motivates it. So many people, with so much to give, have been cruelly murdered, assaulted, robbed, and otherwise victimized. The pain they have felt is tangible and must be acknowledged. But it would be a grave mistake to stop there. The story of disability hate crimes cannot simply be one that ends with recognizing injustice but not doing anything about it. It is just as important to identify ways of addressing this problem, reducing and preventing disability hate crimes in the future. This is the goal of this chapter: to discuss a range of legal, political and social strategies for addressing the problem. The emphasis on political and social strategies in this chapter is not an accident: hate crimes legislation is only one element in creating safer communities. Other strategies must also be adopted which reduce the criminal victimization of disabled people and enhance their access to justice. These include a change in public attitudes towards disability, an end to segregation, improved service provider practices, and support for disabled people who are victims of hate crimes.

For many years, disability activists have been highlighting the ways in which the social exclusion of disabled people creates a climate where they lack safeguards, supports, advocacy and resources to respond to various forms of abuse, aggression and criminal victimization. Many disabled people are isolated from mainstream society. Their marginalization and disempowerment contributes significantly to crime victimization. Some of the factors which contribute to the cultural devaluation of disabled people, raising the risk of criminal victimization, include: negative stereotypes and prejudice about disability; the marginalization, disempowerment and poverty levels experienced by disabled people; and prejudicial perceptions about the lack of credibility of disabled victims.

It is not coincidental that disability hate crimes occur against a backdrop of social exclusion and marginalization. Hate crimes are sometimes described as crimes about power – they are one link in a long chain used to sustain inequality and power imbalances, directed mostly towards marginalized and stigmatized groups (Perry, 2001). In this context, it is important to identify the social, cultural, economic, physical and psychological factors which contribute to a climate in which disabled people become the victims of hate crimes. These factors include the exclusion, isolation and poverty of disabled people and their families; lack of supports, advocacy and safeguards; broader cultural support for violence; the level the problem of hate-motivated violence and pressure politicians to pass legislation, well before courts and police administer and interpret those laws (Jenness and Grattet, 2001). They emphasize the role of social movements in gathering data on hate crimes and publicizing this information, which is then distributed to policymakers, law enforcement agencies and the general public. The implication of this argument is that the disability movement must collect more data on hate crimes and must engage in more lobbying to raise the profile of disability hate crimes. In this respect, the actions of the disability movement in the UK may be a role model for their counterparts in other countries.

Disabled people who are the victims of hate crimes may also need disability accommodations in order to testify in hate crime cases. Courts have arguably done a poor job in dealing with people who have mental health issues as well as people with various cognitive impairments (although there have been some improvements in recent years as a result of improved awareness) (Cooke and Davies, 2001; G. Green, 2001; Gudjonsson et al., 2000; Nathanson and Platt, 2005; Perlin, 1999). A recent UK case highlights this problem: prosecutors abandoned a case because they felt that the victim with psychosis (who had his ear bitten off in the attack) would not be considered a reliable witness. The High Court subsequently criticized the Crown Prosecution Service for its handling of this case and awarded the 25-year-old man £8,000 in compensation because it regarded this as inhuman and degrading treatment (Lombard, 2009). Disability agencies representing people with mental health problems argued that this case highlights the need for further reforms. Prosecutors should receive mental health awareness training and should be trained in how to prevent psychiatric evidence from being used inappropriately in court.

While some jurisdictions have developed innovative programs (for instance, those that involve third party reporting systems when a disabled victim feels unable to contact the police), there is a long way to go in assisting vulnerable witnesses. As this book has shown, there is an alarming rate of sexual assault of disabled people (in particular disabled women). Unfortunately, people with various impairments (but particularly cognitive disabilities) are often doubly victimized in the courts because they are infantilized; various prejudicial stereotypes about their 'child-like' or 'hypersexual' natures also diminish their access to justice when they are the victims of crime (Benedet and Grant, 2007).

It is sometimes assumed that because hate crimes are a legal matter, the most appropriate way to respond to them is also a legal approach. But the prevention of hate crimes requires far more than that. It is interesting to note that one of the most comprehensive guides for responding to hate crimes has been produced by the International Association of Chiefs of Police (2002). Their 22 recommendations for responding to hate crimes recognize the complexities of the causes of hate crime and work to reduce prejudice and bigotry at the individual and the societal level. Their recommendations include increasing public awareness and community involvement in responding to prejudice intolerance and hate crime; developing co-ordinated planning processes, task forces and institutional frameworks to promote community stability and respond to hate groups; and providing adequate support to victims. Other recommendations include reforming school curricula to include diversity training, conflict resolution and information about hate crimes; developing more effective sanctions for perpetrators; encouraging responsible and accurate media coverage of hate crimes; and establishing mechanisms for repairing harm to communities.

This book has highlighted the differences between the perspectives of law enforcement and disability activists when it comes to defining disability hate crimes. It is clear that disability rights activists have a much broader interpretation of these crimes. They deeply believe that there are unique disability-related forms of victimization which need to be recognized as 'hate crimes'. Such crimes include actions which are often considered 'neglect' or 'abuse', such as withholding medications, damaging assistive technology, overmedicating people, and refusing to assist people with activities of daily living. Disabled people who require assistance with intimate care activities such as washing, dressing and using the toilet can be particularly susceptible to crimes associated with those activities; they are frequently targeted for sexual assault and rape. Some disability activists do not regard these crimes as abuse; more and more they are demanding that such crimes be recognized as hate crimes, because the areas where a disabled person needs specific assistance are precisely the ones which are being targeted and exploited in the commission of a crime.

Negative attitudes towards disability which objectify, devalue and dehumanize disabled people have played a major role in making them more vulnerable to hate crimes. A change in attitudes towards disability is therefore absolutely essential. This attitudinal change must start by acknowledging that human differences should be celebrated (not shunned) and that everyone's dignity must be respected. This seems so simple and yet – as Chapter 2 demonstrates – society has a long way to go before disabled people are treated with respect. The hate, intolerance and bigotry described in Chapter 2 must be challenged in order to break down the wider cultural supports for antidisability bias. There is a long cultural history of prejudice and discrimination against disabled people – one that must be challenged and overcome in order to develop a more tolerant and just society.

Like many victims of prejudice, disabled people are often subjected to a range of negative stereotypes which denigrate, stigmatize and isolate them. Such stereotypes rely on false dichotomies between 'us' and 'them' to spread bias, prejudice, fear and intolerance. Disabled people are imagined to be living a life barely worth living and are therefore avoided, devalued, marginalized and disrespected in various ways. These stigmatizing processes occur at both the conscious and unconscious levels and often have cumulative effects which isolate disabled people from their peers, reducing the natural supports which they may have found in a wider social support network (Marks, 1999). Prejudicial attitudes may have significant effects on disabled people's self-esteem. However, disability studies scholars have warned against regarding this as an individual problem – it happens so often and on such a large scale, it is a major social problem (Longmore,

2003). Indeed, such experiences are commonly regarded as a form of 'oppression' by disability studies scholars (Barnes and Mercer, 2002).

Disability is a topic which is often covered in shame – a social dynamic which silences and isolates disabled people, preventing them from having the rights, freedoms and opportunities which they deserve. Breaking down negative images of disability is therefore an important element in reducing the vulnerability of disabled people. It not only increases the supports and safeguards in a person's life, but it may change the way disabled people see themselves. For instance, many people who are considered 'disabled' by others – including people with severe and lifelong illnesses, disorders and diseases – refuse to accept the label themselves because they do not want the stigma which goes with it. Even victims of disability hate crimes have been so reluctant to identify – or be identified – as disabled, that they will not report such crimes to the police, for fear of being stigmatized.

The need for broad changes in attitudes towards disability becomes evident when one considers a sign which was hung from a house in Nephi, Utah, in 2006. After a dispute between neighbors, one of whom has a 13-year-old autistic son, one family hung a sign stating: 'Caution: Retards in Area' (Penrod, 2006). The sign was facing the boy's house. After two visits from the local police chief, and a great deal of media attention, the sign was taken down (Staff *Casper Star Tribune*, 2006). But the fact that it was erected in the first place demonstrates that there is a long way to go in terms of understanding and acceptance.

Many disabled people are isolated from mainstream society. This marginalization and disempowerment contributes significantly to patterns of abuse and victimization. Negative attitudes which objectify, devalue and dehumanize disabled people have historically enabled various human rights abuses including sterilization, institutionalization, and horrifying levels of violence. Disability is commonly assumed to be an abject way of life – one that not only represents 'the other', but which is so horrible, so unimaginable, that one would be better off dead than disabled. And yet disability activists say the direct opposite of this assumption – they highlight the ways in which disabled people can be happy, socially valued and included. Indeed, some studies suggest that disabled students have the same levels of self-esteem as their nondisabled peers (Blake and Rust, 2002).

Andrews and Veronen listed a number of reasons for the increased rates of abuse experienced by disabled people. Some of their reasons include: increased dependency on others for long-term care; denial of human rights which leads to perceptions of powerlessness; the beliefs of perpetrators that they are less likely to be caught; the difficulties some disabled people experience in being believed; lower levels of education, including sexual education, for disabled people; social isolation and risk of manipulation; and physical helplessness or vulnerability in public (Andrews and Veronen, 1993). This list of social factors that influence disabled people's experiences of the criminal justice system indicates that comprehensive social change must be a factor in responding to the problem of disability hate crime.

Of course, disabled people are not the only victims of violence, abuse, and hate crimes – but their experiences of such crimes are an important reminder of the need for broader cultural challenges to bullying, interpersonal violence, and the exploitation of power imbalances in various ways. In this way, challenging disability hate crimes requires more fundamental challenges to exploitative and abusive behaviors in general. It is impossible to address disability hate crimes without having a wider understanding of the need for everyone to feel safe in their homes, in their schools or workplaces, and in their communities. But this means that other abuses of power must also be addressed – such as power imbalances and gender stereotypes which feed in to domestic violence. (And bringing up the issue of domestic violence is not accidental: like the victims of domestic violence, and elder abuse, a large proportion of the victims of disability hate crimes experience their criminal victimization in their homes or residences.)

Given the lack of community (and law enforcement) awareness about disability hate crimes, it should not be surprising that even cases which involve a disabled person being repeatedly victimized may not be recognized as a disability hate crime. A classic illustration of this problem can be found in the case of Dorothy Dixon (Hillig, 2009a, 2009b; Staff *Associated Press*, 2009; Suhr, 2009). She was a 29-year-old African-American developmentally disabled woman from Illinois who was tortured for at least two months and finally murdered by a group of people in January 2008. Dixon had one child, aged 15 months, and was pregnant. Her 15-month-old son lived in the basement with Dixon, and weighed just 15 pounds when authorities discovered Dixon's body. Her unborn child was delivered stillborn on the autopsy table. Dixon was banished to the basement of her own house by her housemates with a thin rug and a mattress on a chilly concrete floor. Her housemates tortured her: they beat her with an axe, a baseball bat and a plunger handle, burned her with boiling water that peeled away her skin, burned her with a hot glue gun, used her for target practice with a BB pistol, and they also burned some of her clothes, so that she walked around naked. When her body was found, deep tissue burns covered one-third of her body (specifically, her face, chest, arms and feet). One of Dixon's housemates, 37-year-old Michelle Riley, had been pocketing her Social Security Disability checks as well. Riley pled guilty to murder, but was not charged with a hate crime, even though disability is included in the hate crime laws in that state. (Federal legislation on disability hate crimes had not been signed into law at the time of the murder.) Four other adults (Judy E. Woods, 44; Benny L. Wilson, 18; LeShelle McBride, 17; and Michael J. Elliott, 20) and one juvenile were also charged with this crime. The 12-year-old juvenile was found guilty of second-degree murder and given 60 days of detention and five years' probation.

Of course, people who are disabled can be victims of a hate crime for a reason other than their disability. For instance, an antigay hate crime might happen to someone who is disabled. Unless there is evidence that the victim was specifically targeted because of their disability, the case will be filed as an antigay hate crime. This was the case with the murder of Michael J. Hatch in Barron County,

Wisconsin, on October 20, 1999. Hatch was Deaf and developmentally disabled. Three people were involved in his murder – Corey Kralewski, Ray Walton and Mary Reed (*State of Wisconsin vs. Raymond C. Walton*, 2000; *State vs. Mary C. Reed*, 1999; *State vs. Corey L. Kralewski*, 1999). They believed that Hatch was gay. Kralewski and Walton beat Hatch to death with tire irons, while Reed watched the murder from a truck. All three voiced their hatred of gay people during the murder. (Importantly, they did not express hatred of disability or Deafness.) After he was dead, Walton and Kralewski stole $40 from the victim and Reed destroyed the murder weapon. Walton was convicted in 2001 of being party to second-degree reckless homicide and theft and was sentenced to 25 years in prison. He appealed his sentence in 2003, on the grounds that he was essentially forced into a plea deal because of a learning disability. His request was denied. Kralewski was sentenced to life imprisonment for first degree intentional homicide, a Class A felony. Reed was sentenced to two years in prison after pleading guilty to aiding a felon (*The Cheteck Alert Courthouse Reporter*, 2006).

Those who study the intersection of disability and other identities (race, sex, gender, class, age, religion, and so on) are often interested in the ways in which perceptions of one identity may interact with another. In this case, Hatch's disability may well have influenced the perpetrators' perception of whether he was an 'easy target'. However, it is inappropriate to speculate about such perceptions without evidence in a criminal case. Without such evidence, it can only be proven that this was an antigay hate crime. At the level of individual cases, it is unwise to speculate about an offender's motives *without any direct evidence*; such speculation has no credibility and would never hold up in court. On the other hand, it would be unwise to completely ignore the connections between the victimization of people because of disablism and other forms of prejudice and hatred such as racism, sexism, homophobia, and anti-Semitism. For instance, two disabled men and their 62-year-old nondisabled companion were assaulted in a park in Orlando, Florida, in 2008 because they refused to pay a 'fee for being white'. The racist underpinnings of this crime were obvious, but the importance of the men's disability identities was never discussed in the press (Staff *Local6.com*, 2008). It is vital that prosecutors neither assume that the disability identity of the victim is central, nor irrelevant, in the perpetrator's motives. Rather, investigating officers and prosecutors must ask (particularly where there are clearly other prejudicial motives): '*Why that particular black person?*' or '*Why that particular gay person?*' or '*Why that particular woman?*' or '*Why that particular Jewish person?*' (and so on).

Other cases where disabled people have been attacked and subjected to racist hate speech involved the cases of Francis Pitia from Ontario, Canada; Janet Stead from Lancashire, England; and Dijuan Davis from Florida, USA. Pitia, 33, whose right leg has been paralyzed since childhood from polio, was beaten with his own crutch during an attack in 2006. Before they were attacked, both Pitia and his friend, Daniel Tolit, were subjected to racist abuse by a group of approximately 10 men. According to Pitia, 'They said, "You black people, Negroes, Negroes", and they come all to me. And then they just try to beat me, beat me' (Staff *CBC*

News, 2006). Pitia was attacked with his crutches, especially in his chest. His face was also attacked, requiring stitches in his mouth. He received a black eye and was unconscious when he was taken to hospital (Khalid, 2006). A similar dynamic occurred in Mascotte, Florida, when a disabled man was seriously injured during a hate crime. Dijuan Davis was subjected to racist slurs before he was beaten and seriously injured in an attack in 2008 (Staff *Click Orlando*, 2008). And Janet Stead, a disabled widow, and her two children were subjected to racist and sexist insults by a local Asian gang. One day, she had vulgar sexual comments shouted at her and on another occasion, a dozen gang members shouted racist abuse at her, made monkey impressions and threw stones at her family (Turner, 2007). Again, it is important to avoid a simple assumption that disablism was a key factor in the motivation of the perpetrators of these crimes, but it cannot simply be assumed that the disability identities of the victims were irrelevant either. The fact that Francis Pitia was hit with crutches – a symbol of his disability identity – surely deserved some attention, for instance.

Another case which raises the issue of intersecting bias involved messages of hate drawn at the Jewish Community Center in DeWitt, New York. This center was subject to graffiti on three consecutive days: obscenities were written on the front door on the first day; swastikas were drawn on the retaining wall the next day; and finally, the handicapped parking sign was covered with hate graffiti on the third day. This third act of vandalism is particularly interesting, because antidisability hatred overlapped with anti-Semitism. It means that the crimes did not just involve anti-Semitism, but also disablist hate. Unfortunately, local police said there were no suspects (Goldberg, 2005).

There is a strong need for additional training and clarification of the reporting procedures in cases where more than one identity is discussed during the commission of a crime. Otherwise, a multi-bias crime may simply be reduced to prejudice against one identity – failing to accurately identify many of the complex power dynamics and motives of a case. It is important to recognize that some of the forms of hate which disabled people experience are also common to other victims of hate crimes. For instance, the Nazi symbol is often used in the commission of anti-Semitic hate crimes, but it also has a long history in eugenics and is sometimes used against disabled people in this way. The Nazis believed that disabled people were 'useless eaters' and should be eliminated as a part of the Final Solution; disabled people were the first group to be systematically exterminated by the Nazis (Friedlander, 1995). Contemporary Nazis and white supremacists sometimes target disabled people in a continuation of this hatred. Paul Alloco, a wheelchair user with multiple sclerosis, experienced such Nazi harassment in 2006 when he was the victim of a hate crime in Shirley, New York (Armario, 2006). Alloco is not Jewish; he was targeted because of his disability. He had been previously taunted because of his disability, but the harassment escalated when two boys, aged 12 and 14, painted swastikas over his house. They were subsequently arrested and charged with first-degree aggravated harassment as a hate crime. The boys had seen the movie *American History X*, which details the life of a white supremacist. The commanding officer of the Hate Crimes Bureau, Det. Sgt. Robert Reeks, commented: 'The intention was to put the Swastika as a hate symbol'.

Another case with white supremacist links occurred in Costa Mesa, California, on July 7, 2006. In that case, Ronald Lee Bray, a white supremacist gang member, spat upon a man in a wheelchair who was outside a 7-Eleven store, pushed the man's wheelchair into a light post, and racially vilified him (Strodl, 2007). Bray raised his arm in a Nazi salute and said 'Heil Hitler'. Bray pleaded guilty to felony charges of committing a hate crime and making a criminal threat with a hate crime enhancement (Carcamo, 2007). He was sentenced to 32 months in prison (Staff *Associated Press*, 2007b). The setting of this crime – Costa Mesa – may not have been a coincidence. It has been a hotbed for Nazi activism for many years and has even been called 'Hatesville, USA' by one commentator because of its connections to Nazi and white supremacist hate groups and militia (Coker, 2006).

Another case which raises the issue of multiple forms of bias was a hate crime committed against New York Governor Paterson during the 2008 presidential election. Paterson is an African-American man who is blind. Timothy W. Day, of Deerfield, New York, was charged with a felony hate crime for aggravated harassment in the second degree as a hate crime for a threat he made about Paterson. The police complaint against Day stated that on September 11, 2008, Day phoned the office of Assemblywoman RoAnn Destito from his home and left a threatening message. The message on her answering machine stated, 'Ah yeah, I just got home from work and I was watching the news and I was kinda amazed about the comment that our Governor made about the woman who is running for vice president with John McCain and I really think you should say something to him. I am so sick of these fucking niggers running around bitching and hollering every time something is said that it's racism. If I ever see that guy in upstate New York … That blind black bastard … I'll fucking kill him' (Oneida County Office of the District Attorney, 2009). Clearly this is a racially motivated hate crime – there is no doubt about that – but the question that remains is whether the placement of the word 'blind' in the last sentence, prior to the word 'black', is enough of a modifier to suggest that there was antidisability bias as well. The fact that his blindness was mentioned highlights the difficult decisions that prosecutors need to make in deciding whether multiple bias was involved or not; in this case, prosecutors considered it did not. Day eventually pleaded guilty to aggravated second-degree harassment in exchange for five years' probation. He was not incarcerated (LaDuca, 2009a, 2009b, 2009c).

Even if a case is identified by prosecutors and law enforcement officers as involving hate, the bias charges are usually dropped in the process of negotiating a plea deal. Prosecutors usually believe that it is harder to prove the motivation (and thus establish the parallel bias crime) and instead simply focus on the first crime. That is a normal and perfectly acceptable prosecutorial decision, to some extent. Prosecutors will often drop certain charges – particularly when negotiations are taking place with a defendant for a plea deal. But if it means that the bias aspects of a disability hate crime are almost always ignored (and in practice this seems to be the case), this *de facto* undermining of disability hate crime legislation certainly deserves critical examination.

One of the important findings from this book is that many hate crimes are inflicted upon disabled people by family members, partners or carers who are employed to look after the welfare of the person. Indeed, the greater the number of carers a disabled person has, the greater the risk of a hate crime being committed. Recent headlines in the media have highlighted the fact that there is a virtual epidemic of abuse and criminal victimization by carers. Some of the stories in the press have included: 'Disabled men in residential care forced into "fight clubs" by carers' (Staff *Herald Sun*, 2009a); 'Women in care "raped, trade sex for smokes" according to a watchdog' (Staff *Herald Sun*, 2009b); 'Two staffers busted for beating autistic woman' (Brosh and Sederstrom, 2007); 'Carer jailed for stealing savings of Royston disabled woman' (Staff *Royston Crow*, 2009); 'Caregiver caught' (Burstein, 2009); 'Caregiver stole from Carrington care home residents' (Gillett, 27 October 2007); 'Carer stole £1,300 from autistic man' (Staff *The Citizen Newspaper*, 14 November 2007); '5 Pinecrest employees arrested in abuse probe' (Bonnette, 2008); 'Ex-aides charged for abuse of autistic boy' (Newhouse, 2009); 'Bankrupt carer jailed after cruel theft' (Staff *M2 Presswire*, 2008); 'Jail for thieving carer' (Staff *Manchester Evening News*, 2008); 'Care manager stole from woman' (Staff *BBC News*, 2009a); 'Carer admits stealing £8k from pensioner' (Staff *BBC News*, 2009b); 'She stole thousands from pair' (Staff *Gloucestershire Echo*, 2006); 'As carer turned crook avoids jail term, OAP asks "Why wasn't she put away?"' (Staff *Hartlepool Mail*, 2007); 'Former care home manager jailed for stealing from vulnerable patients' (Staff *Derby Telegraph*, 2009); 'James Watts jailed for sex crimes at care home' (Staff *North Devon Journal*, 2009); 'Smyrna police charge live-in caregiver with murder' (Staff *Associated Press*, 2007c); 'Caregiver investigated in patients' deaths (Staff *CBS News Los Angeles*, 2009); and 'Cobb caregiver guilty of murder' (Mahone, 2008). This is only a selection of such articles – the list is virtually endless. Other workers have often been silent about these actions – but this pattern of silence (which has enabled crimes to continue) must end. There must be more reporting of abusive or criminal actions committed by service workers, staff or carers who work with disabled people. Other workers can often lead the way in reporting such crimes. Improved reporting rates may be the first step in addressing the epidemic of crime, violence, neglect and abuse in the lives of disabled people.

Unlike many other types of hate crime, disability hate crimes are often committed by people with longstanding relationships with the victim. This characteristic of disability hate crimes seems different from many other hate crimes, where strangers are often the perpetrator of crimes. This pre-existing relationship between perpetrator and victim may demand a different response from law enforcement officers also. Often these officers assume that an act cannot be a hate crime if there is a pre-existing relationship between the victim and perpetrator

(Bell, 2002). However, such an assumption may be flawed in the case of disability hate crimes.

Unfortunately, there is serious lack of awareness among many law enforcement officers about the specific ways in which disabled victims of crime may be terrorized by the perpetrators of hate crime. This lack of awareness is one of the major barriers which must be overcome in order to develop a more accurate picture of the prevalence of disability hate crime. Some of the unique dimensions of crimes that are targeted at disabled people have been explored in the literature on disability and 'abuse'. Though these acts are rarely positioned as 'crimes' within that literature, by incorporating them in hate crime training, law enforcement officers can develop a much better understanding of the dimensions of antidisability crimes. For instance, overmedicating or undermedicating disabled people is a common form of aggression and victimization by caregivers, family members, partners, professionals and 'friends' (Barranti and Yuen, 2008; Cramer et al., 2003; Hunter and Kendrick, 2009; Mitchell and Buchele-Ash, 2000). However, officers who have not been instructed on such matters may not even enquire about them. And alas, such training is very rare indeed – virtually nonexistent, in fact. It should not be surprising then that officers may not ask the right questions or probe all the right areas when they confront cases of disability victimization. And yet people who hate disabled people sometimes actively brag about deliberately overmedicating their victims. One example, posted under the heading of 'Retard meds', should suffice: 'If you switch the meds around on the 'tards, they all strt to dance and yodel a lot. It's fun to give the 'tards lots of dexedrine!' (Anonymous, 2002).

Some of the reasons why disabled people do not report more caregivers for the crimes they commit have been discussed by Powers et al. (2002). These reasons include not knowing who to call, being embarrassed, having no support to deal with the situation, and fear of backlash. Additionally, the low wages which caregivers receive often means there is a shortage of personal assistants and there are no backups available if one is reported and removed. All of these areas need to be addressed: there is a need for alternative sources of support and care to be built into the disability service system, particularly for crisis situations; disabled victims of crime may also need assistance in dealing with psychological issues such as shame following abuse.

Crimes by family members and intimate partners are also alarmingly common. A 2009 survey of 350 community-based social service organizations, including police departments and elected officials in Westchester, New York, found that more than half of these agencies had received reports of domestic violence from a person with disabilities within their group. In almost 9 out of 10 cases, the victim was a woman with a disability and in 71% of cases, the perpetrator was an intimate partner (Editor *Whestchester.com*, 2009; Ferrette, 2009). There are specific types of crimes which can be committed by people who have an intimate connection with the disabled person, such as withholding medication, controlling assistive devices, and refusing to communicate using assistive devices (Gilson et al., 2001).

These behaviors are not just abusive; an increasing number of disability advocates are labeling them as disability hate crimes.

One incredibly disturbing crime by family members occurred in New South Wales, Australia, in 2009. In this case, a 7-year-old girl who had autism was starved to death by her parents, who cannot be named for legal reasons. She had weighed 20.5 kilograms (45.1 pounds) in February 2006, but her weight had dropped to 9 kilograms (19.8 pounds) when she died on November 3, 2007 (Staff *Nine News*, 2009). Her body was found with black vomit and bull ants oozing from her mouth. The smell of urine remained even after the body was washed with cleaning agents. Her mother was found guilty of murder and her father was found guilty of manslaughter (Storer and Nott, 2009). Her mother and father testified that the girl ate a large meal on the eve of her death, and the father said they 'fed her like anything', but doctors testified that she had longstanding starvation and malnutrition, adding that she was probably in a coma for days before her death. One doctor testifying at the trial who specialized in child malnutrition testified that he has seen over 500 cases of child malnutrition but had 'never seen one as malnourished as her' (Staff *Nine News*, 2009). Jurors at the trial were warned before they looked at photos of the dead girl that the images were akin to those in Nazi Germany during the holocaust or those of starving African children (Storer, 2009).

While this crime stands out because of the awful circumstances surrounding the victim's death, this book has discussed numerous cases where family members have robbed, killed, and otherwise harmed disabled people. Unfortunately, however, crimes by family members are even less likely to be reported or prosecuted … the cycle of injustice for victims seems to be particularly resistant to change in this area. Domestic violence laws and elder abuse laws have highlighted the ways in which the family can be a source of criminal victimization; the same dynamics occur in many households with a disabled family member. Some disabled people feel too ashamed or too fearful to report crimes by a family member; they may need support, advocacy and resources (including assistance in finding another place to live) before they feel confident enough to report crimes. Two of the reasons why disabled people do not report crimes are because they fear reprisals, and because they fear losing someone who provides 'care' for them (West and Gandhi, 2006). People need to know that they will be free from further victimization, and that they will not suffer a loss of resources including personal assistance if they do report a crime.

It is clear that many disabled people are not safe in their own homes and they need personal safety courses, assertiveness training, and safety training. However, these responses are not, by themselves, sufficient to address the problems discussed in this book. No genuine solutions to any of the social problems associated with disability can require disabled people to do all the work. Fundamentally, addressing the problem of disability hate crime requires wider social change. Such social change needs to challenge prejudicial attitudes towards disability and must also reduce the social isolation which many disabled people experience. Of course, such changes in attitude must be accompanied by material changes in the lives of disabled people. The background of social exclusion and poverty is the cornerstone of vulnerability upon which other forms of victimization – including hate crimes – occur. Breaking down segregation, closing segregated institutions which have fostered abuse, and addressing the close connection between disability and poverty are also major steps in ensuring that disabled people are not at risk (Sherry, 2000b). Not only is poverty closely associated with disability (both as a cause and effect), but it reduces the options which are available to people to address injustices in their lives. In a cycle of poverty, combined with a cycle of abuse or victimization, it is easy for a person to feel disempowered and trapped. The issue of disability hate crimes therefore necessitates a challenge to wider patterns of social exclusion.

One way of forcing social services agencies to be more active in addressing the criminal victimization of disabled people is for them to be held legally accountable when they fail to respond to such events in a timely manner. In England, a groundbreaking legal ruling against Hounslow Council seems to suggest that social service agencies can be held responsible for responding in a timely manner when their clients report that they are experiencing harassment. (Unfortunately, the ruling was overturned on appeal.) The initial ruling found that Hounslow Council had been made aware of threats, assaults and break-ins against a couple who had learning difficulties, but had negligently failed to protect them from horrendous abuse. The attacks on this couple included forcing them to perform sexual acts, assaulting them in front of their children, spraying their eyes with pepper spray, slashing them with knives, and forcing them to eat feces and drink urine (Chopping, undated; Cumber, 2009; Staff Mencap, 2009). While this particular case was eventually overturned, it may be possible in future for victims of disability hate crimes to sue social services for failing to protect them. Court rulings are increasingly recognizing that social service agencies, including housing agencies, have a duty of care towards vulnerable and disabled residents. Such rulings may encourage more timely and effective responses from such agencies (Mitchell, 2009).

Disability hate crime legislation is still fairly new in many places, so there is a desperate need for more research in this area. For instance, there have been no studies on the most effective treatments for the victims of disability hate crimes. Given that there are unique characteristics of disability hate crimes, such as their hyperviolent and hypersexual nature, such research is urgently needed. Likewise, there are no studies of the secondary disabilities which might develop from disability hate crime victimization (for instance, post traumatic stress disorder following an assault or rape). This is another area requiring more attention. Studies that explore the first stages of harassment and victimization are also needed – so that timely interventions can be developed which prevent abusive behaviors, bullying and antisocial behavior from escalating into more serious crimes. Too many people have died because early and appropriate interventions did not occur. This pattern must stop.

It is clear that police and prosecutors also need additional training on disability hate crimes. Few prosecutors have experience in this area; there is a need for training in order to identify the type of evidence which might indicate that a disability hate crime has been committed and also to examine the impact of such crimes on the victims, their families and their communities. Additionally, crime prevention units also need to develop more effective techniques for responding to disability hate crimes – including how to conduct accessible meetings with a wide range of disabled people. Ensuring physical accessibility is only the first step; equally important are other forms of accessibility (for instance, providing information in accessible ways and challenging disablist attitudes when they arise).

There is a strong temptation, when discussing an issue such as hate crimes, to adopt an 'identity politics' approach: to demonstrate that a particular group (in this case, disabled people) experiences extreme prejudice and criminal victimization, and to demand certain legislative responses, but to ignore more complex issues about how these particular power dynamics relate to other forms of social inequality. So, for instance, the temptation is to present data on 'disablism' as if it were completely distinct from gender, race, class, sex, religion, and other forms of social power. (Or to simply assert that those 'other' forms of social power are only relevant if one is discussing the experiences of particular minorities, such as disabled women, or disabled people from particular ethnic backgrounds.) Such an approach to disability is premised on a very simplistic notion of power which assumes that the power dynamics around disability are vastly different from the power dynamics associated with other forms of social exclusion. Certainly there are some unique power dynamics associated with disability – but there are also many ways in which 'other' forms of power are closely linked to disability. And yet hate crimes advocacy tends to revolve around 'single-issue politics' – limited in scope, wary of all-encompassing causes, and ... therein lies the problem.

In some ways, the data from 'other' forms of power may bolster the evidence about disability hate crime being an important social phenomenon. For instance, a study of hate crimes in the London Borough of Waltham Forest found that 42% of the victims of racist, homophobic or faith-related hate crime were either disabled or found it important to report that a family member was a disabled person. The incident which preceded the hate crime (sometimes called the 'trigger') was disability-related in 13% of all cases, and 'vulnerability' (which often relates to disability) identified in a further 7% of cases (*Disability Now* et al., 2008). But simply noting the presence of disability in such hate crimes is also insufficient. It cannot simply be assumed that disabled people universally experience the same risks, or that 'other' forms of power which disabled people experience (around gender, race, ethnicity, sexual orientation, religion, age, and so on) do not mediate the effects of such criminal victimization. This is an area which urgently requires further study. Unfortunately, police and law enforcement agencies have only begun to collect disability hate crime data relatively recently, and they have not developed a comprehensive profile of those most likely to be targeted. That is an important next step in the research, and will undoubtedly highlight some of the overlaps and contradictions in power relations between disabled people and other socially marginalized groups (and between particular groups of disabled people themselves).

Disability is unevenly socially distributed (it is clustered among poorer people and older people in particular) (Sherry, 2008) so the suggestion in Chapter 3 that disabled people experience higher rates of larceny/theft than other hate crime victims is particularly concerning. It indicates that sections of the community which are already economically disadvantaged and socially isolated are being further targeted for financial crimes, theft and exploitation by ruthless predators. Some of the stories that have been discussed in this book, such as caregivers robbing dying people, or stealing all the money from a disabled person's bank account, seem even more powerful when one considers the strong correlation between poverty and disability (Staff *AAP*, 2009).

Further research should explore some of the connections between the criminal victimization of disabled people and other groups. For instance, the hyperviolent and hypersexual nature of some disability hate crimes has much in common with homophobic hate crimes; financial crimes against disabled people are similar in some ways to the dynamics of elder abuse (which should probably be called 'age-related hate crime'); intimate sexual crimes in disability hate crimes have a lot in common with gender hate crimes. The fact that so many of these crimes occur in the home of the victim is another sickening similarity with elder abuse and domestic violence. Also, the public/private divide which deeply influences discussions around gender, power and sex crimes also permeates discussions of disability hate crimes. There are, undoubtedly, unique dynamics of disability hate crimes (for instance, for those crimes associated with some forms of assistive technology). As further research continues into the problem of disability hate crimes, these similarities and differences should be explored in depth. Another area that requires more attention is the role of protective factors, such as the presence of allies and advocates in the lives of disabled people, which might prevent crimes from happening or might assist people in reporting crimes before they escalate.

This book has explored many aspects of disability hate crimes, but in the end, its message is fairly straightforward. It has demonstrated that disability hate crimes do exist in quite alarming numbers and that the victims of disability hate crimes need far more support. It has also suggested that early interventions can save lives and prevent a cycle of revictimization from occurring. It has argued that it does not help anyone to use euphemisms such as 'bullying' or 'abuse' when the actions being discussed are actually 'crimes'. However, it has also stressed that one of the reasons why disabled people are victimized is their social exclusion; there is a need for broad social change that breaks down disablism in all its forms and promotes the inclusion of disabled people in all aspects of social life. And yet this solution – social inclusion, the eradication of violence, an end to prejudice, and the elimination of disablism – requires quite fundamental shifts in power dynamics within society, shifts that trouble the simple identity politics that underlies a great deal of hate crime legislation. For instance, the elimination of violence in the lives of disabled people arguably requires the elimination of violence in interpersonal relationships more generally ... something that would require fundamental shifts in gender, racial and sexual relations as well. Responses to disability hate crime therefore cannot be limited to the courts – they demand quite profound social changes. Challenging discrimination and prejudice, promoting equality and human rights, and protecting people from violence and other forms of criminal victimization are vital to a safer and more just society, and also provide a foundation for tackling the issue of disability hate crime.

Afterword

In the Preface, I explained how I had been affected by writing this book. It hurt my heart. I was so saddened by these crimes. Sometimes, the violence and brutality just took my breath away. And sometimes, I just felt numb ... just overwhelmed by all the pain. But I hope the book has not just been an overwhelming and depressing narrative; that was never my intention. I did want to stress that there are those who actively *hate* disabled people, but I wanted to indicate that a lot can be done to improve the social dynamics that leave disabled people alone, vulnerable, and isolated. It is these dynamics which we need to change. And we can change them. I have seen one person, acting as an advocate, make a difference in the life of a person who was experiencing criminal victimization. And I have seen disability groups take up cases and campaign around them until justice was done. Individually or collectively, people who read this book can make a difference. You can do something. Whether it is simply providing a phone number for a crime victims support service, or listening when someone needs to tell 'a secret', or reporting a co-worker who is engaging in inappropriate behavior, or attending a meeting where local people share their stories and simply validating their experiences, everyone can do something. And if you are the victim of a hate crime, I want to remind you: you are not the only one who has gone through this kind of experience. You are not to blame, and you can get help. You deserve to be happy and safe. My heart goes out to you.

Bibliography

2 Cr. App. R. (S.) 80 (531) Attorney General's References Nos 108 and 109 of 2005 (Sean Swindon and Michael Peart) Court of Appeal, Criminal Division 2006.

A.I._Obx (2006, 4 May [thread subsequently removed]). *Self-Mutilation: Cutting on Yahoo!* Health. Retrieved 1 June 2009, from <health.yahoo.com/experts/depression/3192/self./comments/?pg=2>.

Adams-Spink, G. (2008, 19 August). *Does Disability Hate Crime Exist?* Retrieved 23 November 2009 from <http://news.bbc.co.uk/2/hi/uk_news/magazine/7570305.stm>.

Agombar, N. (2009, 15 July). *Dishonest Daughter is Disowned by Her Mum.* Retrieved 8 November 2009 from <http://www.gazette-news.co.uk/news/4492259.Dishonest_daughter_is_disowned_by_her_mum/>.

Alcock, E. (1999). *'Living in Fear': The Need to Combat Bullying of People with a Learning Disability.* London: Mencap.

America's Most Wanted (2008, 4 February). *Wheelchair-Bound Woman Dies After Robbery.* Retrieved 17 August 2009 from <http://www.amw.com/fugitives/brief.cfm?id=52506>.

American Psychological Association (1998, 18 August). *Hate Crimes Today: An Age-Old Foe in Modern Dress.* Retrieved 22 August 2009 from <http://www.apa.org/releases/hate.html>.

Andrews, A.B. and Veronen, L.J. (1993). Sexual Assault and People with Disabilities. *Journal of Social Work and Human Sexuality, 8*(2), 137–159.

Anger Central (2002). *I Hate Retards!* Retrieved 11 January 2004 from <http://www.angry.net/groups/r/retards.htm>.

Anonymous (2002, 10 October). *Retard Meds.* Retrieved 15 August 2009 from <http://thingsihate.org/article/447/i_hate_douglas_gordon>.

Armario, C. (2006, September 28). Boys Arrested in Shirley Hate Crime: Two Charged with Painting Swastikas on Home of Neighbor Suffering from Multiple Sclerosis. *Newsday.*

Attorney-General's Reference No. 79 of 2004 sub nom *R. v. Husain (Syed)* (The Court of Appeal Criminal Division Royal Courts of Justice London 2004).

Ayad, M. (2006, 15 September). *Jury Convicts T-ball Coach of Beaming.* Retrieved 15 November 2009 from <http://www.postgazette.com/pg/06258/722075-85.stm>.

Balboni, J.M. and McDevitt, J. (2001). Hate Crime Reporting: Understanding Police Officer Perceptions, Departmental Protocol, and the Role of the Victim. *Justice Research and Policy, 3*(1), 1–27.

Bane (2006, 28 November). *Fuck I Hate Blind People*. Retrieved 19 August 2009 from <http://banedad.blogspot.com/2006/11/fuck-i-hate-blind-people.html>.

Barnes, C. and Mercer, G. (2002). *Disability*. Cambridge: Polity.

Barranti, C.C.R. and Yuen, F.K.O. (2008). Intimate Partner Violence and Women with Disabilities: Toward Bringing Visibility to an Unrecognized Population. *Journal of Social Work in Disability and Rehabilitation, 7*(2), 115–130.

Barrett, K.A., O'Day, B., Roche, A. and Carlson, B.L. (2009). Intimate Partner Violence, Health Status, and Health Care Access Among Women with Disabilities. *Womens Health Issues, 19*(2), 94–100.

Bell, J. (2002). *Policing Hatred: Law Enforcement, Civil Rights and Hate Crime*. New York: New York University Press.

Benedet, J. and Grant, I. (2007). Hearing the Sexual Assault Complaints of Women with Mental Disabilities: Evidentiary and Procedural Issues. *McGill Law Journal, 52*(1), 515–552.

Biesecker, M. and Raynor, D. (2008, 1 March). *Caregivers Abuse Patients, and Usually Get Away with It*. Retrieved 1 March 2008 from <http://www.newsobserver.com/print/saturday/front/story/975411-p2.html>.

Big Van Vader (2005, 12 May). *Dave Chappelle in Psych Facility.wtf*. Retrieved 19 August 2009 from <http://forum.ebaumsworld.com/showthread.php?t=71205>.

Billy Ray Johnson v. Christopher Colt Amox (2006) District Court of Cass County, Texas 5th Judicial District.

Black Hunter (2008, 12 August). *Deaf People*. Retrieved 19 June 2009 from <http://blather.newdream.net/d/deaf.html>.

Blake, T. and Rust, J. (2002). Self-Esteem and Self-Efficacy of College Students with Disabilities. *College Student Journal, 36*(2), 214–221.

Bodinger-De Uriate, C. and Sancho, A.R. (1990). *Hate Crime*. Los Alamitos, CA: Southwest Center for Educational Equity.

Bonnette, T. (2008, 22 October). *5 Pinecrest Employees Arrested in Abuse Probe*. Retrieved 27 October 2008 from <http://www.thetowntalk.com/article/20081022/NEWS01/810220339>.

Bowean, L. (2006, 20 July). 4 Charged in Attack with Prosthetic Leg: Disabled Boy Alarmed that Teens are Released. *Chicago Tribune*.

Bowling, B. (1998). *Violent Racism: Victimization and Social Context*. New York: Oxford University Press.

Brigandi, F. (2008, 12 May). *I Hate Stephen Hawking and His Paper Asshole*. Retrieved 30 August 2009 from <http://biketopia.blogspot.com/2008/05/i-hate-stephen-hawking-and-his-paper.html>.

Brittain, C. (2005, 16 July). Boy Says Coach Paid Him $25 to Injure Player. *Pittsburgh Tribune-Review*. Retrieved 30 December 2009 from <http://www.pittsburghlive.com/x/pittsburghtrib/s_354047.html>.

Brosh, B. and Sederstrom, J. (2007, 19 August). *Two Staffers Busted for Beating Autistic Woman*. Retrieved 12 November 2009 from <http://www.nydailynews.com/news/ny_crime/2007/08/19/2007-08-19_untitled__2autistic19m-1.html>.

Brown, H. (1999). Abuse of People with Learning Disabilities. In N. Stanley, J. Manthorpe and B. Penhale (eds), *Institutional Abuse: Perspectives Across the Life Course* (pp. 89–109). London: Routledge.

Brownlie, E.B., Jabbar, A., Beitchman, J., Vida, R. and Atkinson, L. (2007). Language Impairment and Sexual Assault of Girls and Women: Findings from a Community Sample. *Journal of Abnormal Child Psychology, 35*(4), 618–626.

Brownridge, D. (2006). Partner Violence Against Women with Disabilities: Prevalence, Risk and Explanations. *Violence Against Women, 12*(9), 805–822.

Brownridge, D., Ristock, J. and Hiebert-Murphy, D. (2008). The High Risk of IPV Against Canadian Women with Disabilities. *Medical Science Monitor, 14*(5), PH27–32.

Bryen, D.N., Carey, A. and Frantz, B. (2003). Ending the Silence: Adults Who Use Augmentative Communication and Their Experiences as Victims of Crimes. *Augmentative and Alternative Communication, 19*(2), 125–134.

Bureau of Justice Statistics (2005). *Hate Crime Reported by Victims and Police.* Washington DC: US Department of Justice, Office of Justice Programs.

Burstein, J. (2009, 13 March). *Caregiver Caught: After Two Years, Woman Jailed in Exploitation of Elderly Fort Lauderdale Woman.* Retrieved 7 November 2009 from <http://www.palmbeachpost.com/news/content/state/epaper/2009/03/13/0313exploit.html?cxtype=rss&cxsvc=7&cxcat=0>.

Burton, N. (2008, March 1). Joy as 'Feral' Killers Locked up for Life. *The Northern Echo.*

Capability Scotland and the Disability Rights Commission (2004). 'Hate Crime Against Disabled People in Scotland: A Report'. Edinburgh: Capability Scotland.

Carcamo, C. (2007, January 22). Assailant Faces Prison for Hate Crime. *Orange County Register.*

Casteel, C., Martin, S.L., Smith, J.B., K., G.K. and Kupper, L.L. (2008). National Study of Physical and Sexual Assault Among Women with Disabilities. *Injury Prevention, 14*(2), 87–90.

CCC (2009, 20 April). *Deaf People.* Retrieved 19 August 2009 from <http://bvrz.net/viewtopic.php?f=6&t=532&p=3681&hilit=deaf#p3681>.

Charlie Don't Surf (2008, 25 October). *The People Who Hate.* Retrieved 19 August 2009 from <http://forums.myspace.com/t/4241212.aspx?fuseaction=forums.viewthread>.

Chatila, T. (2008, 7 August). *Two Guilty in Hate Crime Assault.* Retrieved 7 August 2008 from <http://www.sgvtribune.com/rds_search/cl_10071785>.

Chopping, E. (n.d.). *Couple Subjected to 'Horrendous' Abuse Win Groundbreaking Victory.* Retrieved 15 November 2009 from <http://www.disabilitynow.org.uk/latest-news2/news-focus/couple-subjected-to-horrendous-abuse-win-groundbreaking-victory>.

Chuck (2008, 6 July). *Crazy Bipolar Girlfriend Dumped Me and Then Gets Mad About New Girlfriend. What Should I Do?* Retrieved 19 August 2009 from <http://

answers.yahoo.com/my/profile;_ylt=Aka.RVCcY4GzdvnQcxEhvC7D7BR.;_
ylv=3?show=UsyWEb3oaa>.

City News Service (2008, September 25). *Two Gang Members Sentenced to Prison
for Hate Crime Attack on Black Men.* Retrieved 23 November 2009 from
<http://www.lasentinel.net/Two-Gang-Members-Sentenced-to-Prison-For
-Hate-Crime-Attack-on-Black-Men.html>.

Coalition of Community Law Centers Aoteroa Inc. (2009, 21 October).
Aggravating and Mitigating Factors. Retrieved 15 January 2010 from <http://
www.communitylaw.org.nz/Aggravating-Mi.303.0.html>.

Cohen, M., Forte, T., Du Mont, J., Hyman, I. and Romans, S. (2006). Adding
Insult to Injury: Intimate Partner Violence Among Women and Men Reporting
Activity Limitations. *Annals of Epidemiology, 16*(8), 644–651.

Coker, A.L., Smith, P.H. and Fadden, M.K. (2005). Intimate Partner Violence and
Disabilities Among Women Attending Family Practice Clinics. *Journal of
Women's Health, 14*(9), 829–838.

Coker, M. (2006, July 20). Hatesville, USA: Welcome to Costa Mesa. If You're
Colored, Please Leave. *Orange County Weekly.*

Conquer Club (2008, 20 May). *You are Discriminating Against the Blind!* Retrieved
17 August 2009 from <https://www.conquerclub.com/forum/viewtopic.php?
f=8&t=51692>.

Consortium for Citizens with Disabilities (1999). *Disability-Based Bias Crimes.*
Retrieved October 6 1999 from <http:www.c-c-d.org/hate.htm>.

Conti-Ramsden, G. and Botting, N. (2004). Social Difficulties and Victimization
in Children with SLI at 11 Years of Age. *Journal of Speech, Language and
Hearing Research, 47*(1), 145–161.

Cooke, P. and Davies, G. (2001). Achieving Best Evidence from Witnesses with
Learning Disabilities: New Guidance. *British Journal of Learning Disabilities,
29*(3), 84–87.

Cooper, C., Selwood, A., Blanchard, M., Walker, Z., Blizard, R. and Livingston,
G. (2009). Abuse of People with Dementia by Family Carers: Representative
Cross Sectional Survey. *BMJ, 338*, b155.

Cooper, C., Selwood, A. and Livingston, G. (2008). The Prevalence of Elder Abuse
and Neglect: A Systematic Review. *Age and Ageing, 37*(2), 151–160.

Coping with Epilepsy. (2007). *Hooligans Attack Epilepsy Patients During Epilepsy
Awareness Month.* Retrieved 17 August 2009 from <http://www.pr.com/press-
release/60959>.

Copperman, J. and McNamara, J. (1999). Institutional Abuse in Mental Health
Settings. In N. Stanley, J. Manthorpe and B. Penhale (eds), *Institutional Abuse:
Perspective Across the Life Course* (pp. 130–151). London: Routledge.

Cornwall Adult Protection Committee (2007). 'The Murder of Steven Hoskin:
Serious Case Review'.

Court, H. (2009, 15 August). *Man Jailed for Robbing Blind Woman.* Retrieved 3
November 2009 from <http://www.thisiswiltshire.co.uk/news/4547799.Man_
jailed_for_robbing_blind_woman/>.

Craig, K.M. (2002). Examining Hate-Motivated Aggression: A Review of the Social Psychological Literature on Hate Crimes as a Distinct form of Aggression. *Aggression and Violent Behavior, 7*(1), 85–101.

Cramer, E.P., Gilson, S.F. and DePoy, E. (2003). Women with Disabilities and Experiences of Abuse. *Journal of Human Behavior in the Social Environment, 7*(3/4), 183–199.

Crawford, C. (2006, 26 October). *DVD Gang 'Made Break-in Rampage Sequel'*. Retrieved 7 November 2009 from <http://www.news.com.au/story/0,23599,20664319-2,00.html>.

Crown Prosecution Service (2008). 'Hate Crime Report 2007–2008'. London: Management Information Branch, CPS.

Cumber, R. (2009, 6 April). *Tortured Couple Stripped of Compensation*. Retrieved 15 November 2009 from <http://www.hounslowchronicle.co.uk/west-london-news/local-hounslow-news/2009/04/06/tortured-couple-stripped-of-compensation-109642-23323800/>.

Cynical Bastard (2004, 20 June). *Deaf*. Retrieved 19 August 2009 from <http://blather.newdream.net/d/deaf.html>.

D'Auria, C. (2007, October 23). *Two Sentenced in Brutal Sex Attack on Disabled L.I. Man*. Retrieved 15 November 2009 from <http://www.1010wins.com/pages/1123622.php>.

d_i_s_s_i_d_e_n_t (2003). *I Hate Retards*. Retrieved 29 January 2003 from <http://www.geocities.com/d_i_s_s_i_d_e_n_t/ihateretards.html>.

Davis, L.J. (2002). *Bending over Backwards: Disability, Dismodernism, and Other Difficult Positions*. New York: NYU Press.

Davis, M. and Wallace, R. (2006, 25 October). *Teenage Girl 'Tricked Into' DVD Degradation*. Retrieved 23 November 2009 from <http://www.theaustralian.com.au/news/teenage-girl-tricked-into-dvd-degradation/story-e6frg6of-1111112412497>.

Disability Now, The United Kingdom's Disabled People's Council, and Scope. (2008). 'Getting Away with Murder: Disabled People's Experiences of Hate Crime in the UK'. London: Scope.

Dobranski, P. (2008, 19 January). *Sister Beaten with Prosthetic Leg, Police Say*. Retrieved 16 November 2009 from <http://www.pittsburghlive.com/x/pittsburghtrib/news/westmoreland/s_548204.html>.

Dowsley, A. and Healey, K. (2009, 13 April). *Werribee Sex DVD Ringleader's Hate-Filled Rap Song on Web*. Retrieved 7 November 2009 from <http://www.heraldsun.com.au/news/werribee-bully-failed-by-system/story-e6frf7jo-1225697193516>.

Dundon, T. (2007, 8 November). *Vandals Attack a Bus Used to Help Children at a Special School in the City*. Retrieved 3 November 2009 from <http://www.peterboroughtoday.co.uk/news/Heartless-vandals-rob-disabled-children.3455089.jp>.

Editor *Whestchester.com* (2009, 14 November). *Disabled Women also Victims of Abuse, Survey Says*. Retrieved 15 November 2009 from <http://www.

westchester.com/Westchester_News/Health/Disabled_Women_Also_
Victims_Of_Abuse,_Survey_Says_2009111412398.html>.

Edwards, E., Vaughn, J. and Rotabi, K.S. (2005). Child Abuse Investigation and
Treatment for Deaf and Hard of Hearing Children: Ethical Practice and Policy.
The Social Policy Journal, 4(3/4), 53–67.

Elsworth, S. (2008, 10 April). Thief Costs Paralympian $6000 After Leg Stolen.
The Courier Mail.

Emilienburg, L. (2001). *Retarded People: A Blessing or a Crisis.* Retrieved 17
August 2009 from <http://drlight.multics.org/colond/past/colond9.html#3>.

Epilepsy Foundation (2008, 31 March). *Epilepsy Foundation Takes Action Against
Hackers.* Retrieved 17 August 2009 from <http://www.epilepsyfoundation.
org/aboutus/pressroom/action_against_hackers.cfm>.

Equality and Human Rights Commission (2009). *Promoting the Safety and Security
of Disabled People.* London: Equality and Human Rights Commission.

European Blind Union (2003). *Results of Survey on Violence Against Visually
Impaired People: EBU Commission on the Rights of Blind and Partially
Sighted People.* Retrieved 30 December 2009 from <http://www.euroblind.
org/fichiersGB/violence-6.htm>.

Facebook Group (2009, 10 June). *The Werribee DVD Rapists are Scum.* Retrieved
23 November 2009 from <http://www.facebook.com/group.php?v=wall&ref=
search&gid=77583472399>.

Federal Bureau of Investigation (1999). *Crime Data Collection Guidelines
Appendix Three.* Washington, DC: US Department of Justice.

Ferrette, C. (2009, 15 November). *Study Finds High Rates of Abuse Against
Women with Disabilities.* Retrieved 15 November 2009 from <http://www.
lohud.com/article/20091115/NEWS02/911150345/-1/newsfront/Study-finds-
high-rates-of-abuse-against-women-with-disabilities>.

Fitzgerald, P.B., Castella, A.R.D., Filia, K.M., Filia, S.L., Benitez, J. and Kulkarni,
J. (2005). Victimization of Patients with Schizophrenia. *Australian and New
Zealand Journal of Psychiatry, 39*(3), 169–174.

Foreman, C. (2005, 29 July). *Boys Take Stand in T-ball Case.* Retrieved 14
November 2009 from <http://www.pittsburghlive.com/x/dailycourier/news/
s_358349.html>.

Foreman, C. (2007, 21 March). *Convicted Fayette T-ball Coach Sued by Lawyer.*
Retrieved 15 November 2009 from <http://www.pittsburghlive.com/x/
pittsburghtrib/news/fayette/print_498796.html>.

Francis, C. (2009, 22 January). *Cowardly Street Attack on Blind, Handicapped
Man.* Retrieved 8 August 2009 from <www.stuff.co.nz/thepress/4825801a6530.
html>.

Friedlander, H. (1995). *The Origins of Nazi Genocide: From Euthanasia to the
Final Solution.* Chapel Hill, NC: University of North Carolina Press.

Gauthier, R. (2008, 11 April). *Love and Film: I Hate Marlee Matlin.* Retrieved
3 September 2009 from <http://whipitoutcomedy.com/2008/04/11/love-and-
film-i-hate-marlee-matlin/>.

Gerstman, B. (2007, 19 September). Antioch Teen Charged in Attack on Deaf Man. *Contra Costa Times*.

Gill, M.C. (2009). *Intellectual Disability and Sexuality: Challenging Paternalism, Harm Reduction and Incompetence*. Chicago, IL: University of Illinois at Chicago.

Gillett, S. (2007, 27 October). Carer Stole from Carrington Care Home Residents. *Nottingham Evening Post*.

Gilson, S.F., Cramer, E.P. and DePoy, E. (2001). Redefining Abuse Among Women with Disabilities: Enlarging the Scope. *Affilia: Journal of Women and Social Work, 16*(2), 220–235.

Goldberg, D. (2005, October 25, B5). Message of Hate Drawn at Jewish Community Center. *The Post-Standard*. Retrieved 3 January 2007.

Grattan, G. (2004, 21 June). New 'Hate Crime' Laws Will Protect the Disabled. *Belfast Telegraph*.

Green, D.P., Strolovitch, D.A., Wong, J.S. and Bailey, R.W. (2001). Measuring Gay Populations and Antigay Hate Crime. *Social Science Quarterly, 82*(1), 281–296.

Green, G. (2001). Vulnerability of Witnesses with Learning Disabilities: Preparing to Give Evidence Against a Perpetrator of Sexual Abuse. *British Journal of Learning Disabilities, 29*(3), 103–109.

Grossman, S.F. and Lundy, M. (2008). Double Jeopardy: A Comparison of Persons With and Without Disabilities Who Were Victims of Sexual Abuse and/or Sexual Assault. *Journal of Social Work in Disability and Rehabilitation, 7*(1), 19–46.

Gryta, M. (2008, March 27). Dropout Spared Jail for Harassment That Led to Car Crash. *The Buffalo News*.

Gudjonsson, G.H., Murphy, G.H. and Clare, I.C.H. (2000). Assessing the Capacity of People with Intellectual Disabilities to be Witnesses in Court. *Psychological Medicine, 30*(2), 307–314.

Happy Camper (2008, 26 March). *The Best Sign Ever in America*. Retrieved 19 August 2009 from <http://www.purplepride.org/forums/index.php?topic= 43557.msg747230>.

Hassouneh, D., Perrin, N., Hanson, G. and McNeff, E. (2008). Abuse and Health in Individuals with Spinal Cord Injury and Dysfunction. *Journal of Rehabilitation, 74*(3), 3–9.

Hatred, L. (2007, 14 March). *Everybody Hates Cyclists*. Retrieved 17 August 2009 from <http://www.visordown.com/forum/forummessages/mps/utn/272492/v/1/ cp/2/>.

Hellen C. (2004). *Retards in School*. Retrieved 7 January 2004 from <http:// hellncphs.20m.com/Retardsinschool.html>.

Herek, G.M., Gillis, J.R. and Cogan, J.C. (1999). Psychological Sequelae of Hate-Crime Victimization Among Lesbian, Gay and Bisexual Adults. *Journal of Consulting and Clinical Psychology, 67*(6), 945–951.

Herek, G.M., Gillis, J.R., Cogan, J.C. and Glunt, E.K. (1997). Hate Crime Victimization Among Lesbian, Gay, and Bisexual Adults: Prevalence, Psychological Correlates, and Methodological Issues. *Journal of Interpersonal Violence, 12*(2), 195–217.

Hillig, T. (2009a, 27 October). Guilty Plea in Murder of Woman, Her Fetus: Four Others are Awaiting Trial in the Alton Case. *St. Louis Post-Dispatch*.

Hillig, T. (2009b, 27 October). Woman Pleads Guilty in Murder Involving Fetus. *St. Louis Post-Dispatch*.

HonestAbe (2007, 15 April). *I Hate Stephen Hawking*. Retrieved 30 August 2009 from <http://vwww.votemeoff.com/forum.php?show=posts;discussion_id=19;topic_id=95309>.

Horne, B. (2007, 22 January). *Jailed for Rape of Disabled Woman*. Retrieved 2 November 2009 from <http://edinburghnews.scotsman.com/rapeandthelegal system/Jailed-for-rape-of-disabled.3340027.jp>.

Horton, W. (2007, July 5). Disabled Woman too Terrified to Go Home. *South Wales Echo*. Retrieved 25 October 2009.

Houlihan, L., and Metlikovec, J. (2006, 26 October). *Public Outrage Met by Boasts, Laughter*. Retrieved 7 November 2009 from <http://www.heraldsun.com.au/news/victoria/public-outrage-met-by-boasts-laughter/story-e6frf7kx-1111112418619>.

Hsu, C.C., Sheu, C.J., Liu, S.I., Sun, Y.W., Wu, S.I. and Lin, Y. (2009). Crime Victimization of Persons with Severe Mental Illness in Taiwan. *Australian and New Zealand Journal of Psychiatry, 43*(5), 460–466.

Human Rights First (2008). *Hate Crime Report Card 2008*. Retrieved August 17 2009 from <http://www.humanrightsfirst.org/discrimination/pages.aspx?id=158>.

Hunter, S. and Kendrick, M. (2009). The Ambiguities of Professional and Societal Wisdom. *Ethics and Social Welfare, 3*(2), 158–169.

illuxtris (2009, 17 May). *Vomits*. Retrieved 19 August 2009 from <http://illuxtris.livejournal.com/217322.html>.

International Association of Chiefs of Police (2002, January). *Hate Crime in America Summit Recommendations*. Retrieved 12 November 2009 from <http://www.theiacp.org/PublicationsGuides/LawEnforcementIssues/Hatecrimes/tabid/191/>.

Ja, C. (2008, 17 March). *Paralympic Swimmer Brendan Burkett's Leg Stolen*. Retrieved 17 August 2009 from <http://www.news.com.au/story/0,23599,23387687-421,00.html?from=public_rss>.

Jamieson, R.L. (2006, 1 July). *'Trash' Fire Turns Out to Be a Man*. Retrieved 13 November 2009 from <http://www.seattlepi.com/jamieson/276153_robert01x.html>.

Jeff (2003, 11 June). *I Hate Stevie Wonder*. Retrieved 3 September 2009 from <http://steviewonder.free.fr/forum/index.php3?forum=main&archive=28>.

Jenness, V. and Grattet, R. (2001). *Making Hate a Crime: From Social Movement to Law Enforcement*. New York: Russell Sage Foundation.

Jesus Christ (2004, 17 February). *Cripples, Retards, and the Other Untouchables*. Retrieved 30 December 2009 from <http://www.ubersite.com/m/25797>.

Johnson, A. (2009, 17 February). *Woman Tells of Hoodie Stabbing Ordeal*. Retrieved 15 November 2009 from <http://www.clickliverpool.com/news/local-news/122909-woman-tells-of-hoodystabbing-ordeal.html>.

Jones, D. (2008, 13 March). *'I Hate Gary Coleman' Group on Facebook*. Retrieved 3 September 2009 from <http://www.facebook.com/search/?q=i+hate+gary+coleman&init=quick#/group.php?gid=5004984723>.

Jones, L.A. (2008, July 24). South Seattle Man Accused of Harassing Autistic Child, Threatening Arson. *The Seattle Times*.

KDS (2009, 21 May). *Kojima Website Image a Fake*. Retrieved 19 August 2009 from <http://www.cgreviews.com/site/blogs/blog1.php/2009/05/21/kojima-website-image-a-fake>.

Kelly, J. (2009, 9 May). *A Comment Complaint*. Retrieved 19 August 2009 from <http://www.thelastgaffe.com/genres/nonfiction/an-open-letter-to-everyone-who-never-comments-on-my-articles/>.

Kelsey, N.L. (2007, 1 April). *Wheelchair Bound Man's Dog Kidnapped in Pennsylvania*. Retrieved 15 November 2009 from <http://www.associatedcontent.com/article/199365/wheelchair_bound_mans_dog_kidnapped.html>.

Kerr, A. and Shakespeare, T. (2002). *Genetic Politics: From Eugenics to Human Genome*. Cheltenham: New Clarion Press.

Kestin, S., Franceschina, S. and Maines, J. (2009, 27 September). *Convicted Felons Could Be Working in Your Mother or Father's Nursing Home*. Retrieved 12 November 2009 from <http://www.sun-sentinel.com/news/felons-elderly-disabled-b092809,0,3847233.htmlstory>.

Khalid (2006, July 25). *Racism at Its Worst: Disabled Black Refugee Beaten by His Own Crutch*. Retrieved 23 November 2009 from <http://baheyeldin.com/writings/culture/racism-at-its-worst-disabled-black-refugee-beaten-by-his-own-crutch.html>.

Kidd, B. (2009, 3 June). *Offences (Aggravation by Prejudice) (Scotland) Bill Scottish Parliament Debates*. Retrieved 18 January 2010 from <http://www.theyworkforyou.com/sp/?id=2009-06-03.18098.0>.

KNBC.com (2007, 25 April). *4 Arrested in Beating of Man with Cerebral Palsy*. Retrieved 8 August 2009 from <http://www.KNBC.com/print/13133712/detail.html>.

LaDuca, R. (2009a, 2 April). *Deerfield Man Pleads Guilty to Threatening Gov. Paterson*. Retrieved 9 November 2009 from <http://www.uticaod.com/news/x549590145/Deerfield-man-pleaded-guilty-to-threat-on-governor>.

LaDuca, R. (2009b, 15 May). *Deerfield Man Who Threatened Gov. Paterson: 'I Lost My Temper'*. Retrieved 9 November 2009 from <http://www.uticaod.com/news/x342399949/Deerfield-man-who-threatened-Gov-Paterson-I-lost-my-temper>.

LaDuca, R. (2009c, 14 March). *Police: Deerfield Man Made Threat on Governor*. Retrieved 9 November 2009 from <http://www.uticaod.com/news/x549590145/Deerfield-man-pleaded-guilty-to-threat-on-governor>.

Lamb, L. and Redmond, M. (2007). *Learning Disability Hate Crime: Identifying Barriers to Addressing Crime*. London: Care Services Improvement Partnership, Valuing People Support Team.

Lane, F.J. (2006). 'Law Enforcement Officers' Endorsement of the Bias Categorization of Crime Scenarios: A Prospective Study of Differences Between Disability and Other Protected Categories'. Ph.D. Thesis in Rehabilitation Science, University of Florida, Florida.

Lawrence, F.M. (1999). *Punishing Hate: Bias Crimes Under American Law*. Cambridge: Harvard University Press.

Levin, J. (2007). *The Violence of Hate: Confronting Racism, Anti-Semitism, and Other Forms of Bigotry*. Boston, MA: Pearson Education.

Levin, J. and McDevitt, J. (2002). *Hate Crimes: America's War on Those Who Are Different*. Boulder, CO: Westview Press.

Levine, J. (2006). Press Release: Homeless Veteran Attacked Outside Campaign Office, Spokane Washington 23 June (Vol. 2007).

Lewin, B. (2007). Who Cares About Disabled Victims of Crime? Barriers and Facilitators for Redress. *Journal of Policy and Practice in Intellectual Disabilities, 4*(3), 170–176.

Lil satre (2009, 12 February). *I Hate Retards*. Retrieved 23 November 2009 from <http://forums.somethingawful.com/showthread.php?threadid=3200132>.

Lobo (2006, 10 November). *How to Kill a Spastic*. Retrieved 19 August 2009 from <http://www.ubersite.com/m/95602>.

Lockyer, B. (2001). *Reporting Hate Crimes: The California Attorney General's Civil Rights Commission on Hate Crimes*. Sacramento, CA: California Attorney General's Office.

Lombard, D. (2009, 29 January). *Judge Strikes Blow for Equal Treatment for People with Mental Health Problems*. Retrieved 13 November 2009 from <http://www.communitycare.co.uk/Articles/2009/01/29/110580/high-court-reverses-cps-decision-on-man-with-mental-health-issues.htm>.

Longmore, P.K. (2003). *Why I Burned My Book and Other Essays on Disability*. Philadelphia, PA: Temple University Press.

Macdonald, K. (2008). *Prosecuting Disability Hate Crime*. London: The Crown Prosecution Service.

Maddox (2004, 12 October). *Christopher Reeve is (was) an Asshole*. Retrieved 30 August 2009 from <http://www.thebestpageintheuniverse.net/c.cgi?u=creeve>.

Madfreemindmuch (2007, 19 August). *I Hate Helen Keller! Xanga Webring*. Retrieved 19 August 2009 from <http://www.xanga.com/groups/group.aspx?id=585470&s=2>.

Mahone, D. (2008, 11 September). *Cobb Caregiver Convicted of Murder*. Retrieved 23 November 2009 from <http://www.ajc.com/metro/content/metro/cobb/stories/2008/09/11/caregiver_disabled_murder.html>.

Mallon, G.P. (2001). Sticks and Stones Can Break Your Bones: Verbal Harassment and Physical Violence in the Lives of Gay and Lesbian Youth in Child Welfare Settings. *Journal of Gay and Lesbian Social Services, 13*(1–2), 63–81.

Maltz, M.D. (1999). *Bridging Gaps in Police Crime Data*. Paper presented at the Workshop on Uniform Crime Reporting Imputation, sponsored by the Bureau of Justice Statistics and the Federal Bureau of Investigation Uniform Crime Reporting Program.

Maniglio, R. (2009). Severe Mental Illness and Criminal Victimization: A Systematic Review. *Acta Psychiatrica Scandinavica, 119*(3), 180–191.

Marinos, V., Griffiths, D., Gosse, L., Robinson, J., Olley, J.G. and Lindsay, W. (2009). Legal Rights and Persons with Intellectual Disabilities. In F. Owen and D. Griffiths (eds), *Challenges to the Human Rights of People with Intellectual Disabilities* (pp. 124–153). London: Jessica Kingsley.

Marks, D. (1999). *Disability: Controversial Debates and Psychosocial Perspectives*. London: Routledge.

Martin, S.E. (1996). Investigating Hate Crimes: Case Characteristics and Law Enforcement Responses. *Justice Quarterly, 13*(3), 455–480.

Martin, S.L., Ray, N., Sotres-Alvarez, D., L.L., K., Moracco, K.E., Dickens, P.A., et al. (2006). Physical and Sexual Assault of Women with Disabilities. *Violence Against Women, 12*(9), 823–837.

Matsuda, M.J., Lawrence, C.R.I., Delgado, R. and Crenshaw Williams, K. (1993). *Words That Wound: Critical Race Theory, Assaultive Speech, and the First Amendment*. Boulder, CO: Westview Press.

Mattthews, J. (2005, 24 October). *Nice State Quarter, Assholes!* Retrieved 19 August 2009 from <http://www.thephatphree.com/features.asp?StoryId=1615>.

McMahon, B.T., West, S.L., Lewis, A.N., Armstrong, A.J. and Conway, J.P. (2004). Hate Crimes and Disability in America. *Rehabilitation Counseling Bulletin, 47*(2), 66–75.

McPhail, B.A. (2000). Hating Hate: Implications of Hate Crime Legislation. *Social Service Review, 74*(4), 635–653.

Medoff, M.H. (1999). Allocation of Time and Hateful Behavior: A Theoretical and Positive Analysis of Hate and Hate Crimes. *The American Journal of Economics and Sociology, 58*(4), 959–973.

Mencap (2007). '"Don't Stick It", Stop It. Bullying Wrecks Lives: The Experiences of Children and Young People with a Learning Disability'. London: Mencap.

Mental Welfare Commission for Scotland (2008, April). *Justice Denied: A Summary of Our Investigation into the Care and Treatment of Ms A*. Retrieved 2 November 2009 from <http://www.mwcscot.org.uk/web/FILES/Publications/Justice_Denied_Summary_FINAL.pdf>.

Michael, J.A. (2007, August 2). Mentally Challenged Man and His Advocate Target of Racist and Anti-Gay Vandalism. *Between the Lines Newspaper*.

Miletic, D. (2006, October 25). Outcry Over Teenage Girl's Assault Recorded on DVD. *The Age*.

Minchin, R. (2008, January 8). Teenager Convicted of Murder 'for Sport'. *Press Association Regional Newswire for English Regions*.

Mind (2007). *Another Assault*. Retrieved 25 October 2009 from <www.mind.org. uk/anotherassault>.

Mishra, R. (2001, 12 November). In Attacks on Disabled, Few Verdicts Despite Evidence: Law Enforcement Drops Most Cases. *Boston Globe*.

Mitchell, E. (2009, 25 February). *Landmark Court Decisions for Adult Protection*. Retrieved 15 November 2009 from <http://www.communitycare.co.uk/ Articles/2009/02/25/110797/Landmark-court-decisions-for-adult-protection.htm>.

Mitchell, L.M. and Buchele-Ash, A. (2000). Abuse and Neglect of Individuals with Disabilities: Building Protective Supports Through Public Policy. *Journal of Disability Policy Studies, 10*(2), 225–243.

Montijo and Lilibeth (2009, 21 October). *Mesa Man Assaulted Woman in Wheelchair, Police Say*. Retrieved 15 November 2009 from <http://www. azcentral.com/community/mesa/articles/2009/10/21/20091021abrk-dvassault. html>.

Moody, G. (2007, 10 October). *Update: Teens Who Raped Disabled Woman Sentenced*. Retrieved 2 November 2009 from <http://www.yourlocalguardian. co.uk/news/1746365.0/>.

Moore-Bridger, B. (2009, 20 January). Family Condemns 'Soft' Jail Sentences for Acid Rape Gang. *London Evening Standard*. Retrieved 2 November 2009 from <http://www.thisislondon.co.uk/standard/article-23623393-family-condemns-soft-jail-sentences-for-acid-rape-gang.do>.

Morrish, A. (2009, 20 February). Disabled Woman Abused and Tipped out of Scooter. *The Bourne Local*.

Murdergoround09 (2004, 7 February). *i hate retarded people*. Retrieved 17 August 2009 from <http://local.ubersite.com/m/25122>.

Mysterious Rhinestone Cowboy (2009a, 17 August). *I Really Hate Retarded People*. Retrieved 17 August 2009 from <http://isitnormal.com/story/retarded-people-piss-me-off-28131/>.

Mysterious Rhinestone Cowboy (2009b, 17 August). *Retarded People Piss Me Off*. Retrieved 17 August 2009 from <http://isitnormal.com/story/retarded-people-piss-me-off-28131/>.

Nannini, A. (2006). Sexual Assault Patterns Among Women With and Without Disabilities Seeking Survivor Services. *Women's Health Issues, 16*(6), 372–379.

Narain, J. (2006, 29 August). Police Probe Nursing Home Rape of Severely Disabled Woman. *Mail Online*. Retrieved 2 November 2009 from <http:// www.dailymail.co.uk/news/article-402769/Police-probe-nursing-home-rape-severely-disabled-woman.html>.

Nathanson, R. and Platt, M. (2005). Attorneys' Perceptions of Child Witnesses with Mental Retardation. *The Journal of Psychiatry and Law, 33*, 5–42.

National Coalition for the Homeless (2007). *Hate, Violence and Death on Main Street USA: A Report on Hate Crimes and Violence Against People Experiencing Homelessness 2006.* Retrieved 17 August 2009 from <http://i.a.cnn.net/cnn/2007/images/02/19/nch.2006.pdf>.

National Coalition for the Homeless (2009, August). *Hate, Violence, and Death on Main Street USA: A Report on Hate Crimes and Violence Against People Experiencing Homelessness 2008.* Retrieved 17 August 2009 from <http://www.nationalhomeless.org/publications/hatecrimes/hate_report_2008.pdf>.

Newhouse, E. (2009, 20 October). *Ex-Aides Charged for Abuse of Autistic Boy.* Retrieved 15 November 2009 from <http://www.greatfallstribune.com/apps/pbcs.dll/article?AID=/20091020/NEWS01/910200301>.

North Wales Police Heddlu Gogledd Cymru Freedom of Information Team (2009). *2009/629 – Investigations – Murder of Christopher Foulkes of Rhyl on 08/03/2007.*

Nosek, M.A., Hughes, R.B., Taylor, H.B., and Taylor, P. (2006). Disability, Psychosocial, and Demographic Characteristics of Abused Women with Physical Disabilities. *Violence Against Women, 12*(9), 838–850.

Nosek, M.A., Howland, C.A. and Young, M.E. (1998). Abuse of Women with Disabilities: Policy Implications. *Journal of Disability Policy Studies, 8*(1–2), 158–175.

Obinna, J., Krueger, S., Osterbaan, C., Sadusky, J.M. and DeVore, W. (2006). *Understanding the Needs of the Victims of Sexual Assault in the Deaf Community.* Minneapolis, MN: Council on Crime and Justice.

Oneida County Office of the District Attorney (2009). *Re: People v. Timothy Day.* Utica, NY: Personal Communication, October 19.

Orr, D. (2008, 30 January). *We Must Protect Disabled People Against This Wave of Barbaric and Hateful Crimes.* Retrieved 15 November 2009 from <http://www.independent.co.uk/opinion/commentators/deborah-orr/deborah-orr-we-must-protect-disabled-people-against-this-wave-of-barbaric-and-hateful-crimes-775617.html>.

Oschwald, M., Renker, P., Hughes, R.B., Arthur, A., Powers, L.E. and Curry, M.A. (2009). Development of an Accessible Audio Computer-Assisted Self-Interview (A-CASI) to Screen for Abuse and Provide Safety Strategies for Women With Disabilities. *Journal of Interpersonal Violence, 24*(5), 795–818.

Pagey/Bowser (2008, May 5). *Quotes from My Life.* Retrieved 19 August 2009 from <http://blogs.myspace.com/index.cfm?fuseaction=blog.ListAll&friendID=78719290>.

Pearson, A. (2008, January 9). *Two Admit Murdering Brent Martin for 'Sport',* <www.journallive.co.uk>.

Penrod, S. (2006, 21 July). *Family Upset about Sign in Neighbor's Yard.* Retrieved 23 November 2009 from <http://www.ksl.com/?nid=148&sid=374518>.

Perlin, M.L. (1999). 'Half-Wracked Prejudice Leaped Forth': Sanism, Pretextuality, and Why and How Mental Disability Law Developed as it Did. *Journal of Contemporary Legal Issues, 10*, 3–36.

Perlin, M.L. (2000). *The Hidden Prejudice: Mental Disability on Trial*. Washington, DC: American Psychological Association.

Perlin, M.L. (2002). 'Things Have Changed': Looking at Non-Institutional Mental Disability Law Through the Sanism Filter. *New York Law School Law Review*.

Perry, B. (2001). *In the Name of Hate: Understanding Hate Crimes*. New York: Routledge.

Pirez, V. (2007, 30 November). *I hate. retards and autistic children. My Hate Blog: Retards*. Retrieved 30 December 2009 from <http://www.myhateblog. com/2007/11/30/i-hate-retards-and-autistic-children/>.

Pitt, V. (2009, 4 November). *One in 11 Disabled People are Victims of Hate Crime*. Retrieved 15 November 2009 from <http://www.communitycare. co.uk/Articles/2009/11/04/113061/One-in-11-disabled-people-are-victims-of-hate-crime.htm>.

Potok, M. (2001). 'Discounting Hate: Ten Years After federal Officials Began Compiling National Hate Crime Statistics, the Numbers Don't Add Up'. *Southern Poverty Law Center Intelligence Report, Winter*, 6–15.

Poulsen, K. (2008, 28 March). *Hackers Assault Epilepsy Patients Via Computer*. Retrieved 17 August 2009 from <http://www.wired.com/print/politics/security/ news/2008/03/epilepsy>.

Powers, L.E., Curry, M.A., Oschwald, M., Maley, S., Saxton, M. and Eckels, K. (2002). Barriers and Strategies in Addressing Abuse: A Survey of Disabled Women's Experiences. *The Journal of Rehabilitation, 68*(1), 4–13.

Powers, L.E., Renker, P., Robinson-Whelen, S., Oschwaldd, M., Hughes, R., Swank, P., et al. (2009). Interpersonal Violence and Women with Disabilities. *Violence against Women, 15*(9), 1040–1069.

Powers, L.E., Saxton, M., Curry, M.A., Powers, J.L., McNeff, E. and Oschwald, M. (2008). End the Silence: A Survey of Abuse Against Men with Disabilities. *Journal of Rehabilitation, 74*(4), 41–53.

Pulkkinen, L. (2008). *Neighbor Sentenced for Directing Drunken Tirades at Autistic Boy*. Retrieved 1 August 2009 (subsequently made a private post) from <http://www.seattlepi.com/local/395505_levinson10.html>.

R. v. Clements (Norman Edward) (The Court of Appeal Criminal Division Royal Courts of Justice London 2009).

R. v. Cutts (Shirley) (The Court of Appeal Criminal Division Royal Courts of Justice London 2006).

R. v. De Weever (Rawle) (The Court of Appeal Criminal Division Royal Courts of Justice London 2009).

R. v. Frith (Helen) (The Court of Appeal Criminal Division Royal Courts of Justice London 2008a).

R. v. Frith (Helen) (The Court of Appeal Criminal Division Royal Courts of Justice London 2008b).

R. v. Grocock (Sharon Lesley) (The Court of Appeal Criminal Division Royal Courts of Justice London 2008).

R. v. Healy (Joseph) (The Court of Appeal Criminal Division Royal Courts of Justice London 2009).

R. v. Irvine (Caroline Laura) (The Court of Appeal Criminal Division Royal Courts of Justice London 2008).

R. v. Kunz (Hugh) (The Court of Appeal Criminal Division Royal Courts of Justice London 2008).

R. v. Liu (Su Hua) and Tan (Lun Xi) (The Court of Appeal Criminal Division Royal Courts of Justice London 2006).

R. v. Morgan (Nicholas) (The Court of Appeal Criminal Division Royal Courts of Justice London 2009).

R. v. Redhead (David) (The Court of Appeal Criminal Division Royal Courts of Justice London 2006).

R. v. W (Andrew S) (The Court of Appeal Criminal Division Royal Courts of Justice London 2009).

Radio New Zealand (2009, 10 November). *'Despicable' Theft from Child with Cerebral Palsy*. Retrieved 15 November 2009 from <http://www.radionz. co.nz/news/stories/2009/11/09/1245d36c49d2>.

Rand, M.R. and Harrell, E. (2009). 'Special Report – National Crime Victimization Survey: Crime Against People with Disabilities 2007'.

Raynes, B., Chamberlain, S. and Smith, C. (2009). 'Serious Case Review External Summary Child Sarah 15/06/2003 – 26/11/2007'. Bath, England: Reconstruct London for the Flintshire Safeguarding Children Board.

Reiter, S., Bryen, D.N. and Shachar, I. (2007). Adolescents with Intellectual Disabilities as Victims of Abuse. *Journal of Intellectual Disabilities, 11*(4), 371–387.

Rich, J. (2007, 29 January). *Blind Woman Mugged for Sixth Time*. Retrieved 29 January 2007 from <http://news.ninemsn.com.au/article.aspx?id=182103&print=true>.

Roberts, B. (2008, 18 October). *Werribee Sex DVD Maker Aims to Direct Films*. Retrieved 7 November 2009 from <http://www.heraldsun.com.au/news/ victoria/sex-film-teen-aims-to-direct/story-e6frf7kx-1111117784122>.

Robinson, C. (2007, 7 December). *Carer Jailed for Stealing from Patient; Vulnerable Pensioner Fleeced of £3,650*. Retrieved 7 November 2009 from <http://www.journallive.co.uk/north-east-news/todays-news/2007/12/07/ carer-jailed-for-stealing-from-patient-61634-20215503/>.

Rosenblatt, M. (2008). *I Exist: The Message from Adults with Autism in England*. Bristol, UK: The National Autistic Society.

Rosindale, L. (2009, 18 August). *'I FUCKING HATE MARLEE MATLIN AKA JODI LERNER' Group on Facebook*. Retrieved 3 September 2009 from <http://www.facebook.com/search/?q=I+hate+marlee+matlin&init=quick#/ group.php?gid=118754807449&ref=search&sid=30118467.707017504.1>.

Ross, D. (2008, January 12). Pattern of Hate Crime Against Disabled 'Upsetting'. *The Herald*.

Sam (2008, 9 February). *Most Useless Person Ever*. Retrieved 1 August 2009 from <http://groups.myspace.com/helenkellersucks>.

Sanai, R. (2008). *Even Sapir Clubhouse for Disabled Kids Overcomes Local Resistance and Arson*. Retrieved 28 December 2008 from <https://www.haaretz.co.il/hasen/spages/1001638.html>.

Saxon, M., Curry, M.A., Powers, L.E., Maley, S., Eckels, K. and Gross, J. (2001). 'Bring My Scooter So I Can Leave You'. *Violence Against Women, 7*(4), 393–417.

Saxton, M., McNeff, E., Powers, L., Limont, M. and Benson, J. (2006). 'We're All Little John Waynes': A Study of Disabled Men's Experiences of Abuse by Personal Assistants. *Journal of Rehabilitation, 72*(4), 3–13.

Scottish Executive (2004). *Working Group on Hate Crime Report*. Edinburgh: Scottish Executive.

Self-Advocates Becoming Empowered. (2005, 5 September). *Ricky Whistnant*. Retrieved 13 November 2009 from <http://www.peoplefirstofnh.org/SABE/RickyWhistnant.htm>.

Shakespeare, T., Gillespie-Sells, K. and Davies, D. (1996). *Untold Desires: The Sexual Politics of Disability*. New York: Cassell.

Sherry, M. (2000a). *Hate Crimes Against People with Disabilities*. Brisbane, Australia: Women with Disabilities Australia.

Sherry, M. (2000b). Hate Crimes and Disabled People. *Social Alternatives, 19*(4), 23–30.

Sherry, M. (2003a). *Don't Ask, Tell or Respond: Silent Acceptance of Disability Hate Crimes*. Ontario: Disabled Women's Network.

Sherry, M. (2003b). *Exploring Disability Hate Crimes*. Paper presented at the 16th Annual Meeting of the Society for Disability Studies.

Sherry, M. (2004). Exploring Disability Hate Crimes. *Review of Disability Studies, 1*(1), 51–59.

Sherry, M. (2006). *If I Only Had A Brain*. New York: Routledge.

Sherry, M. (2007). (Post) Colonizing Disability. *Wagadu: A Journal of Transnational and Women's Studies, 3*, 10–23.

Sherry, M. (2008). *Disability and Diversity: A Sociological Approach*. New York: Nova Science.

Shrimsley, R. (2007, 7 November). A Mockery of the Law and the Disabled. *Financial Times*. Retrieved 17 August 2009 from <http://www.ft.com/cms/s/0/205a3854-8d65-11dc-a398-0000779fd2ac.html>.

Shtargot, S. (2007, July 21). Werribee DVD Youths Plead Guilty, Avoid Jail. *The Age*.

Skanlyn. (2009, 28 March). *Children of a Lesser God: I HATE DEAF PEOPLE*. Retrieved 19 August 2009 from <http://skanlyn.xanga.com/697149927/children-of-a-lesser-god/>.

Slappy (2000, 24 March). *Why We'll Never Cure the Cripples*. Retrieved 17 August 2009 from <http://www.angelfire.com/journal/slappy/rants/rant6.html>.

Smith, D. (2007). Disability, Gender and Intimate Partner Violence: Relationships From the Behavioral Risk Factor Surveillance System. *Sexuality and Disability, 26*(1), 15–28.

Sobsey, D. (1994). *Violence and Abuse in the Lives of People with Disabilities: The End of Silent Acceptance?* Baltimore, MD: Paul H Brookes.

Spiral_Abraxis (2004). *I Hate Crippled People*. Retrieved 17 August 2009 from <http://www.ubersite.com/m/46408>.

St. Louis-Sanchez, M. (2009, 15 October). *Vandals Leave Disabled Clients with No Wheels*. Retrieved 7 November 2009 from <http://www.gazette.com/news/services-63846-organization-clients.html>.

Staff *AAP* (2009, 23 July). *Blind Woman Robbed, Punched*. Retrieved 3 November 2009 from <http://www.news.com.au/story/0,23599,25848153-1702,00.html>.

Staff *Associated Newspapers* (2008, 15 October). *Disabled Girl, 16, 'Gang Raped and Then Burned'*. Retrieved 2 November 2009 from <http://www.metro.co.uk/news/article.html?Disabled_girl,_16,_%91gang_raped_and_then_burned%92&in_article_id=359093>.

Staff *Associated Press* (2005, 15 June). Teen Gets Probation for Role in Incident that Led to Man's Death. *The Hartford Courant*.

Staff *Associated Press* (2003, 3 November). Man Guilty of Kidnapping Suspect in Unsolved Murders. *The Bismark Tribune*. Retrieved 3 November 2009 from <http://www.bismarcktribune.com/news/local/article_c45eebfc-f3a2-5aaf-8d6f-006e462296d3.html>.

Staff *Associated Press* (2007a, September 10). Antioch Police Allege Hate Crime in Beating of Deaf Man at Party. *The Union Tribune*.

Staff *Associated Press* (2007b, January 23). Orange County Man Admits Attack on Handicapped Black. *Orange County Register*.

Staff *Associated Press* (2007c, 11 December). *Smyrna Police Charge Live-In Caregiver with Murder*. Retrieved 23 November 2009 from <http://www.freerepublic.com/focus/f-news/1938114/posts>.

Staff *Associated Press* (2007d, 16 July). *Thugs Attack Amputee with His Artificial Leg, Cops Say*. Retrieved 17 November 2009 from <http://www.nydailynews.com/news/ny_crime/2007/07/16/2007-07-16_thugs_attack_amputee_with_his_artificial.html>.

Staff *Associated Press* (2009, 26 October). Woman Pleads Guilty in Torture Slaying. *Associated Press Newswires*.

Staff *Associated Press KAIT Jonesboro AR* (2006, 3 January). *SeMo Teen Gets Six Months in Jail for Prosthetic Leg Attack*. Retrieved 17 August 2009 from <http://www.kait8.com/Global/story.asp?S=5885944&nav=0jsh>.

Staff *BBC News* (2003, 24 February). *Blind Man Thrown in Canal*. Retrieved 3 November 2009 from <http://news.bbc.co.uk/2/hi/uk_news/england/2793659.stm>.

Staff *BBC News* (2006a, January 26). *Athlete's Stolen Leg is Returned*. Retrieved 17 August 2009 from <http://news.bbc.co.uk/go/pr/fr/-/2/hi/uk_news/wales/4652268.stm>.

Staff *BBC News* (2006b, 30 March). *Carer Jailed Again for Stealing*. Retrieved 13 November 2009 from <http://news.bbc.co.uk/2/hi/uk_news/england/beds/bucks/herts/4860838.stm>.

Staff *BBC News* (2006c, November 17). *Killers Lose 'Slave' Death Appeal*. Retrieved 3 November 2009 from <http://news.bbc.co.uk/2/hi/uk_news/england/south_yorkshire/6159034.stm>.

Staff *BBC News* (2007a, 13 July). *Blind Man Robbed in Street Attack*. Retrieved 3 November 2009 from <http://news.bbc.co.uk/2/hi/uk_news/england/humber/6896978.stm>.

Staff *BBC News* (2007b, 31 July). *Men Tip Woman Out of Wheelchair*. Retrieved 3 November 2009 from <http://news.bbc.co.uk/2/hi/uk_news/england/hereford/worcs/6923561.stm>.

Staff *BBC News* (2009a, 16 September). *Care Manager Stole from Woman*. Retrieved 23 November 2009 from <http://news.bbc.co.uk/2/hi/uk_news/wales/8259269.stm>.

Staff *BBC News* (2009b, 17 September). Carer *Admits Stealing £8k from Pensioner*. Retrieved 23 November 2009 from <http://news.bbc.co.uk/2/hi/uk_news/wales/8259269.stm>.

Staff *Berrow's Worcester Journal* (2009, 9 October). *Sick Attack on Buses for Disabled*. Retrieved 3 November 2009 from <http://www.berrowsjournal.co.uk/news/4672776.print/>.

Staff *Braintree and Witham Times* (2009, 15 July). *Braintree: Woman Stole Over £20k from Mother and Elderly Neighbour*. Retrieved 8 November 2009 from <http://www.braintreeandwithamtimes.co.uk/news/4493995.Braintree_Woman_stole_over_20k_from_mother_and_elderly_neighbour/>.

Staff *Casper Star Tribune* (2006, 25 July). *Police Remove Sign Targeting Autistic Boy*. <http://trib.com/news/state-and-regional/article_6198b3ac-41f8-51cc-b22d-9c878db22c7e.html>.

Staff *CBC News* (2006, 21 July). *Man Beaten with His Own Crutch*. Retrieved 23 November 2009 from <http://www.cbc.ca/canada/toronto/story/2006/07/21/sudan-beating.html>.

Staff *CBC News Canada* (2009, 8 October). *Assault Should Cost Driver His Job: Mother*. Retrieved 13 October 2009 from <http://www.cbc.ca/canada/prince-edward-island/story/2009/10/06/pei-bus-driver-assault-584.html>.

Staff *CBS News Los Angeles* (2009, 17 November). *Caregiver Investigated in Patients' Deaths*. Retrieved 23 November 2009 from <http://cbs2.com/local/Dameria.Lawhorn.Nurses.2.1318699.html>.

Staff *Click Orlando* (2008, 12 October). *Disabled Man Beaten in Apparent Hate Crime*. Retrieved 23 November 2009 from <http://www.clickorlando.com/news/17697408/detail.html>.

Staff *Daily Mail* (2007a, 15 June). *350,000 Pensioners 'Are Abused by Carers, Families and Friends'*. Retrieved 8 November 2009 from <http://www.thisislondon.co.uk/news/article-23400539-350000-pensioners-suffer-abuse-in-own-home.do>.

Staff *Daily Mail* (2007b, 26 October). Yob Who Urinated on Dying Woman is Jailed for Three Years. *Mail Online*.

Staff *Derby Telegraph* (2009, 26 June). *Former Care Home Manager Jailed for Stealing from Vulnerable Patients*. Retrieved 23 November 2009 from <http://www.thisisderbyshire.co.uk/news/care-home-manager-jailed-stealing-vulnerable-patients/article-1113003-detail/article.html>.

Staff *Echo Reporter* (2008, 5 June). Son Stole £8,000 from Deaf Parents. *South Wales Echo*. Retrieved 7 November 2009.

Staff *Edinburgh Evening News* (2007, 7 July). *Off-Duty Police Officer Foils Rape Attempt on Disabled Woman*. Retrieved 2 November 2009 from <http://edinburghnews.scotsman.com/latestnews/Offduty-police-officer-foils-rape.3302165.jp>.

Staff *eNews Park Forest* (2007, 12 October). *80 Year Old Man Robbed, Pushed to Ground: Charges Include Robbery, Aggravated Battery, Hate Crime*. Retrieved 15 November 2009 from <http://www.enewspf.com/index.php?option=com_c ontent&task=view&id=1220&Itemid=2>.

Staff *Gloucestershire Echo* (2006, 30 March). She Stole Thousands from Pair. *Gloucestershire Echo*. Retrieved 7 November 2009.

Staff *Hartlepool Mail* (2007, 5 May). *As Carer Turned Crook Avoids Jail Term, OAP Asks 'Why Wasn't She Put Away?'* Retrieved 24 November 2009.

Staff *Herald Sun* (2009a, 11 March). *Disabled Men in Residential Care Forced into 'Fight Clubs' by Carers*. Retrieved 13 November 2009 from <http://www.heraldsun.com.au/news/world/disabled-men-forced-into-fight-clubs/story-e6frf7lf-1111119095176>.

Staff *Herald Sun* (2009b, 24 September). *Women in Care 'Raped, Trade Sex for Smokes' According to a Watchdog*. Retrieved 13 November 2009 from <http://www.heraldsun.com.au/news/women-in-care-raped-trade-sex-for-smokes-according-to-a-watchdog/story-e6frf7jo-1225778968210>.

Staff *Local6.com* (2008, 31 March). *Disabled Men, Woman Beaten Over Not Paying 'Fee' for Being White*. Retrieved 23 November 2009 from <http://www.clickorlando.com/news/15747448/detail.html>.

Staff *M2 Presswire* (2008, 17 November). *Bankrupt Carer Jailed After Cruel Theft*. Retrieved 23 November 2009 from <http://www.tmcnet.com/usubmit/-uk-government-bankrupt-carer-jailed-after-cruel-theft-/2008/11/18/3795089.htm>.

Staff *Mail Online* (2009, 17 February). *Agony of Disabled Woman Living in Fear After Sick Gang Butchers her Yorkshire Terrier. Then Tortures HER for an Hour*. Retrieved 15 November 2009 from <http://www.dailymail.co.uk/news/article-1147822/Agony-disabled-woman-living-fear-sick-gang-butchers-Yorkshire-terrier--tortures-HER-hour.html>.

Staff *Manchester Evening News* (2008, 16 July 2008). *Jail for Thieving Carer*. Retrieved 23 November 2009 from <http://www.manchestereveningnews.co.uk/news/s/1058371_jail_for_thieving_carer_?>.

Staff Mencap (2009, 17 June). *Legal Ruling Protects Vulnerable Adults*. Retrieved 23 November 2009 from <http://www.mencap.org.uk/page.asp?id=3234>.

Staff *Mirror.co.uk* (2009, 13 October). *Thug Beats Blind Man Unconscious*. Retrieved 3 November 2009 from <http://www.Mirror.co.uk/news/top-stories/2009/10/13/thug-beats-blind-man-115875-21743275/>.

Staff *Newark Post* (2009, 28 October). *Home Invaders Rob Man in Wheelchair*. Retrieved 15 November 2009 from <http://newarkpostonline.com/articles/2009/10/28/news/doc4ae888f12bb72772715356.txt>.

Staff *Nine News* (2009, 19 May). *Starved Girl Weighed 9kg at Death: Court*. Retrieved 23 November 2009 from <http://news.ninemsn.com.au/national/815506/jurors-to-hear-confronting-evidence>.

Staff *North Devon Journal* (2009, 5 November). *James Watts Jailed for Sex Crimes at Care Home*. Retrieved 23 November 2009 from <http://www.thisisnorthdevon.co.uk/news/James-Watts-jailed-sex-crimes-care-home/article-1487035-detail/article.html>.

Staff *Northern Echo* (2008, 17 January). Man Who Urinated on Disabled Woman Loses Appeal. *The Northern Echo*.

Staff *Pittsburgh Post Gazette* (2007, 21 March). *Lawyer Sues for Fees in T-Ball Case*. Retrieved 30 December 2009 from <http://www.post-gazette.com/pg/07080/771254-85.stm>.

Staff *Reporter Europe Intelligence Wire* (30 March 2006). Blind Man Robbed in Street Attack. *Europe Intelligence Wire*.

Staff *Royston Crow* (2009, 30 October). *Carer Jailed for Stealing Savings of Royston Disabled Woman*. Retrieved 7 November 2009 from <http://www.royston-crow.co.uk/content/crow/news/story.aspx?brand=ROYWestOnline&category=News&tBrand=HertsCambsOnline&tCategory=newslatestROY&itemid=WEED30+Oct+2009+15%3A09%3A18%3A923>.

Staff *Seattle Times* (2008, 4 October). Man Accused of Harassing Autistic Boy Faces Hate-Crime Charge. *The Seattle Times*. Retrieved 30 December 2009 from <http://seattletimes.nwsource.com/html/localnews/2008227153_levison04m.html>.

Staff *Seattle Times* (2008a, 4 October). Man Accused of Harassing Autistic Boy Faces Hate-Crime Charge. *The Seattle Times*.

Staff *Seattle Times* (2008b, 24 July). South Seattle Man Accused of Harassing Autistic Child, Threatening Arson. *The Seattle Times*.

Staff *Skegness Standard* (2007, 31 July). *Pair Tip Disabled Woman Out of Her Wheelchair*. Retrieved 3 November 2009 from <http://www.skegnessstandard.co.uk/news?articleid=3072423>.

Staff *Sky News* (2008, 24 September). *Girl Murdered for Being Disabled*. Retrieved 9 November 2009 from <http://news.sky.com/skynews/Home/UK-News/Naomi-Hill-Mother-Joanne-Hill-Jailed-After-Murdering-Daughter-By-Drowning-Her-In-The-Bath/Article/200809415105564?>.

Staff *Taranaki Daily News* (2009, 13 October). *Jail for Two Involved in Opunake Riot*. Retrieved 3 November 2009 from <http://www.stuff.co.nz/taranaki-daily-news/news/2957357/Jail-for-two-involved-in-Opunake-riot>.

Staff *The Age Newspaper* (2004, 13 February). *Appeal for Two Lost Legs*. Retrieved 17 August 2009 from <http://www.theage.com.au/articles/2004/02/12/1076548159293.html>.

Staff *The Citizen Newspaper* (2007, 14 November). Carer Stole £1,300 from Autistic Man. *The Citizen Gloucestershire*.

Staff *The Danbury News-Times*. (2009, 14 July). Naugatuck Teens Accused of Robbing, Flipping Handicapped Man out of Wheelchair. *The Danbury News-Times*.

Staff *WABC-TV/DT* (2006, 17 January). *Blind 92-Year-Old Woman Robbed, Again*. Retrieved 8 November 2009 from <http://abclocal.go.com/wabc/story?section=news/local&id=3820744>.

State of Washington, Respondent, v. Marilea R. Mitchell (2009).

State of Wisconsin vs. Raymond C. Walton (Case No. 2000F000060 Barron County 2000).

State v. Mary C. Reed (Case No. 1999CF000127 Barron County 1999).

State vs. Corey L. Kralewski (Case No. 1999CF000126 Barron County 1999).

Stefan, S. (2001). *Unequal Rights: Discrimination Against People with Mental Disabilities and the Americans with Disabilities Act*. Washington, DC: American Psychological Association.

Storer, G. (2009, 20 May). *Bull Ants in Starving 7-Year-Old's Mouth: Trial*. Retrieved 23 November 2009 from <http://www.illawarramercury.com.au/news/local/news/general/bull-ants-in-starving-7yearolds-mouth-trial/1517478.aspx>.

Storer, G. and Nott, H.N. (2009, 23 June). *Parents Guilty of Starving Daughter*. Retrieved 23 November 2009 from <http://news.smh.com.au/breaking-news-national/parents-guilty-of-starving-daughter-20090623-cuy1.html>.

Strodl, K. (2007, January 24). Man Sentenced for Hate Crime. *Huntington Beach Independent*.

Suhr, J. (2009, 26 October). *Woman Pleads Guilty in Ill. Torture Slaying*. Retrieved 15 November 2009 from <http://www.google.com/hostednews/ap/article/ALeqM5iabbCpwynpg96u3aP6B2PtXoXvoAD9BJ1VF00>.

Teotonio, I. (2007, 21 January). *Stolen Gold Paralympic Medal Found*. Retrieved 17 August 2009 from <http://www.thestar.com/article/173306>.

Teplin, L.A., McClelland, G.M., Abram, K.M. and Weiner, D.A. (2005). Crime Victimization in Adults with Severe Mental Illness. *Archives of General Psychiatry, 62*(8), 911–921.

The Cheteck Alert Courthouse Reporter (2006, 20 December). Appeal of 1999 Beating Death Rejected. *The Chetek Alert*.

The National Autistic Society (2009). *A Response from The National Autistic Society: NAS Comments on the Anti-Social Behaviour Bill Part 2 (Housing)*. Retrieved 25 October 2009.

The Ref (2004, 31 May). *Looking Out for the Little Guy or Why I Hate Midgets*. Retrieved 19 August 2009 from <http://www.ubersite.com/m/34610>.

The State of New Jersey v. Jennifer Dowell, Brandon Cruz, Marni Soloman, William Mackay, Christal Lavary, Daniel Vistad, et al. (2000). 334 N.J. Super. 133, 756 A.2d 1087: Monmouth County Court.

Thomas, K. and McKenzie-McLean, J. (2009). *Thugs Attack Disabled, Blind Man*. Christchurch, New Zealand.

Times Online Law Reports (2008). *Threshold for Sadistic Murder*. Retrieved 17 August 2009 from <http://business.timesonline.co.uk/tol/business/law/reports/article4333064.ece>.

Tjaden, P. and Thoennes, N. (1998). *Prevalence, Incidence, and Consequences of Violence Against Women: Findings from the National Violence Against Women Survey*. Washington DC: National Institute of Justice, Centers for Disease Control and Prevention.

Today Tonight (2006, 24 October). *Today Tonight Werribee Students DVD*. Retrieved 7 November 2009 from <http://www.youtube.com/watch?v=dKqcGyE_WJ8>.

Turner, K. (2007, 25 July). *Family Hounded out by Racists*. Retrieved 23 November 2009 from <http://www.lancashiretelegraph.co.uk/news/1573035.print/>.

Turner, L. (2008, 4 June). Man Jailed for Stealing from Deaf Parents. *Press Association Newswire*. Retrieved 7 November 2009.

Valk, A. (2007, 9 July). *Murder Hunt after Disabled Man 'Tipped out of Wheelchair'*. Retrieved 23 November 2009 from <http://www.northamptonchron.co.uk/news?articleid=3014956>.

Vicious Headbutt (2004). *Retards 2*. Retrieved 7 January 2004 from <www.murderize.com/Editorials/Headbutt/retards2>.

Violent Acres (2006, 17 November). *Retard Genocide*. Retrieved 23 November 2009 from <http://www.violentacres.com/archives/40/retard-genocide/>.

Watson, S.T. (2007, 16 August). Teens Face Hate Crime Charges After Crash. *The Buffalo News*.

Weber, M.C. (2007). *Disability Harassment*. New York: NYU Press.

West, B. and Gandhi, S. (2006, Winter). Reporting Abuse: A Study of the Perceptions of People with Disabilities (PWD) Regarding Abuse Directed at PWD. *Disability Studies Quarterly, 26*(1). Retrieved 15 November 2009 from <http://www.dsq-sds.org/article/view/650/827>.

Whillock, R.K. (1995). The Use of Hate as a Strategem for Achieving Political and Social Goals. In R.K. Whillock and D. Slayden (eds), *Hate Speech* (pp. 28–54). Thousand Oaks, CA: Sage.

Whitfield, G. (2008, 22 January). *Teenager Convicted of Murder 'for Sport'*. Retrieved 17 August 2009 from <http://www.journallive.co.uk/north-east-news/breaking-news/2008/01/22/teenager-convicted-of-murder-for-sport-61634-20380520>.

Williams, J. and Keating, F. (1999). The Abuse of Adults in Mental Health Settings. In N. Stanley, J. Manthorpe and B. Penhale (eds), *Institutional Abuse: Perspectives Across the Lifecourse* (pp. 152–172). London: Routledge.

Willott, S., Rabone, L., Offen, L. and Pratap, S. (2004). Justice and Empowerment for People with Learning Disabilities Who Have Been Abused. *Clinical Psychology, 34,* 25–28.

Wright, S. (2009, 18 July). 'Highly Dangerous' Bradford Man Locked Up. *Telegraph and Argus,* from <http://www.thetelegraphandargus.co.uk/news/local/localbrad/4500237.Teenager_locked_up_for_rape_may_never_be_freed/>.

xxxotic (2005, 23 December). *I Fucking Hate.* Retrieved 19 August 2009 from <http://www.extremebullshit.com/main-bullshit/t-i-fucking-hate-10333/page2.html>.

Index